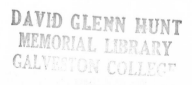

MARIONETTES ONSTAGE!

MARIONETTES ONSTAGE!

Leonard Suib & Muriel Broadman

HARPER & ROW, PUBLISHERS

New York, Evanston, San Francisco, London

CREDITS

Don Avery and the *Puppetry Journal*, for selected excerpts.
The Performing Arts Program of the Asia Society and Kazuko
Hillyer International, Inc., for photographs.

FIRST EDITION

Library of Congress Cataloging in Publication Data
Suib, Leonard.
    Marionettes onstage!
    Bibliography: p.
    Includes index.
    1. Puppets and puppet-plays. I. Broadman, Muriel, joint
author. II. Title.
PN1972.S77   791.5′3   75-6363
ISBN 0-06-014166-2

75 76 77 78 79 10 9 8 7 6 5 4 3 2 1

CONTENTS

Acknowledgments   vii

Foreword   ix

PART ONE   THE NEW MARIONETTE

Introduction   3

SECTION 1 PREPARING THE MARIONETTES

Cardboard Construction   5
Making Kandu   5
Giving Kandu Life   21
Making Ruff   38
Giving Ruff Life   44

SECTION 2 PREPARING THE SHOW

A Stage for Kandu   47
Kandu's Props   51
Lighting Kandu   53
Kandu's Music and Sound Effects   54

SECTION 3 PUTTING ON THE SHOW

"Kandu the Magnificent and His Talking Wonder Dog Ruff"   55
Touring Kandu   62

PART TWO   BECOMING A PUPPETEER

Introduction   67
Playscripts   69

v

Expanding the Cast of Players 80

Performing 94

Marionette Stages 96

Scenery 110

Props 119

Lighting 121

Music and Sound Effects 128

Marionette Magic 142

Multi-Media 150

Direction 154

Putting on the Show 158

Safety 164

PART THREE PUPPET THEATER MANAGEMENT

Introduction 169

Where Do You Go from Here? 171

Opportunities to Perform 175

Selling the Show 176

Business Procedures 195

Incorporating and Funding 213

Future of Puppetry 220

Appendix 1 223

Appendix 2 225

Appendix 3 227

Bibliography 229

Glossary 233

Index 239

ACKNOWLEDGMENTS

The authors are indebted to those family members and friends whose cooperation has been of immeasurable assistance in the preparation of *Marionettes Onstage!*—the late Joseph Suib, painter and sculptor, Shirley and Sally Suib, who helped with patterns and costumes, and Nancy, Peter, and Sidney Suib, who worked on diagrams and in other areas. William Haas, Jr., checked over the lighting section. Jack Leskoff was generous with his knowledge of music, as was Elizabeth McCormick with her theatrical lore. Paul Yurcik contributed his services in organizing the material. Special thanks are due to Bob Daly for his photographs. Thanks to Don Avery for allowing us to use material from *The Puppetry Journal.* And we are grateful to W. A. Dwiggins and to all the other puppeteers of the world on whose traditions our new marionettes and stages have been created.

FOREWORD

The world of puppetry is a world of enchantment. At one time or another we have all ventured into it either as the magic makers or as the spectators contributing our involvement. We lose reality's sense of scale as we watch. We enter, we believe, we participate in this world in which anything can happen.

The performers are hand, rod and stick, shadow, and stringed puppets—and the stringed puppet or marionette is the elite of the puppet theater. Although *Marionettes Onstage!* is concerned principally with stringed puppets, much of its information is applicable to other forms of puppetry as well.

The marionette theater offers all that "live" theater does and more. Because the master puppeteer functions in every capacity, he can develop a totality, a unity in his presentation that the live theater seldom realizes. But a puppet justifies its existence only if it can do its thing better than a human counterpart. What a human being can do better, a live actor should. But a puppet has skills that no real person can match. It can juggle impossible balls, fly, leap through the air, vanish, reappear, come apart, join together again. It can transform itself from

a queen to a bird, from a witch to a horse, from a frog to a prince. A flower can grow before our eyes, dance, become a fairy.

A marionette is a tool to say or do something with—not an end in itself. The guiding hand is yours, not only in the sense of the ideas you give your creature but in the literal sense of manipulation. Your puppet is an extension of yourself into areas where you cannot go without it. *You* create *it*. *You* pull the strings.

Most puppetry is performed for young audiences, but it's a false notion that it can be appreciated only by children. If your material and treatment are adult-oriented, there's no age barrier to your audiences. Gluck, Haydn, de Falla, and Respighi are among those who have composed marionette operas for adults. Goethe's *Faust* was originally conceived for puppets, as were works of Maeterlinck and George Sand. Plays as "adult" as O'Neill's and Shakespeare's have been successfully presented with marionettes. In nightclubs throughout the country it's not uncommon to see marionette extravaganzas complete with chorus lines, satirical impressions, and topical revues. The gamut of subjects is wide, ranging from stripteasers to current political figures—and all for adult consumption.

Which audience is for you, and what do you want to say? Do you want to tell a fairy tale? Present a vaudeville or variety show? A political satire? A comment on the human condition? You can create the medium in which to say whatever is important to you, and you'll be at your best with what interests you most.

There's an unfortunate impression abroad, shared even by many puppeteers, that stringed puppets are "so difficult and complicated and take so long to make." In teaching the different forms of puppetry to classes of children and adults, we have seen students discouraged before they started when they came to marionettes. Even art students with a background in drawing have often been unable to turn a flat sketch into the three-dimensional figure that is a marionette. Marionettes are cumbersome to create, they say, and need an elaborate workshop. "Balancing" them is fraught with complexities. Marionettes are heavy and a strain on the puppeteer's back and arms. And learning to manipulate the strings is an extensive course of study.

It's true that many of the customary processes are intricate, and many a would-be marionette beginner has been justifiably discouraged. But we shall demonstrate a new method of making a marionette that simplifies the construction and the manipulation.

With the new marionette we have devised, there's no longer any reason not to enjoy the unique pleasures of the stringed puppet. The principle on which the new marionette is created is a simple one: Cut-out modular pieces based on front and side silhouettes are interlocked to form a three-dimensional image. All pieces are joined together with the simplest of means, and the only tools necessary are a pair of scissors and a small pair of pliers. Once the basic idea is grasped, there is no conventional marionette that can't be created easily with these modules. This new marionette is approximately one-quarter the weight of a conventional marionette. The only figures at all comparable in lightness are those made of plastic foam (e.g. Styrofoam), which has serious disadvantages. Our marionette comes with its balance built in, so this problem never arises.

If you've had no experience with stringed puppets or have had unsatisfactory results from attempts made along conventional lines, this new construction and simplified method of manipulation will be a delight.

We'll start you out with foolproof plans to enable you to create a marionette with readily available household materials. Step by step you'll learn everything you'll need to know about its complete construction. You'll learn how to string it and make it do whatever is necessary for a performance. We'll give you a suggested script to start you and your marionette on your way, as well as some ideas on how to demonstrate your freshly developed abilities to an audience. We'll even give you plans for an optional second puppet, should you wish to make your presentation more elaborate.

However, Part One—"The New Marionette" —won't put too heavy a burden on you by throwing at you expositions of skills you won't need for these first puppets, or other information before you're ready for it. It's important that your first marionettes be fun for you, or you won't be enthusiastic about going on to more complicated projects that will yield greater enjoyment.

Part Two—"Becoming a Puppeteer"—will show you how to make other marionettes and more elaborate stages and will cover additional manipulative techniques, a discussion of scripts, and whatever else you should know to become as proficient as the most skilled marionette master.

Part Three—"Puppet Theater Management" —discusses the practical aspects of puppetry as a profession. Whether you opt for being a highly skilled amateur or decide to turn your hobby into a livelihood, you owe it to yourself to know what all this pleasure is costing in dollars and cents and what it will cost to share it if you play a school or a hospital, for instance. Part Three will show you how to budget your production, how to "sell" it, and the tricks professional puppeteers use when they take their shows on the road.

So dip into Part One—but beware! You may become a marionette addict and never be the same again.

PART ONE

THE NEW MARIONETTE

INTRODUCTION

Whether you're a novice in puppetry or a veteran, Part One of *Marionettes Onstage!* is an introduction to an entirely new way of thinking about marionettes and constructing them. You'll be given plans for building two figures that are light in weight, flexible in simulating "live" movement, and perfectly balanced. And they need no elaborate tools or supplies.

The plans are for Kandu the Magnificent, a magician, and his Talking Wonder Dog Ruff. When you've cut out the patterns and assembled the pieces, the concept of designing a puppet on a combination of frontal and profile outlines will be clear, not merely as a theory but as a fact that you understand from having developed the puppet with your own hands.

Kandu is a specific magician, but when you've made him you'll know essentially how to create any human marionette. Ruff is a dog, but when he is finished you'll know essentially how to create any animal marionette.

Because your journey into the world of the marionette should be pleasurable, we don't necessarily recommend that you begin with the first words of Part One and conscientiously follow every direction all the way to the end of it. Not at all. We suggest you start with Kandu. His patterns must be duplicated precisely if he is to function well. When he's assembled, if you want to have fun making him move, you needn't costume him, or put "skin" on his "bones," or even paint him. You may skip all this and go directly to "Giving Kandu Life" and go back and costume him, or a replica of him, when your fancy dictates. By the same token, you need feel under no moral obligation to start on Ruff immediately after completing Kandu, if you're happy exploring what you and Kandu can do together. In the script that comes at the end of Part One, with full stage directions, the entire portion dealing with Ruff can be eliminated until you've constructed Kandu and learned his manipulation. The script has been designed to be episodic so that you can skip any tricks you find particularly difficult, and they can be inserted later when you've mastered them.

Following the same line, if you're in a rush to perform, you needn't stop to build a stage. You can give a little informal performance almost anywhere. But if you want a theatrically more effective presentation, we have plans for two stages that can't be simpler, plus two others that require more construction and will give a better show.

You'll have to follow carefully the patterns and assembling directions and learn basic stringing and manipulation, but everything else set down here may be considered more as guides or suggestions than constricting rules. Knowing how to build and use marionettes can free you creatively and enable your imagination to soar.

However, when you complete all the constructions and learn all the techniques that Part One covers, you'll have a good basic knowledge of the art of the marionette. The mini-play at the end of Section 1 provides a vehicle for rehearsing a wide range of skills and lets you exhibit them and share your pleasure with others.

La-deez and gentlemen! Girls and boys! Children of all ages! Step right up and let us introduce to you Kandu the Magnificent! See how a performing wizard grows from scraps of cardboard and cloth before your very eyes! See Kandu step before the curtain and take his place in the spotlight! See incredible feats of legerdemain that have no equal on any continent or in any clime! And the best part of all —the magician is *you*!

SECTION 1

PREPARING THE MARIONETTES

CARDBOARD CONSTRUCTION

The construction of our magician and his dog has been simplified to where it will present no difficulties if you go along with us one step at a time. Each figure is constructed by putting together in various combinations modular pieces that can be cut from a pattern by anyone—even by children who can use scissors without hurting themselves.

Start with sheets of cardboard—any kind of cardboard, from the lightweight tops and bottoms of suit boxes to the generally heavier shirt cardboard from laundries. You can purchase special supplies from an art store, but this shouldn't be necessary in most instances. The thicker the cardboard, the sturdier the marionettes will be, but don't use heavier cardboard than you can cut without difficulty. You'll need approximately the equivalent of three shirt cardboards for Kandu and about the same amount for his dog Ruff.

So that you can make Kandu and Ruff without unnecessary complications, we've provided full-scale patterns.

MAKING KANDU
TRACING THE PATTERNS

Let's do Kandu first and leave Ruff until later. And although it's possible to complete each step of Kandu's construction before going on to the next, it might be more interesting for you to complete Kandu a few sections at a time before going on to other sections. As Kandu begins to take shape in your hands, you will be stimulated to continue by your pleasure in completing his components.

To begin with Kandu's head and body, we have to transfer the patterns for his head, chest, waist, and pelvis (Figures 1, 2, and 3) to cardboard. One way to do this is to lay tracing paper on top of the pattern and go over the outline exactly with a soft pencil. Don't forget to trace interior details of slots (for interlocking), thick dots (for hinging joints), and triangles (for manipulation strings) into your drawings. Turn the tracing paper over when you're through so that the penciled outline is now face down. This goes on top of your cardboard, so that with your pencil you can go over

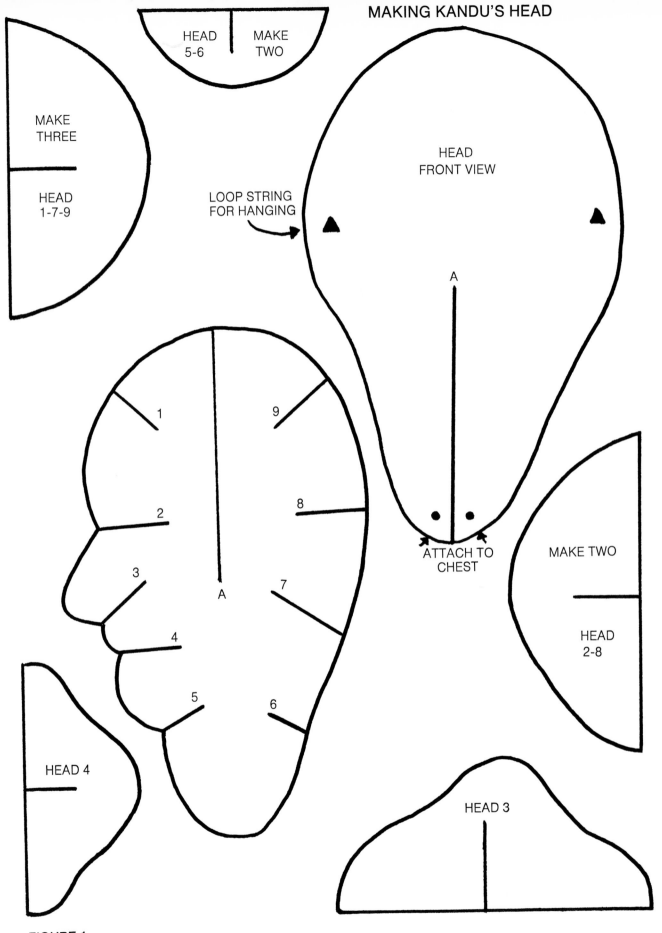

MAKING KANDU'S HEAD

HEAD 5-6   MAKE TWO

MAKE THREE

HEAD 1-7-9

LOOP STRING FOR HANGING

HEAD FRONT VIEW

A

1   9

2   8

3

A   7

4

5   6

ATTACH TO CHEST

MAKE TWO

HEAD 2-8

HEAD 4

HEAD 3

FIGURE 1

the outline which shows through to the other side of the tracing paper. Pressing on the outline will transfer some of the original graphite of your pencil from the paper to the cardboard. Do this for each module (pattern piece).

There's another way to achieve the same result. After you've made your modular tracings, put the tracing paper right side up on the cardboard, with a sheet of carbon paper in between, carbon side down. Trace over your original lines to transfer the pattern to the cardboard.

Whichever method you use, be sure to label each module immediately to avoid confusion when you put the pieces together afterward.

CUTTING OUT THE MODULES

With scissors, cut the cardboard modules out as accurately as you can. Cut each piece free of the cardboard before cutting the slots. Each slot should be cut to the same thickness as the cardboard, and it's important that the slot be the exact length shown on the pattern.

The dots and triangles indicate where holes should be made in the cardboard. They need be no larger than for heavy thread to pass through.

The holes can be made in several ways. The best way to make a reinforced hole is with a grommet stapler, which punches a hole and simultaneously sets a metal ring around it. A grommet stapler is a relatively inexpensive gadget, obtainable in most stationery and variety stores. However, if you don't want to use one, the holes can be made with a hole punch, an awl, an ice pick, a heavy needle, or any other sharp instrument. If you don't use a grommet stapler, it's advisable to strengthen the area around the hole by brushing or spraying on shellac.

ASSEMBLING KANDU'S HEAD, CHEST, WAIST, AND PELVIS

When all this has been done, Kandu's head and body are ready to be put together. The cut-out modular pieces are assembled like a three-dimensional jigsaw puzzle. The modules should be interlocked to the full length of their slots. No tools are necessary except a small pair of pliers.

Kandu's Head. Collect the eleven modules making up the *head.* They include a large *front view* and a *side view* of the same size, each with a slot marked "A." Interlock both slots at right angles to each other to get a three-dimensional egg-shaped form. The remaining nine modules have slots that correspond and interlock with the slots on the *side view.*

Kandu's Chest. Collect the eight *chest* modules. The "B" *side view* slot interlocks with the "B" slot of the *front view.* The "A" and "C" *side view* modules interlock with their corresponding slots on the *chest front view.* Make sure all "front" pieces face in the right direction. The *chest* section is now composed of four modules, to which the remaining four interlock, as indicated.

Kandu's Waist. Collect the six *waist* modules. The *front view* and *side view* interlock at Slots "B." When Modules "A" and "E" and "C" and "D" are interlocked, as indicated, the *waist* is completed.

Kandu's Pelvis. The six *pelvis* modules are all that are left. The *front view* and *side view* modules interlock through Slot "B." Continue assembling the *pelvis* as with the other body units.

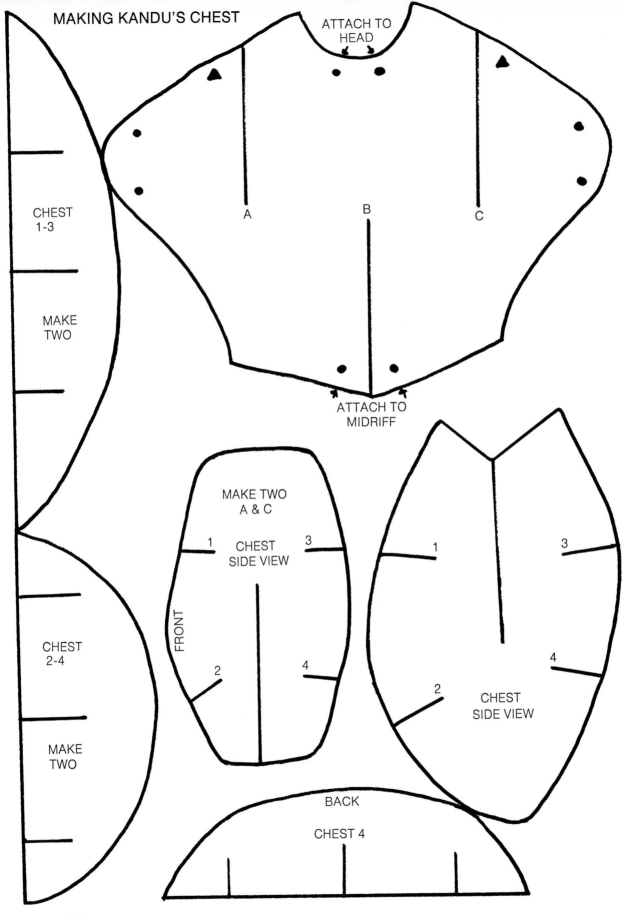

MAKING KANDU'S CHEST

ATTACH TO HEAD

A

B

C

ATTACH TO MIDRIFF

CHEST 1-3

MAKE TWO

CHEST 2-4

MAKE TWO

MAKE TWO A & C

CHEST SIDE VIEW

FRONT

1

2

3

4

1

2

3

4

CHEST SIDE VIEW

BACK

CHEST 4

FIGURE 2

MAKING KANDU'S MIDRIFF & PELVIS

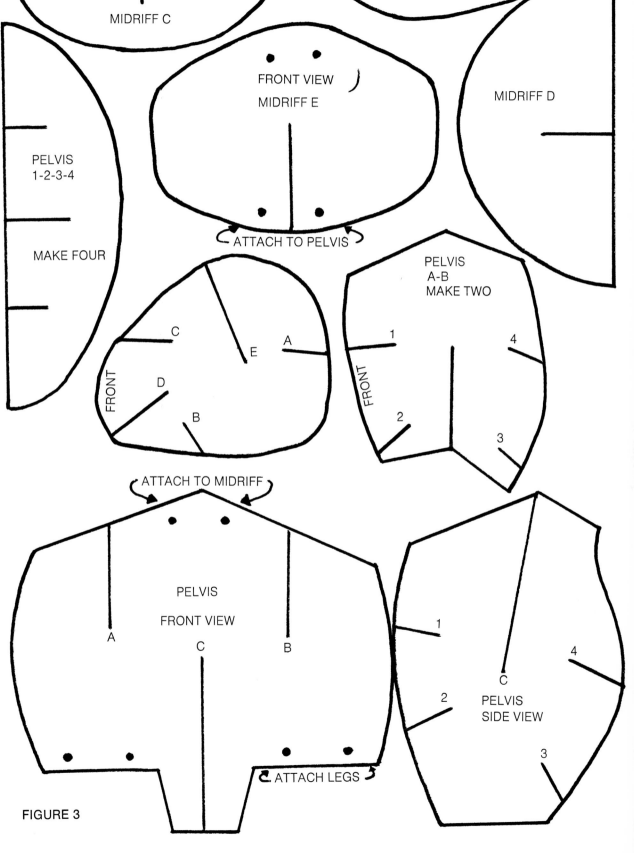

MIDRIFF C

A-B MAKE TWO
MIDRIFF

FRONT VIEW
MIDRIFF E

MIDRIFF D

PELVIS
1-2-3-4

MAKE FOUR

ATTACH TO PELVIS

C

E

A

FRONT

D

B

PELVIS
A-B
MAKE TWO

1

4

FRONT

2

3

ATTACH TO MIDRIFF

PELVIS

FRONT VIEW

A

C

B

ATTACH LEGS

1

C

4

2

PELVIS
SIDE VIEW

3

FIGURE 3

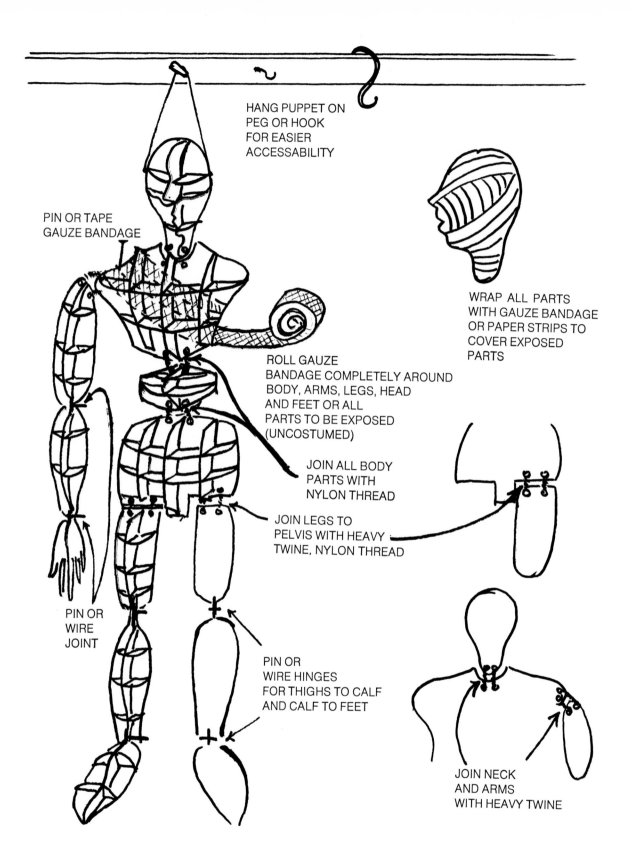

HANG PUPPET ON
PEG OR HOOK
FOR EASIER
ACCESSABILITY

PIN OR TAPE
GAUZE BANDAGE

WRAP ALL PARTS
WITH GAUZE BANDAGE
OR PAPER STRIPS TO
COVER EXPOSED
PARTS

ROLL GAUZE
BANDAGE COMPLETELY AROUND
BODY, ARMS, LEGS, HEAD
AND FEET OR ALL
PARTS TO BE EXPOSED
(UNCOSTUMED)

JOIN ALL BODY
PARTS WITH
NYLON THREAD

JOIN LEGS TO
PELVIS WITH HEAVY
TWINE, NYLON THREAD

PIN OR
WIRE
JOINT

PIN OR
WIRE HINGES
FOR THIGHS TO CALF
AND CALF TO FEET

JOIN NECK
AND ARMS
WITH HEAVY TWINE

FIGURE 4

CONNECTING KANDU'S HEAD AND BODY SECTIONS

Now the four sections can be joined together.

The small end of the egg-shaped *head*, which is the neck, has two holes. The top of the *chest* has two. When the face and the front of the *chest* are in the proper relationship to each other, the four holes are aligned. (Figure 4.) These are joined, two and two, with heavy twine, upholstery thread, fish line, or any other heavy-duty thread. Each thread goes through one neck hole and one *chest* hole and is knotted on itself. Leave enough thread for a secure triple knot—and for your fingers. It's important not to have the thread loop so loose the body joints are too far apart, which would result in sloppy movement, or so tight that movement is restricted unnaturally.

At the bottom of the *chest* there are two holes, both of which attach the same way to the two holes at the top of the *waist*. Again, take care to allow enough thread for your fingers to make the loops and to make the loops neither too loose nor too tight. The aim is always to simulate genuine body action as closely as possible.

The two holes at the base of the *waist* now are fastened to the two at the top of the *pelvis*, and you can begin to see where your efforts are leading.

You can see also why we suggest you create Kandu in sections. Not only is he fascinating, even in his unfinished state, but you have no modular pieces left over to become mixed up with the modules you're going to prepare for his legs and arms.

KANDU'S LEGS

So now let's do Kandu's legs.

As with Kandu's head and torso, we have

Figure 5. A photo of the completed cardboard puppet uncostumed but strung and ready for action. *Photo: Bob Daly*

to transfer the *leg* modules from Figure 6 to cardboard. The patterns show only the left side, but remember, Kandu has a right leg as well. To make the right *leg*, make two left side modules in each instance, then turn one over and mark the identification on the reverse side. The holes are to be punched where indicated and the slots cut. With the *legs*, everything is done as before, with one exception. You'll see that the *calf front view* and Modules 1 through 6 have slots that are to be cut double the thickness of the cardboard instead of the single thickness of all the rest of the slots. In assembling Kandu's legs, we suggest you work one at a time.

11

MAKING KANDU'S LEG

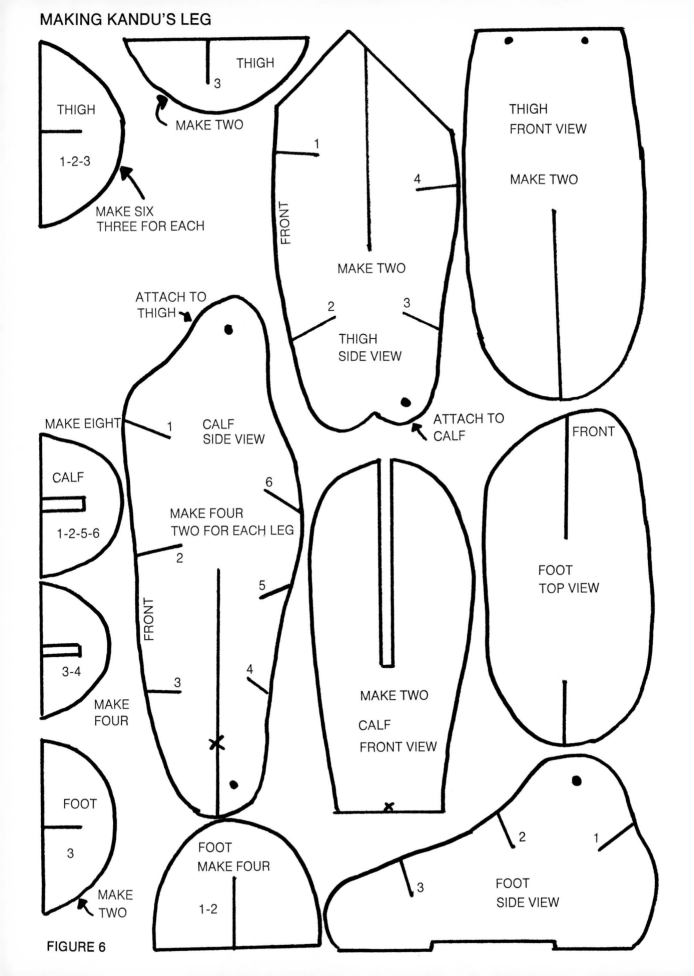

THIGH

THIGH

MAKE TWO

1-2-3

MAKE SIX
THREE FOR EACH

FRONT

1

4

THIGH
FRONT VIEW

MAKE TWO

MAKE TWO

2

3

THIGH
SIDE VIEW

ATTACH TO
THIGH

ATTACH TO
CALF

MAKE EIGHT

1

CALF
SIDE VIEW

6

CALF

MAKE FOUR
TWO FOR EACH LEG

FRONT

FOOT
TOP VIEW

1-2-5-6

2

5

3-4

FRONT

MAKE TWO

CALF
FRONT VIEW

MAKE
FOUR

3

4

X

FOOT

3

MAKE
TWO

FOOT
MAKE FOUR

1-2

X

FOOT
MAKE FOUR

2

1

3

FOOT
SIDE VIEW

FIGURE 6

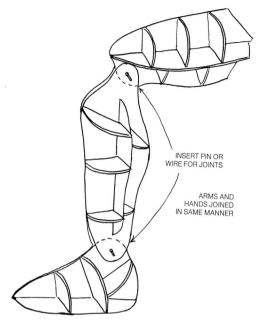

INSERT PIN OR
WIRE FOR JOINTS

ARMS AND
HANDS JOINED
IN SAME MANNER

FIGURE 7

Kandu's Thigh. Using the same method as formerly, interlock the *front view* with the *side view*, and then interlock the four corresponding modules.

Kandu's Calf. Take two *side view* modules, place one upon the other, and interlock the two *together* as a unit to the full length of their slot with the full length of the *calf front view* double-thickness slot. Modules 1 through 6 interlock with the *side view*.

Kandu's Foot. Interlock the *top view* and the *side view*. These are the only two modules that need to have the lock reinforced by glue, masking tape, or some similar material. The three remaining *foot* modules interlock with their corresponding *side view* slots.

To put Kandu's left *leg* together, match up the hole in the bottom of the *thigh* and the one in the top of the *calf*. The single thickness of *thigh side view* goes between the two cardboard parts that combine to make up the

calf side view. Through the holes, insert a hinge made of a heavy straight pin, a paper clip, or a short length of strong wire. Bend the ends of the wire or whatever else you're using to keep the hinge from falling out. You may want the pliers for this. (Figure 7.)

Give additional support to this primary joint by shellacking the cardboard around it. If the joint doesn't move freely, in a natural way, put talcum powder in and around the hinge. Or insert a cardboard sliver between the two parts of the *calf side view* immediately below the joint. If the grommet stapler was used to make the holes, the shellac, the talcum powder, and the sliver aren't necessary.

The hole at the bottom of the *calf* and that at the top of the *foot* are similarly hinged with metal, with the single thickness of the "foot" cardboard going between the double thickness of the *calf side view*. A sliver wedge above the hinge, or talcum powder, may be necessary.

When both *legs* are assembled, they can be joined to Kandu's body. The holes at the bottom of the *pelvis* and the top of the thighs are strung together with thread loops. Make sure that front and back and right and left are laid out correctly—unless you want Kandu to see where he's been instead of where he's going.

KANDU'S ARMS

And now for Kandu's *arms*. His left and right *arms* are traced onto cardboard from Figure 8, exactly as with his *legs*. Also as with his *legs* you'll see that some modules—in this instance *lower arm side view* and lower arm Modules 1 through 4—have double slots. We'll do Kandu's left *arm* first and then reverse for the right.

Kandu's Upper Arm. The *front view* and *side view* interlock, and then the remaining four modules are interlocked, as indicated.

13

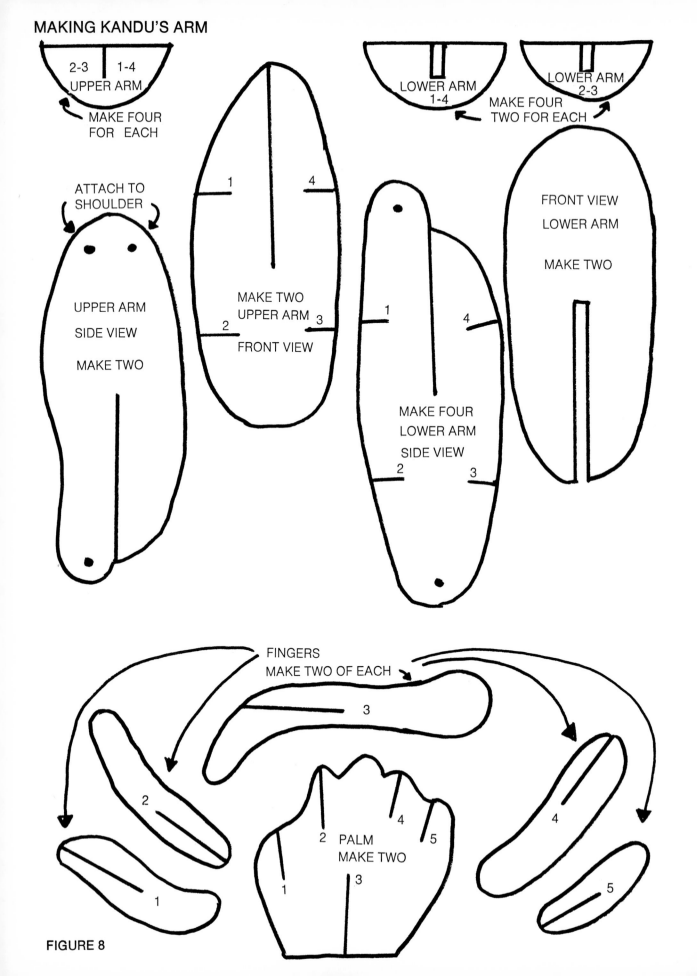

MAKING KANDU'S ARM

2-3 | 1-4
UPPER ARM

MAKE FOUR
FOR EACH

LOWER ARM
1-4

LOWER ARM
2-3

MAKE FOUR
TWO FOR EACH

ATTACH TO
SHOULDER

1   4

UPPER ARM

SIDE VIEW

MAKE TWO

MAKE TWO
UPPER ARM

2   3

FRONT VIEW

1   4

MAKE FOUR

LOWER ARM

SIDE VIEW

2   3

FRONT VIEW

LOWER ARM

MAKE TWO

FINGERS
MAKE TWO OF EACH

3

2

1

PALM
MAKE TWO

2

4

5

1   3

4

5

FIGURE 8

Kandu's Lower Arm. Lay one *side view* piece over an identical module and interlock them as a unit with *lower arm front view.* The four remaining modules interlock with the *side view.*

Kandu's Hand. The *palm* and five *fingers* are interlocked, as indicated. The lock of Module 3 (middle *finger*) and the *palm* is the only one needing reinforcing by glue or tape.

To assemble the units of Kandu's left *arm,* we hinge the bottom of the *upper arm* to the top of the *lower arm* with metal. The bottom of the *lower arm* joins the #3 *finger* of the *hand,* the same way as the *calf* and *foot.*

The complete left *arm* assembly is now joined at the top of the *upper arm* to the left shoulder of the *chest* with thread or string. The thread through the top hole of the shoulder and the *arm* should be fairly tight. The lower thread should be loose enough to enable Kandu to raise his arm easily above his head. And when both arms have been joined, presto!

KANDU'S SKELETON

Now Kandu is all together. Actually, what you've created up to this point is an armature, a frame or support that is mobile and agile. In itself the armature is a working puppet and it can be strung and manipulated. In fact, if you're in a hurry to get to manipulation, you need go no further in providing Kandu with skin and clothing. He's quite a handsome fellow just as he is, but a coat of paint would give him a more dashing air. He could be painted all one color, or giving each of his many squares a different color could turn him into Harlequin. Or black and white Mondrianlike divisions are always smart.

But if you want to continue Kandu's evolution as a magician, we have to finish off his anatomy and clothe it. A puppet exists to com-municate, and there are numerous details that can be applied to make Kandu more effective in this respect.

HANGING KANDU

Before you proceed further with Kandu, you might want to set him up in a position that will make him easy to work on. He has a hole on either side of his head, and if you run a six-inch loop of string through them, you can hang him from it at a convenient working height. (Figure 9.)

KANDU'S SKIN

So far, Kandu's head is merely a roughly shaped egg, and all his internal structure is naked to the world. For a more realistic look he'll need skin over his modular bones. However, since he'll appear onstage in formal attire, he'll need skin only on the parts that show: his head and neck and his lower arms and hands. We'll cover his feet and ankles also, because while he'll be wearing shoes and stockings, it will be easier to paint these on than to have to make them.

Kandu's skin can be made of virtually any wrapping—fabric, paper, gauze bandage, or anything else. Two factors could influence your selection—the final texture you're aiming for and what's handy around the house. If you have something very special in mind, you may want to buy a particular kind of covering, but you'll need only a relatively small amount, even for a two-foot-tall marionette.

Cut your skin fabric into strips approximately an inch wide. You can use one-inch gauze bandage just as it comes. If you use any other lightweight soft material—an old pillow case or curtain, for example—cut the material along the grain (that is, along the direction of

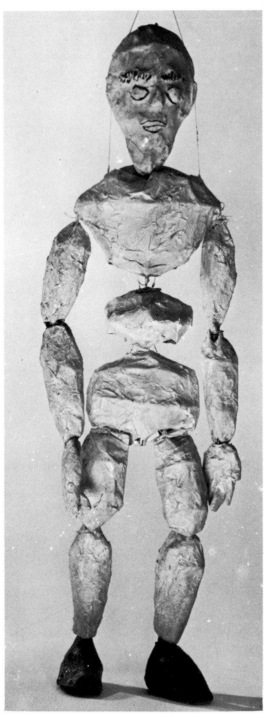

Figure 9. The cardboard puppet can be covered with papier mâché or gauze bandage. *Photo: Bob Daly*

the threads in the weave). Start at one end of a body segment, attaching the beginning of the cloth strip with pins or a piece of masking tape. Wind the fabric tightly (but don't crush the cardboard!) and smoothly to the other end of the body segment. You don't need too many layers of fabric. Finish off with masking tape or pins to hold the end of the strip in place. (See Figure. 4) Before going on, check to see that the fabric doesn't interfere with the complete mobility of the joints. If there is any impediment to Kandu's action, rewind the stripping. When you're satisfied you've done a good job, then, and not before, you're ready for gluing.

Any household cold-water glue will serve. Just paint the glue over the top of the fabric with a brush, while the puppet is hanging from a support. Begin with the head and work down to the feet. Let the glue sink below the surface, set, and dry. It's much easier to wind the stripping dry and glue afterward than to glue as you go along, which is the customary method. This way only the marionette will get glued, not you, and you can correct any mistakes as you go along, before they become problems.

KANDU'S FACE

Now Kandu's head is a skin-covered egg. The egg has to be molded into the likeness of a human face. We'll suggest a simple face for him, but there are variations you may wish to explore in Part Two.

For the face to be more human, it needs brow ridges, eyes, cheekbones, a nose, a mouth, a chin, and ears. Kandu's face doesn't have to be a literal reproduction of a human being's, but if you have trouble finding a model for him, this is easy to solve. Look into a mirror and caricature what you see there. Or work from a magazine photograph or a poster.

16

It would be wise at this juncture to determine Kandu's characterization. Is he to be young or old? Handsome or funny-looking? Does he possess any unique quality that should be reflected in his appearance? Since his face and voice are closely related, your decision about the former will be influenced by the kind of voice you can give him. (See page 38 on Kandu's voice.)

How do you create features? By building up the "egg." By applying additional material to the areas you want to bulge out. Toilet or facial tissue is excellent for this purpose. Make small wads of it, soak them in water, squeeze out the excess water, and press the wads, one at a time, onto the face where you want to build it up. Smooth the wads out with your fingers and shape them into the bones that underlie the skin on a human face. Keep adding wads until the face takes on the appearance you wish.

Inasmuch as Kandu is to possess affability and charm, give him the kind of features that suggest these to you. If you think a Roman nose endearing, give him a dilly. If Grecian noses appeal to you, or little button pug noses, this is one of the ways you can make your Kandu different from any other.

You can make Kandu even more particularly your own by the facial hair, if any, you give him. His eyebrows can be built up. So can a mustache or a goatee or a beard, a forked one. The hair of his head can be built up the same way, or it can be made from a variety of other materials. See Part Two and Figure 10.)

As you work on the face, from time to time turn the head toward a single overhead light source and examine your progress from different angles. The single light source will create sharper shadows than diffused or multidirectional lighting, and it will show you where you need "filling."

When you've built up Kandu's features to where you are satisfied, take a thin, dry piece of tissue and plaster it dry across the wet wads. Smooth everything out with your fingers and paint it with glue. Let all the paper dry thoroughly.

If the wadded areas are not smoothed in enough to the surrounding facial parts, you can use white tempera paint to fill in, and use it as thickly as you can.

PAINTING KANDU

Kandu is now ready to be painted. If you're going to give him head or facial hair of something other than the paper-sculpted surface, something that has a color you want to keep, don't apply it until after the paint is dry to keep it from being messed up.

As a preparation to painting, brush or spray on a thin coat of shellac to seal the surface of Kandu's skin to cut down on the amount of paint required.

Tempera (poster paint) is fine for Kandu's skin and hair. Usually one coat is enough, but if it doesn't cover adequately, let the first dry before putting on the second coat. Tempera colors are darker wet than dry, so take this into consideration. It's a sound idea to experiment with all color mixtures on a separate test sheet before painting Kandu. Let the test color dry thoroughly. If the result is not satisfactory and you adjust the mix, repeat the test until the dry results are perfect.

Where Kandu's skin is not to be covered by costume or hair, it should be painted in flesh tones. If his flesh is to be Caucasian, don't make the common mistake of painting him too pink. So-called white skin is a peachy combination of red and white with a splash of raw sienna. Oriental skin is not yellow; to give a realistic tone, use the same mix as for "white" but with slightly less red and slightly more sienna. Similarly, "black" skin is not black; it comes in tones of brown that range from *café au lait* to very dark brown. These "blacks" can be obtained by mixing burnt umber with either white or a bit of black to make the basic brown lighter or darker.

After the flesh tones dry, paint irises and whites on the eyeballs and paint the eyebrows, the mustache, beard, and head hair, if they are paper-sculpted. To avoid the masklike effect of having the face all one flat and uninteresting color, you can apply make-up to Kandu very much the way an actor applies stage make-up. To give life and sparkle to the lips, dampen them with a brush dipped in clear water and then blend a little red into the wet area. If the color doesn't dry brightly enough, intensify it with additional red. A flush along the cheekbones can be added the same way.

If you want to put shadows under the cheekbones, the lower lip, or the eyes, dampen the

areas and blend a little umber in—or a touch of black if the skin is dark brown to begin with.

When Kandu looks just right to you, give his skin a thin coat of shellac to retain the finish. Otherwise, if he gets wet, the tempera paint will wash off.

There's one more step in his make-up. Wherever you want highlights—the lower lip, the cheekbones, the eyeballs—put on a dab of glossy varnish. These are small touches, but they brighten up a face.

Kandu's head is now finished, if you've sculpted his hair.

KANDU'S HAIR

If you've left off Kandu's hair so far because you want a different effect from that "built-in" hair would give, now is when to get around to it.

Hair can be made of any number of materials. (See Part Two, Figure 10.) Some of these, like sponge and plastic foam, can be glued directly to Kandu's scalp with any white household glue. A wig of yarn is effective and easy to make. Take the heel of a stocking and shape it to the head. If it fits snugly enough, it won't need to be glued on. This has the advantage of enabling you to change the hair style easily if you want to create a different character for the same puppet. Use enough yarn when you sew loops onto the stocking heel so that the head of hair looks full (Figure 10). When you have sewn on enough loops, you can cut them open. If the finished wig isn't tight to the head, glue or pin it on.

Eyebrows, mustache, and beard of yarn or other material can be glued directly onto Kandu's face, or they can first be attached to a base of muslin or some similar fabric and then glued on.

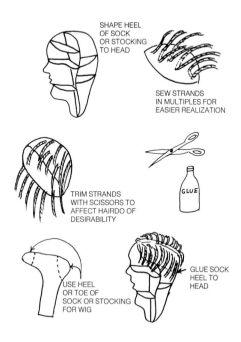

SHAPE HEEL OF SOCK OR STOCKING TO HEAD

SEW STRANDS IN MULTIPLES FOR EASIER REALIZATION

TRIM STRANDS WITH SCISSORS TO AFFECT HAIRDO OF DESIRABILITY

GLUE

USE HEEL OR TOE OF SOCK OR STOCKING FOR WIG

GLUE SOCK HEEL TO HEAD

FIGURE 10

18

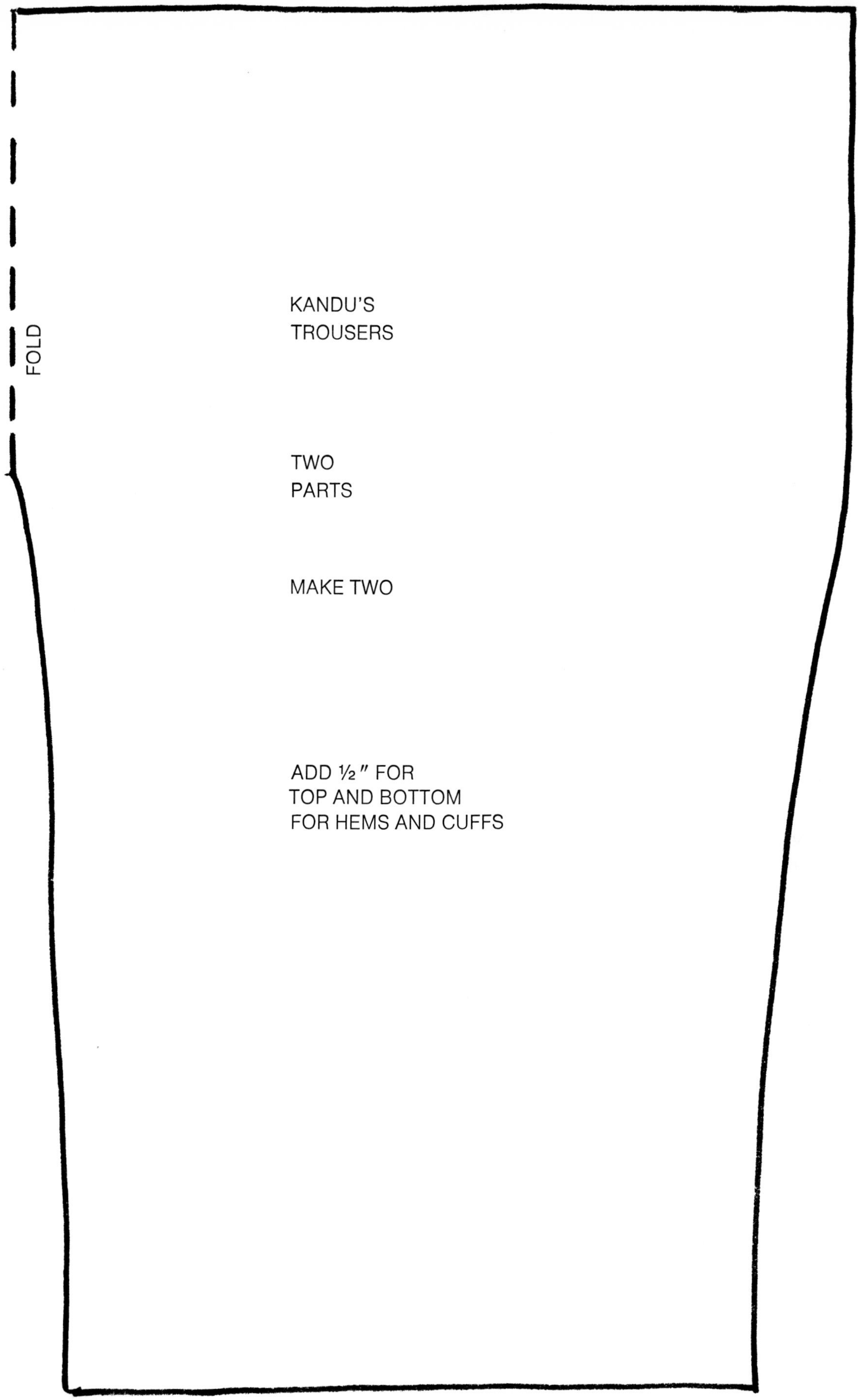

KANDU'S
TROUSERS

TWO
PARTS

MAKE TWO

ADD ½″ FOR
TOP AND BOTTOM
FOR HEMS AND CUFFS

FIGURE 11

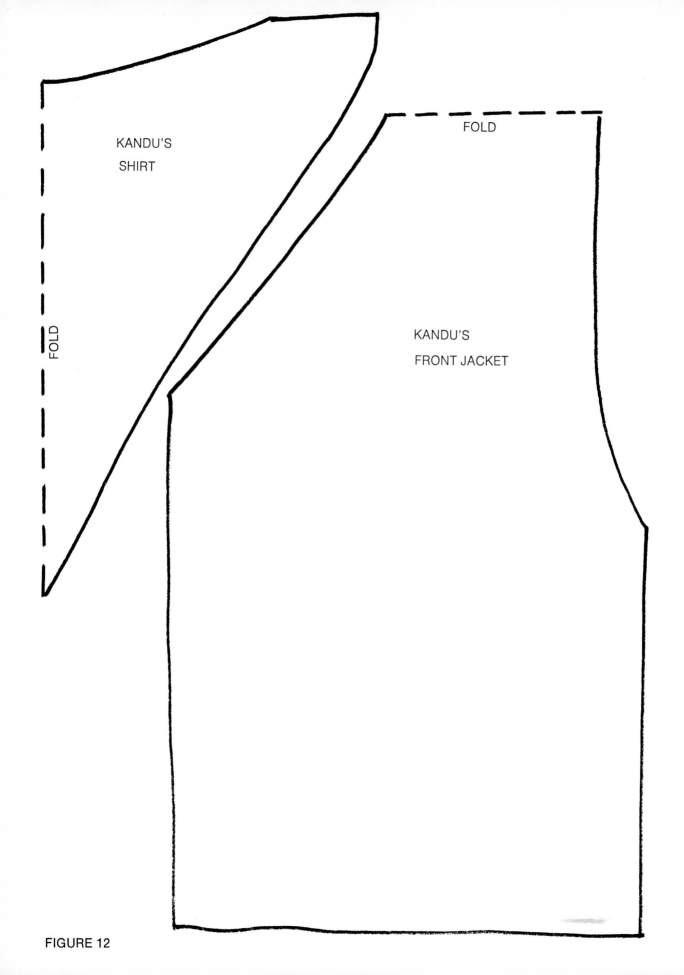

KANDU'S
SHIRT

FOLD

FOLD

KANDU'S
FRONT JACKET

FIGURE 12

KANDU'S FEET

Painting Kandu's lower legs and feet black will take care of them with dispatch. If you want him to have shiny shoes, draw lines to indicate the top of his shoes and varnish the feet below the lines.

COSTUMING KANDU

Kandu has on his stage make-up, but obviously he can't appear in public without his costume and all the paraphernalia that go into the making of a magician. Our Kandu is to be a man of the world—smooth, debonair, and very much the master of his craft. He'll want to go onstage impeccably clad in his top hat, black tie, dinner jacket, and cape (Figures 11 through 17). Of course, these can't be ordinary dress clothes. They're designed to enable him to perform his routines. He's going to pull a rabbit out of his hat, produce a bouquet of flowers from his lapel, do a card trick, and bring on a bird from nowhere.

Patterns are provided for Kandu's garments. His suit and cape can be cut from any smooth, dressy black fabric. A ribbon stripe of satin down the side of each leg and a facing of satin on the lapels will add panache. His dashing black cape can be lined with a bright red satin, with stripes, or another design emphasizing vertical lines. The cape pattern includes secret pockets for the magical tricks. Figure 15 indicates how the lining should be attached.

Since only the front and cuffs of the shirt will show, the shirt pattern is for these parts only (Figure 12). The shirt can be tailored or ruffled. A pattern is also supplied for the tie.

If you've never done any sewing before, don't be daunted. These days there are a variety of substitutes for needle and thread and several brands of glue work fine for hems, cuffs, and such.

Be sure to iron his clothes before you dress Kandu. You may also want to spray them with Scotchgard or some other similar preparation to keep them clean as long as possible.

To dress Kandu, slip his trousers on. Add his shirt front and then the vest. With a few stitches, tack all three garments together where the stitches won't show when he's fully clothed. Fasten the shirt cuffs to the inside of the jacket cuffs and then put the jacket on Kandu. A couple of tacking stitches here and there will hold the jacket to the vest. The tie need be tacked to the collar only.

If you care to add to Kandu's costume, optional accessories could include cufflinks, a watch chain, and other jewelry. Spangles and sequins sewn or glued on the costume will turn Kandu into an even more theatrical wizard.

Kandu's feet and ankles have already been painted black for shoes and socks. If you wish, you can glue on small buckles, buttons, tassels, or shoestring bows.

The hat with its rabbit and the other magical properties will be dealt with under "Props."

GIVING KANDU LIFE

Marionettes are different from all other puppets in that they alone are worked by strings. They alone rely on gravity to hold them to the earth, just as do actual living beings. It is this that gives their movements an almost uncanny resemblance to those of real people and animals. Other forms of puppets are frequently made with only a head, torso, and arms—and sometimes even less. A marionette nearly always exists as a total being, with all its limbs movable, so that the puppeteer can transmit a wide spectrum of agile movements to his creature.

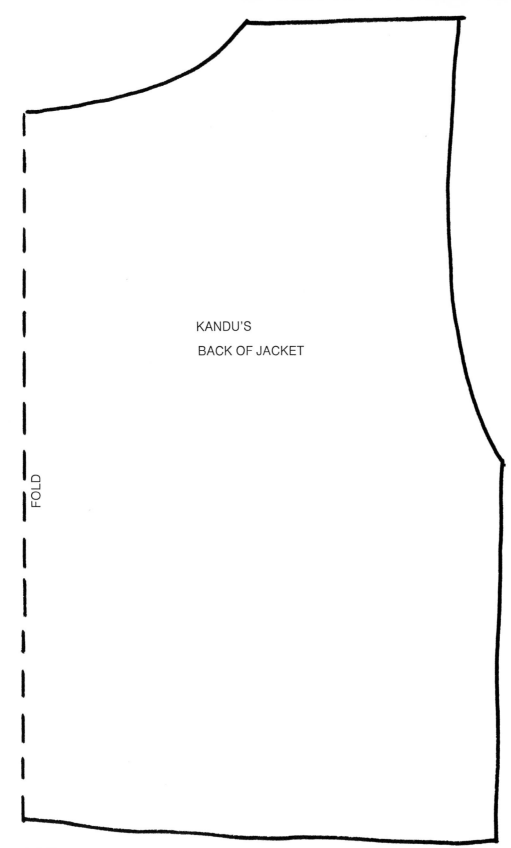

KANDU'S

BACK OF JACKET

FOLD

FIGURE 13

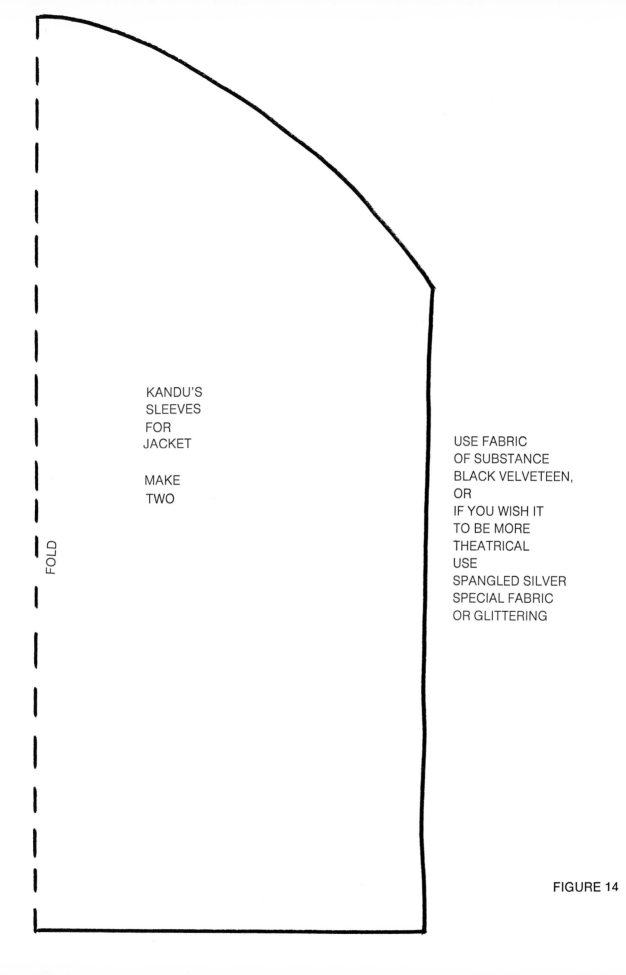

KANDU'S
SLEEVES
FOR
JACKET

MAKE
TWO

FOLD

USE FABRIC
OF SUBSTANCE
BLACK VELVETEEN,
OR
IF YOU WISH IT
TO BE MORE
THEATRICAL
USE
SPANGLED SILVER
SPECIAL FABRIC
OR GLITTERING

FIGURE 14

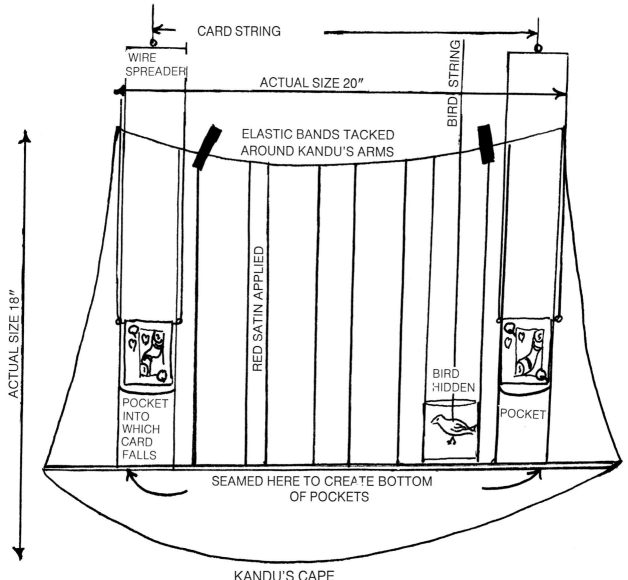

KANDU'S CAPE
ONE FOURTH FULL SIZE

ON BLACK FABRIC APPLY RED SATIN STRIPES
TO ADD COLOR AND DISTRACTION

(BIRD IS DUPLICATE OF ONE IN CAGE)

FIGURE 15

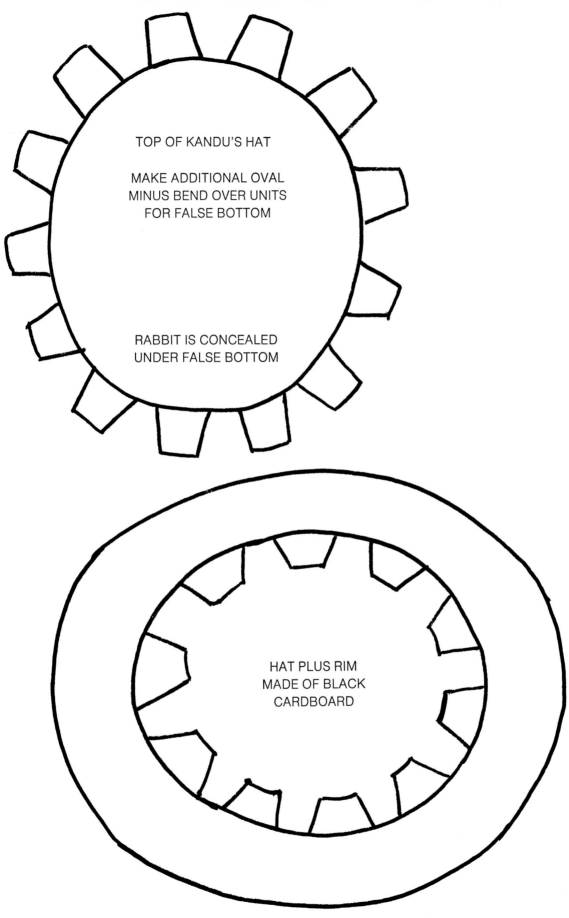

TOP OF KANDU'S HAT

MAKE ADDITIONAL OVAL
MINUS BEND OVER UNITS
FOR FALSE BOTTOM

RABBIT IS CONCEALED
UNDER FALSE BOTTOM

HAT PLUS RIM
MADE OF BLACK
CARDBOARD

FIGURE 16

↑

Add 1¼ " for CROWN or measure the girth of completed head to attain the proper size after allowing for hair style

Hat should fit snuggly

Adjust all sizes to your marionette when completed

KANDU'S
HAT

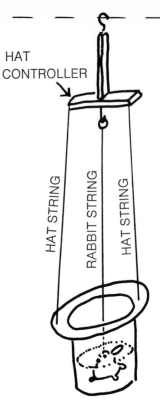

HAT
CONTROLLER

HAT STRING

RABBIT STRING

HAT STRING

KANDU'S
TOP HAT
SHOWING RABBIT
UNDER FALSE
BOTTOM

FIGURE 17

Your muscles pull your bones to move your body. The strings on the marionette are its muscles, and the stringing must be done so that the marionette can do everything required of it. You, the puppeteer, must control its body as well as your own, to make it virtually an extension of yourself.

For the novice puppeteer, stringing the marionette is at once the most frightening and thrilling part of creating a puppet. The controls appear complicated. And even if the stringing is done properly, can someone who is all thumbs work them? The answer is *Yes*. Of course manipulation of marionettes requires skill, but it's a skill acquired with only a little practice when you use the simplified system shown in the figures.

KANDU'S CONTROLLER

The controller is the operating mechanism of the marionette. Kandu's is the "double airplane," so called because it looks like two

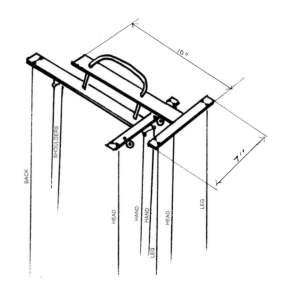

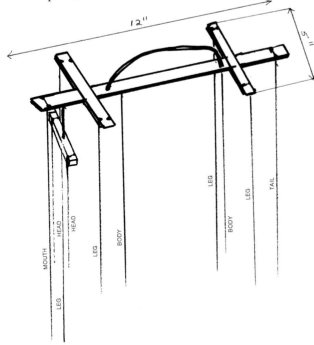

planes, one above the other and a couple of inches forward. Figure 18A shows how to construct the controller. If you wish to notch the wood strips where they cross each other so that they dovetail and fit flush, the controller will look more professional but it will work no better than strips nailed together with brads. Make sure the crossbars are firmly attached. Put notch saw cuts in the back ends of the crosspieces (Figure 19). The two "T's" are then placed one on top of the other with the top unit about two inches forward. Drill two quarter-inch holes through the two T-bars. Then loop heavy twine (Venetian-blind cord is ideal; heavy shoe laces are also serviceable.) between the two bars, knotting it in such a fashion that at least one and one-quarter inches of space exists between the two bars. It is from this U-shaped loop that Kandu hangs when he is not onstage.

Two screw eyes are fastened to the forward part of the bottom T-bar and two screw eyes to the lower bar, about two and one half inches from the back. (See Figure 19.)

The controller should be painted a dull black to have low visibility and reflect a minimum of light. This is essential if your manipulation is to be in full view of the audience.

If splinters or cracks develop in the controller, they should be sanded smooth or otherwise repaired immediately to prevent the strings from catching in the rough spots and breaking or tangling.

KANDU'S STRINGS

For the strings that will move Kandu, use black nylon or heavy upholstery cotton. Black is the least conspicuous color because it absorbs a maximum of light. Several puppeteers have experimented with white strings against a white background, but they failed to take into consideration that the white strings reflected more light than the black, and when spotlights were focused on the stage the additional light emphasized the white strings more.

Kandu has the nine basic strings of every puppet in addition to those that enable him to do his tricks. We'll deal with the special ones later. Now we have to prepare him for normal activities: walking, sitting, kneeling, bowing, and moving his head and arms.

STRINGING KANDU (Basic Strings)

The first thing to do in stringing a puppet is to suspend the double airplane controller from any stable hanger. Make an "S" hook (a heavy wire shaped in the form of an "S"). Wire from a metal clothes hanger is ideal for this purpose. This "S" hook is looped around any fixed sturdy object, about five feet off the ground (one end of a bureau, secretary, bookcase, etc.). See to it that the hook is firmly placed, one end on the furniture and the other to the heavy twine of the controller.

Now take a string approximately six feet long and run it through the two screw eyes that are

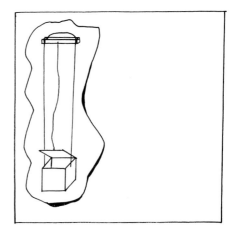

FIGURE 20

about two and one half inches from the back of the controller. Each end of the string is attached to a shoulder of the puppet. The stringing is attached to the puppet and not to the costume. You may have to penetrate the costume with a heavy needle to find the holding place indicated on the pattern by a triangle. As you string Kandu, test each effort as you go along to check whether the movement is realistic. The strings should be fairly taut. Adjustments should be made at the controller, where notches have been provided.

Make sure Kandu is facing forward and that the crossbar pieces of the controller are also forward. In all people marionettes the shoulders carry the weight of the entire figure, so it's important that this string that holds up the puppet be sturdy and unfrayed.

Another six-foot string goes through the two screw eyes in the front of the controller. Each end goes to a hand. The part of the hand that is attached determines how Kandu will use his hand. For general use, it's best to put one end to the right thumb and the other to the middle finger of the left hand. This allows for different gestures with each hand.

All the rest of the strings are about three feet long.

The head strings are next, one to each side of the head. At this stage, because Kandu is a magician, insert a strong piece of wire through the head about where the ears are set. (See Figure.40) This wire should be about six inches long, with loops on either end, and it must be wider than the brim of the top hat. Attach the head strings to the wire loops and to the crossbar made for the head. If your puppet wears no hat, then of course the wire rod is unnecessary and the strings attach directly to the head where the triangles are indicated on the pattern.

A string from Kandu's spine (*waist* section) goes to the back end of the controller, and two strings from the upper crossbar go to the front of the knees. These add up to a total of nine, the basic strings that give Kandu movement.

STRINGING KANDU (Special Strings)

Kandu will be performing several marvelous feats of magic, so special stringing is essential to work them. One special string goes to the flower in Kandu's lapel (see pages 51–53 in "Props"), the other end being attached to the forward part of the controller. This string should be looser than the others so that it will not agitate the flower and call attention to it prematurely. Two other strings for the disappearing cards are needled to the cards through the cape and go to the forward part

FIGURE 21

of the controller. These three strings are attached to small leather flaps that have been anchored to the controller (Figure 19). Another optional special string is for a little bird concealed in a pocket of the cape. This three-foot string, however, goes to a loose ring on a cup hook screwed into the forward part of the controller (Figures 19 and 26). For easy identification, these four special strings can be marked on the controller.

MANIPULATING KANDU

With the stringing completed, Kandu can be said to be truly born. He was created to be a performer, but his muscles, the strings, are moved by your hands and he can do nothing without you. Study him and acquaint yourself with the location of each string on the controller, and you're halfway home in manipulation.

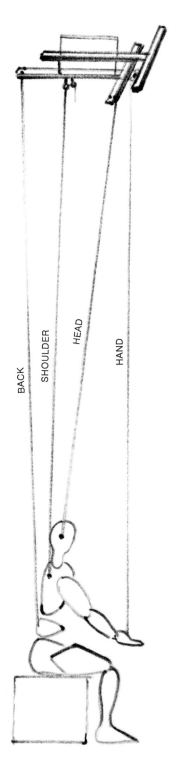

FIGURE 22

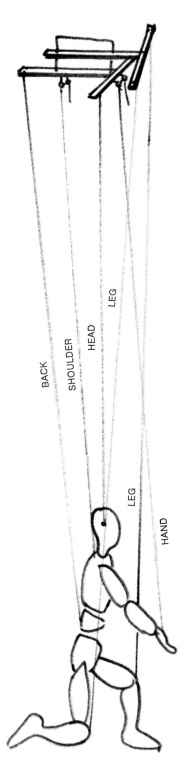

FIGURE 23

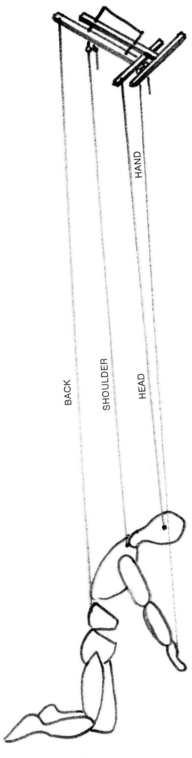

BACK

SHOULDER

HEAD

HAND

FIGURE 24

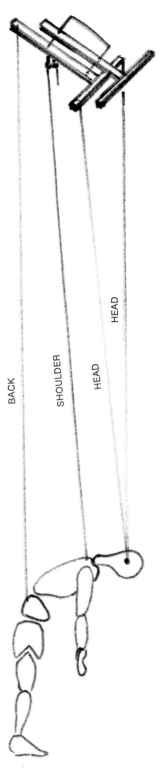

BACK

SHOULDER

HEAD

HEAD

FIGURE 25

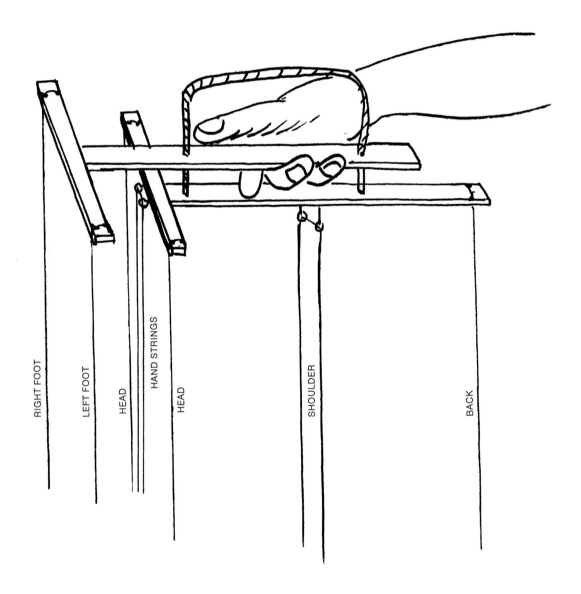

RIGHT FOOT

LEFT FOOT

HEAD

HAND STRINGS

HEAD

SHOULDER

BACK

GRIPPING CONTROLLER ABOVE
SHOULDER STRINGS GIVES THE
BEST BALANCED CONTROL

FIGURE 26

Learning how to handle the controller is the first step. Follow the directions here and in the diagrams (or photographs) if you are right-handed. If you are left-handed, reverse them.

For all movements, your right hand, palm down, grips the controller at the point where the shoulder strings (the ones through the screw eyes) are attached (See Figure 26.) This is your leverage point and all movements center here. This right hand will control the head, bowing, and walking. The left hand is reserved for all special and detailed movements. And now let's learn the basic actions.

Walking (Figure 27). Raise the upper part of the controller in a sideways rocking movement, and the legs will respond. This is marching in place. To move forward, lift the controller while pushing it forward simultaneously. Keep your hand directly over the puppet, moving forward with your body as the puppet advances. Be sure Kandu's feet touch the ground when he walks, as he would in real life. If he doesn't learn to keep his feet on the ground as quickly as you'd like, tape a three-quarter-inch washer on the sole of each shoe near the toe. This will help him find the floor. Walking is perhaps the most difficult action to learn, but there's no excuse for slovenly, inept manipulation.

Sitting (Figure 22). This is relatively easy. Hold the leg strings taut and allow the rest of the puppet to drop by gravity. In practicing sitting, it will be helpful if Kandu has a rock or chair (scaled to his size) to sit on, though he should learn to sit on the floor too.

Kneeling (Figures 23 and 24). Use the left hand to lift the string of one leg slightly, thrust the controller forward, dip it, and Kandu will go down on one knee. To make him go down on

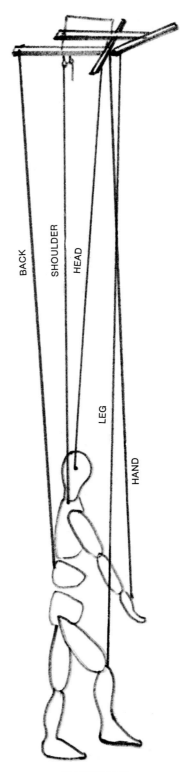

FIGURE 27

33

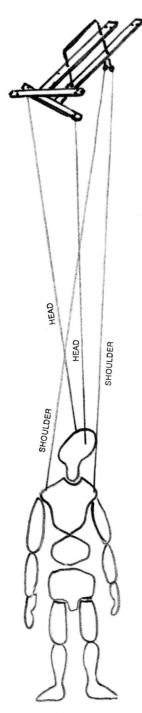

FIGURE 28

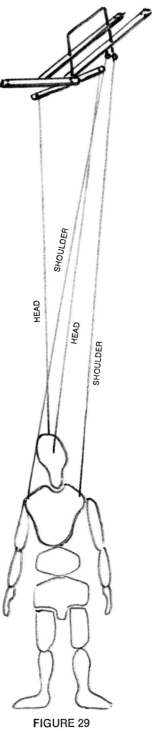

FIGURE 29

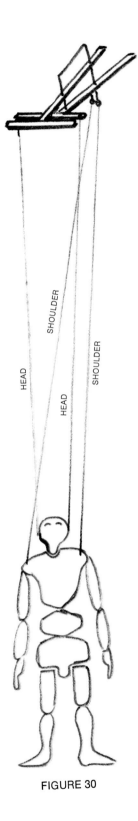

FIGURE 30

both knees, give a full dip and thrust the controller forward. To return him to a standing position, lift one leg string at a time to imitate human movement. Don't have Kandu jump up from a double kneeling position.

Bowing (Figure 25). Merely dip the complete controller, holding the back string taut and keeping Kandu's feet firmly on the ground.

Head Movements (Figures 28, 29, and 30). Dip the controller downward slightly and the head will nod affirmatively or sleepily. Dip the controller from side to side to show a negative response. When Kandu speaks, move the head in unison with the words.

Arm Movements (Figure 31). To gesture in accordance with speech, reach your left hand around to lift one or the other of the strings attached to Kandu's hands. Whether the speech is positive or negative, calm or impassioned, will determine how strong your movement should be and its direction. If the gesture expresses doubt, a dip down and sideward up movement is effective. To reach for something, lift one or both arm strings toward a specific object, simultaneously turning the complete controller to left or right if a change in direction is desired.

PRACTICING MANIPULATION

Most puppeteers find it helpful to practice before a full-length mirror so that they can see what they're doing and how it looks to someone else. Don't be discouraged if you don't attain full mastery of the techniques in one or two sessions. The practice is fun in itself, and there's no substitute for the satisfaction you'll derive as you see yourself becoming more proficient daily.

35

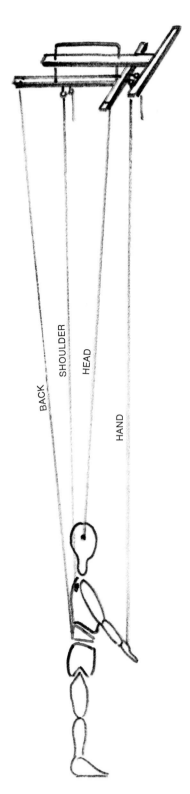

BACK
SHOULDER
HEAD
HAND

FIGURE 31

Tangled strings are the novice puppeteer's greatest dread. Wrapping, or putting a marionette to bed properly, is the answer to most of the problem. When putting a marionette away, hang it from its hanging strap to make sure that all strings are taut. Then put the marionette feet first into a laundry bag or a bag made specifically for it. The bag should enclose the entire marionette, except for the strings and controller. Release the hanging strap, which has been suspended all this time, and carefully wind all the strings around the controller, usually on the diagonal from cross-piece to cross-piece, since this requires less winding (Figure 32). When the controller reaches the puppet in the bag, secure the bag's tie cords around the controller with a bow knot or other easily opened knot. Wrap the same way each time to establish good working habits.

Of course, problems will arise. You can follow all the rules and still end up with tangles. A string may break and wind around the others. Or catch on a splinter of the controller, or foul up in the crevices of the crossbar. But these are easily straightened out, provided only one string—or even two—is out of order. The only time you have a real problem with strings is when they are *all* fouled up. If you wrap your marionette carefully, this can only happen through an accident beyond your control. For example, a child backstage can get at your puppet strings and create havoc. Sometimes the best way to untangle them is to go back to the beginning, provided the shoulder strings are still in good order. All except the shoulder and hand strings have been attached to notches and can be easily disassembled. Hang the puppet from its hanging strap, slip the individual

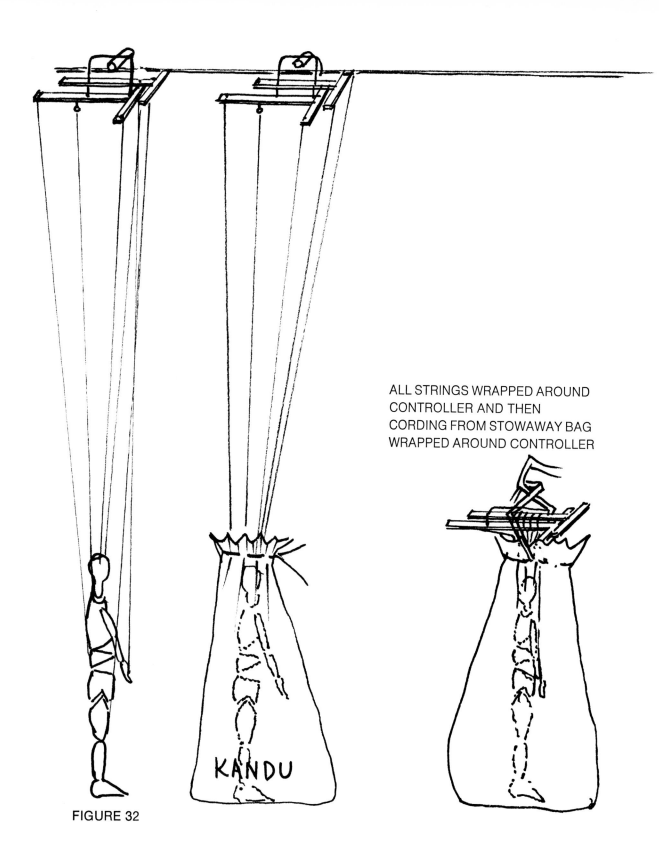

ALL STRINGS WRAPPED AROUND
CONTROLLER AND THEN
CORDING FROM STOWAWAY BAG
WRAPPED AROUND CONTROLLER

KANDU

FIGURE 32

strings from their notches, and let them drop. When they've all been disconnected, with only the shoulder and hand strings remaining, it should be a simple matter to pull out one string at a time and slip it back into its proper notch: leg string to leg bar, back string to back end of controller, and head strings to head bar. Special strings besides the basic nine will have to be dealt with similarly.

KANDU'S VOICE

If you have introduced Kandu in your own natural voice, or your own voice modified somewhat for theatrical purposes, you'll want Kandu's voice to be different enough so that the audience will regard the marionette as a creature apart from you—his own man, with his own existence. Creating such an illusion is the supreme thrill of the puppeteer.

KANDU'S VOCAL RANGE

Before you decide on the voice for Kandu, which, of course, must emanate from your throat, it's a good idea to try out a variety of voices. Whether to make Kandu's voice higher or lower than yours, or with a different resonance, depends on how long you can sustain the characterization without experiencing discomfort. If Kandu is to be "spoken for" by a woman, she might want to conceive of him as youngish, with a relatively light voice. Or he could be an old man with a cracked voice, which might be more comfortable for her natural register. For a man to do Kandu, his range could be from falsetto to bass. A child speaking for Kandu could interpret him as also being a child essaying an adult role. Whichever, the voice should be in accord with Kandu's face, and one or the other may have to be modified.

KANDU'S ACCENT, LAUGH, ETC.

Accents can be fun if they are consistently maintained and if they are in good taste. You want to entertain your audience, not offend any ethnic group. But if your presentation is honest and your accent is used to lend added charm or mystery to Kandu, then try an accent and see how it goes.

If you want Kandu to laugh, cough, or sneeze —practice! There are few stunts more difficult for the beginner than to laugh or sneeze convincingly on cue.

MAKING RUFF
TRACING, CUTTING OUT, ASSEMBLING, AND CONNECTING

Now that you have completed Kandu, Ruff's construction will be comparatively simple.

Trace and cut out Ruff's modular pieces, as you did with Kandu. As before, the *head* is a good starting place in assembling the complete dog.

Ruff's Head and Neck (Figure 33) consist of three basic pieces plus six interlocking modules. The "A" piece interlocks through the mouth and the "B" piece interlocks with the neck. Modules 1 through 6 complete the *head* and *neck* as one unit.

Ruff's Chest (Figure 33) is made up of eight pieces. The *chest side view* consists of two identical pieces, one directly on top of the other, with a slot marked "C." Slot "C" interlocks with the "C" slot on the *top view*, which needs a double thickness cut to accommodate it. The two remaining identical *side view* modules, marked "A" and "B," respectively, interlock with the "A" and "B" slots on the *top view*. The smaller Modules 1, 2, and 3 interlock with their corresponding slots.

MAKING RUFF—TRACING PATTERNS

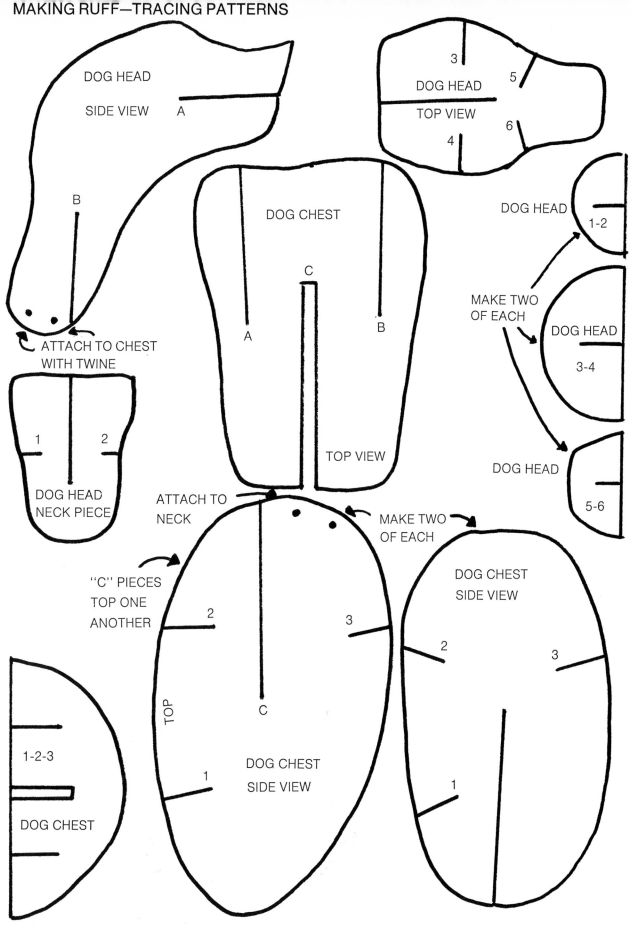

DOG HEAD
SIDE VIEW   A

B

ATTACH TO CHEST
WITH TWINE

1   2

DOG HEAD
NECK PIECE

DOG CHEST

C

A   B

TOP VIEW

ATTACH TO
NECK

"C" PIECES
TOP ONE
ANOTHER

2

TOP

3

C

1

DOG CHEST
SIDE VIEW

1-2-3

DOG CHEST

3
DOG HEAD
TOP VIEW   5

6

4

DOG HEAD
1-2

MAKE TWO
OF EACH

DOG HEAD
3-4

DOG HEAD
5-6

MAKE TWO
OF EACH

DOG CHEST
SIDE VIEW

2   3

1

FIGURE 33

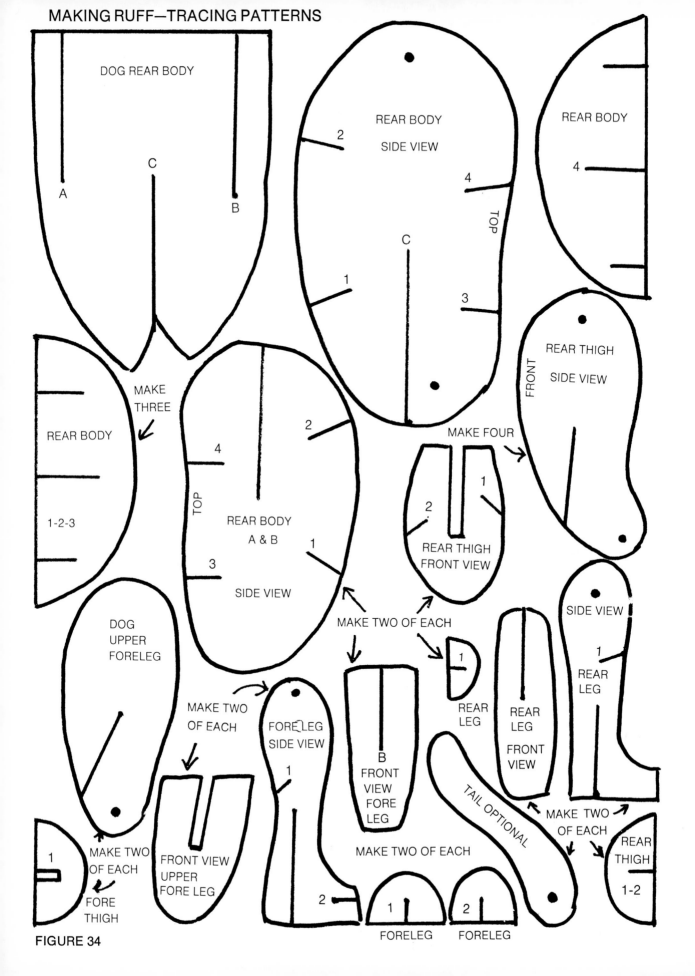

MAKING RUFF—TRACING PATTERNS

FIGURE 34

To join Ruff's *neck* to his *chest*, place the assembled *head* unit so that the holes in the *neck* line up with the holes in the *chest* and join the sections together with string.

Ruff's Rear Body (Figure 34) is composed of eight pieces. The three *side views* interlock with the *top view*, as indicated, and then the four other modules interlock number to number.

After the *rear body* is assembled, join it to the *chest* unit, remembering to hinge the *rear body* insertions into the double thickness of the *chest* pieces.

Ruff's Rear Thigh (Figure 34; don't forget—cut two!) is composed of five pieces; *front view*, two *side views* that combine to make one module of double thickness, and two interlocking modules of single thickness with a double-thickness slot. Assemble each *thigh* by interlocking the modules as indicated.

Ruff's Rear Lower Legs (Figure 34) are each composed of three pieces: a *front view*, a *side view*, and one interlocking module, to be assembled in the usual manner.

To join the *thigh* and the *lower leg*, make the customary wire hinge. The combined *leg* assemblage is then attached to the *rear body* the same way.

Ruff's basic structure is now complete, except for his *forelegs* and *tail*.

Ruff's Upper Forelegs (Figure 34) are each composed of four pieces: a double-thickness *side view*, a *front view*, and an interlocking module, to be assembled as usual.

Ruff's Lower Forelegs (Figure 34) are also each composed of four pieces: a *front view*, a *side view*, and two interlocking modules. Assemble as indicated.

The *upper* and *lower foreleg* are hinged together by wire and then hinged as units to the chest, with each double *upper foreleg* module enclosing a single-thickness *chest* piece at the joint.

Ruff's Tail doesn't need a cardboard skeleton. The fabric tail cut from the pattern for his covering (Figure 35) just gets sewed to Ruff's rear end where a tail should go.

Check all movable parts to see that they are free-moving. Loosen the wires if more flexibility is necessary. All joint areas should be shellacked, and, when dry, a little talcum powder should be applied to them to reduce friction. If you want more mobility, put an extra sliver of cardboard between the double pieces to spread them farther apart.

COVERING RUFF

Now it's time to give Ruff his coat. Decide what kind of dog he is to be. If you want to make him as shaggy as an English sheepdog, a fake fur or a high pile or looped fabric (as is common in bathroom mats and seat covers) is good. Terrycloth (turkish toweling) works well for a short-hair.

Trace the patterns (Figures 35 and 36) onto see-through paper and then cut them out. Lay your fabric out on a flat surface. If the fabric has a heavy pile, put the pile side down and work from the wrong side. Place the paper patterns on the fabric and pin them into position. Cut the fabric around the patterns.

Now put a looped string through the two triangular holes in the top of the *chest* and *rear body* and suspend Ruff at a convenient working height.

Lay the fabric pieces over the parts of Ruff's skeleton they are to cover. Sew each piece snugly to itself around the body, legs, etc., with the seams on the inside of the body. The fabric pieces don't attach to the cardboard or to each

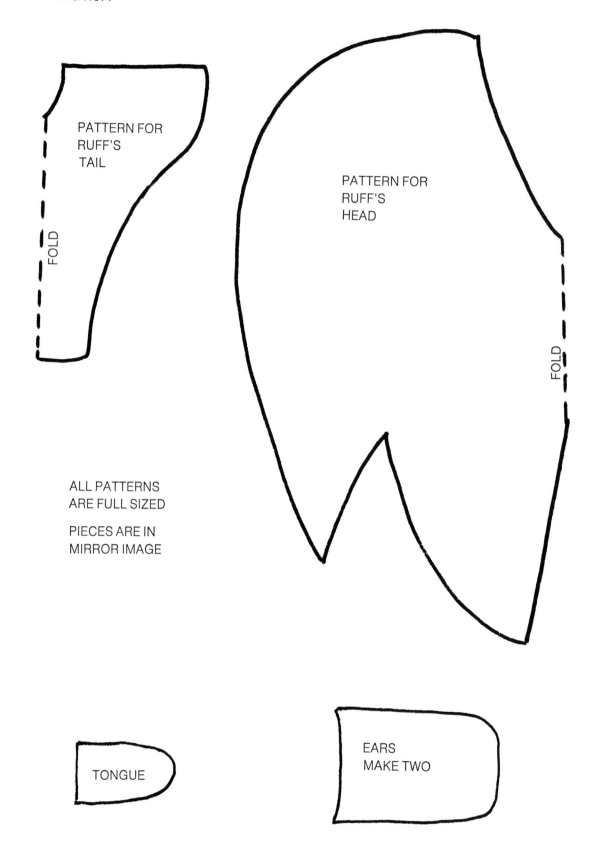

PATTERN FOR
RUFF'S
TAIL

FOLD

PATTERN FOR
RUFF'S
HEAD

FOLD

ALL PATTERNS
ARE FULL SIZED

PIECES ARE IN
MIRROR IMAGE

TONGUE

EARS
MAKE TWO

FIGURE 35

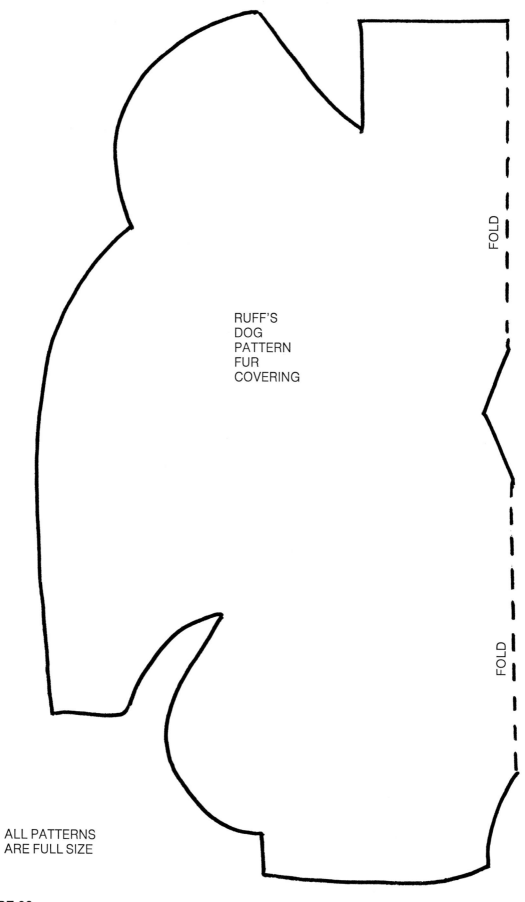

RUFF'S
DOG
PATTERN
FUR
COVERING

FOLD

FOLD

ALL PATTERNS
ARE FULL SIZE

FIGURE 36

Sally and Shirley Suib are putting Ruff together after cutting the parts from the patterns. *Photo: M. Richardson*

other. Ruff's joints are concealed by overlapping fabric edges. When covering the joints, be careful not to curtail Ruff's freedom of movement.

Leave the hanging strings exposed. If necessary, make a small hole in the fabric for them to come through.

Ears and tongue can be attached after the head is covered and buttons for eyes sewed on or glued. Add the tail and presto! Kandu's best friend is complete.

GIVING RUFF LIFE
RUFF'S CONTROLLER

Since Ruff will walk on four legs most of the time and has a tail to wag, his controller differs from Kandu's (Figure 18). Only one long stick with two crossbars is necessary, plus a small dropped bar for the head. A screw eye goes into the forward end of the long stick.

STRINGING RUFF

All Ruff's strings are cut to three feet, except for the six-foot *ear* string. After the *chest* and *rear body* strings are in place, the length of the other strings is adjusted to them.

All strings attach to the covering, not to the cardboard skeleton.

Ruff's first strings are from the long stick of the controller to the top of the *chest* and the top of the *rear body*. One string for each *leg* attaches above the middle joint from an end of a crossbar.

The *tail* string attaches to the back end of the long stick.

A string from each side of the *head* just behind the base of the ears attaches to the ends of the dropped bar. The six-foot-long string goes from the tip of one ear through the screw eye and down to the tip of the other ear.

44

Peter Suib working both Kandu and Ruff at home.

MANIPULATING RUFF

A four-legged animal puppet never gives an entirely lifelike movement, but skillful manipulation results in acceptable movement.

Walking. Wobble the controller in a rocking side-to-side manner, advancing it as you do.

Galloping. Rock the controller forward and back, raising first the front legs off the ground and then the back, advancing it as you do.

Sitting. Relax the rear end of the controller —and Ruff's rear end. Keep his front feet and rump on the floor.

Sitting Up. Raise the forward end of the controller and relax the rear end perpendicularly.

Head Movements. Use the same techniques for Ruff's head movements as you do for Kandu's.

Ear Movements. Lift one or both ear strings to perk up the ears.

Tail Movements. Waggle the tail string.

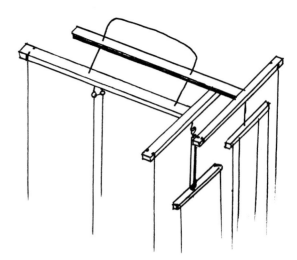

FIGURE 37

RUFF'S VOICE

As you analyzed Kandu's appearance and characterization in order to develop an appropriate voice for him, you must do as much for Ruff. Your experience with real dogs has made you aware of the many ways dogs can use their voices to communicate, as well as their ears and tails and assorted body movements. Of course he can bark, but he can also whine, whimper, yip, growl, snarl, and scream. He won't need his full vocabulary for his part as written, but he will be barking. If you go on to expand his role subsequently, then you'll work on the other sounds he'll be making.

Ruff is an exhibitionist. He deliberates to make his effects. But is he a large dog with a big bark or a small dog with a tiny bark? He barks proudly when he gives the correct answer to a question put to him as a test. An affirmative bark to a conversational inquiry would have another inflection. No "dialogue" for Ruff has been indicated when he investigates the box, but if you want him to whine or whimper and you can manage it while Kandu is making his spiel to the audience, fine! Ruff's voice should have whatever nuances a human voice would take on according to the requirements of the script.

Practice barking until you can manage a *r-r-ruff!* that belongs to Ruff and satisfies you. Ruff is full of life—but the life is yours.

46

SECTION 2

PREPARING THE SHOW

Kandu and Ruff are not dolls. They are marionettes—by definition, performers. It's not enough for you to have created them and learned how to make them move and talk. They require a theater in which to come fully to life and a vehicle through which they can express themselves. How simple or elaborate you want their performance to be and how much time and effort you are willing to put into it—these considerations will affect your next steps into the marionette's world.

A STAGE FOR KANDU

No theatrical venture has value until it's presented to an audience, so Kandu will need a performing area. The simplest way to present Kandu to an audience is in any cleared space —in a living room, a hospital ward, or a library —without any formal stage apparatus. There may be circumstances that could make this kind of presentation desirable. But since Kandu is a magician, he should be allowed to present his tricks with the superior showmanship and protection for his secrets only a stage can provide.

Here, in the order of increasing complexity— and theatrical effectiveness—are four stages that will serve to frame the performance and focus attention on it. The last two have an important additional advantage: They raise the performance to a level where an audience beyond the first row can see it.

In this part of the book, even the most complicated of these stages is relatively easy to construct. Part Two deals with stages that are professional in their plans and in the types of marionette production they will allow you to present.

Stage #1. The "Mop Handle" and Drapery. This most rudimentary of stages can be improvised anywhere. All you need are two straight-back chairs the same height, across which and between you rest a broomstick, a mop handle, or any similar rod. Drape a length of opaque fabric (a large towel, etc.) across the rod, and the job is done. You stand on one side of the drapery and work the marionettes on the other side (Figure 38).

For hanging the puppets offstage, a hat rack or clothes tree is an excellent device.

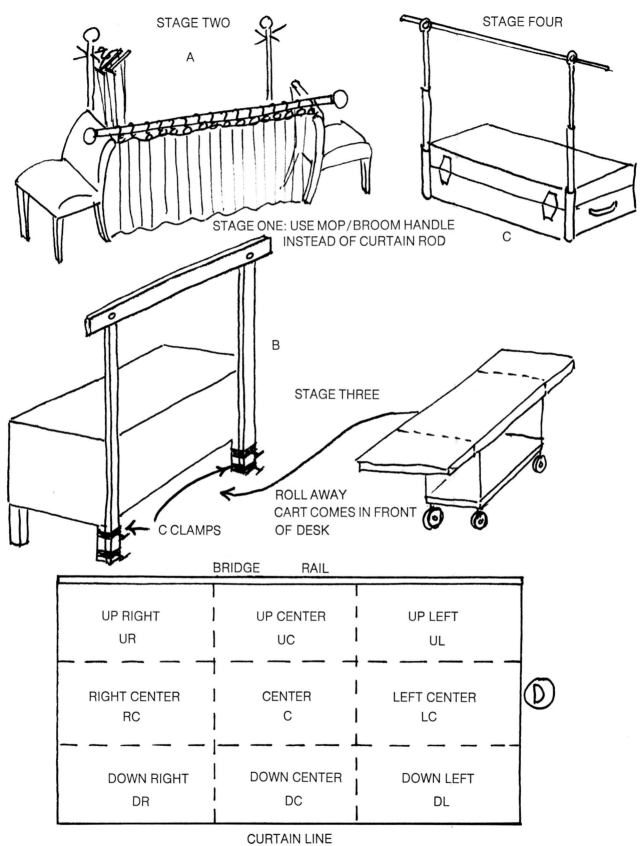

STAGE TWO

A

STAGE FOUR

STAGE ONE: USE MOP/BROOM HANDLE
INSTEAD OF CURTAIN ROD

C

B

STAGE THREE

ROLL AWAY
CART COMES IN FRONT
OF DESK

C CLAMPS

BRIDGE   RAIL

UP RIGHT UR	UP CENTER UC	UP LEFT UL
RIGHT CENTER RC	CENTER C	LEFT CENTER LC
DOWN RIGHT DR	DOWN CENTER DC	DOWN LEFT DL

D

CURTAIN LINE

FIGURE 38

Stage #2. The Curtain Rod and Chairs. This stage is merely a more sophisticated version of Stage #1. Instead of a mop handle you have a round, heavy-duty, extensible metal curtain rod, with an approximate diameter of three fourths of an inch. With this you have a curtain already pleated or gathered and fastened to curtain hooks or rings permanently in place on the rod. As with Stage #1, the rod goes across and between two chair backs of the same height (Figure 38). Stage #2 has obvious advantages: The rod collapses for storage and transportation, it's adjustable in length, and it saves scrounging around for makeshift materials. With this set-up, you and Kandu are ready to perform at the drop of a suggestion.

Stage #3. The Desk-and-Table (or Two-Table) Combination. Start with a strong table solid enough to take your full weight. Most tables are thirty inches high, and one with a surface four or five feet long by twenty-four or thirty inches wide will allow you to move around on it a little without having to worry about falling off and will give you enough room to work. For the marionettes' performing area, put another table or desk in front of the first piece of furniture. This need not be so strong, since it will not have to support any substantial weight. The table on which you stand should be protected from scratches by a heavy fabric throw. The desk needn't be covered unless the marionettes or props could mar it. However, a fabric floor for the stage gives the marionettes' feet a better purchase.

Between the two pieces of furniture goes a portable bridgerail. A bridgerail is a structure that separates the playing stage area from the manipulating area and provides a support from which to hang curtains, marionettes, and miscellaneous equipment. When curtained, it at least partially conceals the puppeteer from the audience.

The bridgerail is fastened to whichever of the two pieces has the better legs for the purpose. It's an inverted "U"-shaped construction consisting of three lengths of one-by-three (inch) wood. ("One-by-three" is standard lumberyard terminology.) Two of the three lengths, each about five feet long, are fastened to the legs of one of the stage units (Figure 38). Each is fastened to its leg with four "C" clamps, two on each side of each upright. You can protect the furniture leg by putting a thin strip of plywood or heavy cloth between the leg and the clamps. Two feet of the uprights are below the tabletop and three feet extend above. The third one-by-three is as long as required to connect the two uprights, and it's held to them by nails (if you anticipate one use only) or by hinges (if repeated use is expected). The cross-piece can also be made of a round rod of wood or metal. See Figure 38 for modifying the construction.

This desk-and-table stage has advantages and disadvantages. On the pro side, it raises the performance two and a half feet off the floor so that it can be seen by many more than Stages #1 and #2 accommodate, and it makes it unnecessary to travel with bulky, heavy equipment. Particularly if you'll be playing in schools or libraries, you can nearly always count on sturdy desks and tables being available. On the other hand, there may be times when desks and tables are not available to you. And there's one more factor: A six-foot puppeteer standing on a thirty-inch table requires a ceiling height of at least eight and a half feet. Some houses and apartments don't come that high.

THE STAGE CURTAIN

The curtain can be suspended from the bridgerail as a permanent installation, or it can be made removable. Whether permanent or not, at the end of your show it can be rolled neatly around the cross-piece and stored.

Any opaque material that drapes softly makes a good curtain. Velveteen is fine. A light fabric like muslin will serve if it's lined. The color of your curtain will depend on what goes in front of it. The curtain must not distract from the performance or be so similar to the costumes and props as to make it difficult to see them. Because Kandu will be dressed in black, a gray curtain would fill the bill in this instance.

Twice the width of the cross-piece will give full folds. One and one half times the width will give less fullness, of course, but can get by. Less fabric will look skimpy. Allow for an extra thickness of material at the top for reinforcement under the tacks or pins or hooks that attach the curtain to the cross-piece. Paste or sew a hem and, if necessary, weight it.

If the cross-piece is wood, the curtain can be thumbtacked to it for temporary use, or carpet-tacked or stapled to it for permanence. If the cross-piece is a round rod, attach the curtain to rings large enough to slide over the rod easily, and you can adjust evenly spaced folds quickly with your fingers.

If you want to use the curtain for a variety of shows, it's a good idea to keep it unadorned. But if it's only for Kandu, you can decorate it with occult symbols—zodiac signs, for instance —and perhaps some glitter here and there. But remember—the curtain is there to enhance Kandu's performance, not overpower it.

Stage #4. The trunk (Figure 38). The basic element of this stage is a small trunk— a foot-locker type with a flat top you can stand on. The trunk will contain all your equipment (lighting units, etc.) as well as your marionettes. This stage is very compact, so you must plan everything that goes into it with space-saving in mind. For efficiency, everything has its designated spot in the trunk and all put-together pieces are clearly marked so that no time is wasted in assembling them or taking them apart for packing. Figure 38 gives detailed instructions for modifying a trunk into a portable, versatile performing apparatus.

With this set-up, the puppeteer stands on the trunk (which is approximately eighteen inches high) and the marionettes perform on the floor in front. If you are giving a party show and a row or two of children sit in a semicircle on the floor before you, this stage is excellent. There are other kinds of informal presentations where it also works, and it is particularly serviceable when the performance is held on a platform or proscenium raised stage.

This is not a good stage for use in a hospital ward or other situations where beds or other equipment would block the view of the audience. However, one or more sturdy tables or desks could make an impromptu platform on which the trunk and you could stand. Provided the ceiling is high enough to accommodate the thirty inches of the table plus the height of the trunk plus your own height, this, then, becomes a most satisfactory portable stage for a little marionette show.

STAGE AREAS

For purposes of direction, any stage can be thought of as being divided into nine areas. All directions are from the viewpoint of the performers. (See Figure 38.)

CONDITION OF THE STAGE

The condition of your stage will contribute to the impression you make on other people. It should always be clean and in good repair,

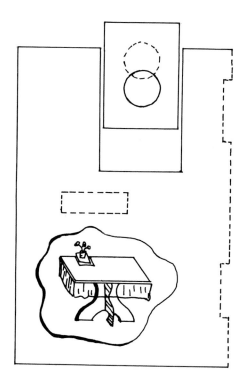

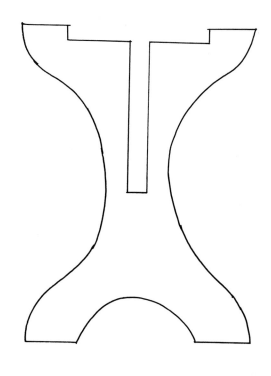

and when you are finished with your performance and gone, there should be no scratched
furniture, dented floors, or torn carpet to indicate you were ever there. Only the memory of
a splendid performance should remain.

KANDU'S PROPS
THE TABLE

Every magician needs a full complement of
paraphernalia, including a special table on
which to demonstrate his astounding skill.
Kandu, of course, has his own table. Notice
that the plans in Figure 39 are scaled to Kandu's
proportions so that the table is believable. Using
the same basic interlocking construction as for
Kandu and Ruff, construct the prop from sturdy
corrugated cardboard, similar to that used in
packing cases. After cutting out the patterns

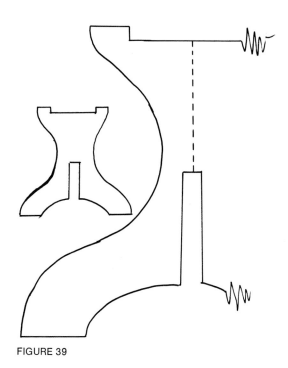

FIGURE 39

51

FIGURE 40

you have traced from page 51, finish off the raw edges of the cardboard by covering them with masking tape. Shellac the cardboard to seal it and then paint it with tempera or a rubber-based prepared paint. Red or black would be theatrically effective. After the paint has dried, tack, glue, or staple a three-inch skirt to the edge of the tabletop to conceal the working of the trick.

The heart of the table is a spin-around piece that changes a flower and its container into a different potted plant. These small pots of flowers can be bought inexpensively in almost any variety store or florist's shop, but there's nothing difficult about making them yourself. One pot is glued to the top surface of the spin-around piece, the other to the under side (Figure 39).

OTHER PROPS

The mysterious hand that lies on the table, two miniature birds, the birdcage, the magic box, and the bouquet can be home-made or

52

come from a hobby or specialty shop. Patterns are included on pages 24–29 (Figure 40), but if you buy the props, keep them in scale with Kandu.

For the card trick, you want two identical Queens of Hearts, which you can make "normal" life-size so that they can be seen at a distance, or which you can take from a pinochle deck (which has two of everything).

Kandu's hat is actually a puppet in itself. It has a false bottom and a white rabbit less than two inches high that fits inside, costing little to buy and less to make (Figure 17).

Directions for stringing and manipulating these props are given on page 26.

LIGHTING KANDU

Without light Kandu and Ruff can't be seen. But with the wrong kind of light, their show would lack sparkle and some of their best tricks could fall flat. Natural daylight is wrong for their performance, except in a little demonstration to show how the production works. Even very simple lighting of the right kind greatly enhances the show, giving it a professional look, intensifying the action, and adding dramatic impact.

A couple of standing lamps with bullet-type heads holding a 100-watt bulb in each are adequate for Kandu's act. Collapsible music stands without the music rack, or photographers' tripods that lights can be clamped to, can be substituted for the lamps if you will be touring. If these lamps or stands are placed one on either side of the stage, about two feet to the side and two feet in front, they will light the performing area. Particular care should be taken to keep the light on the marionettes, not the manipulator.

If both lamps are hooked up to household extension cords with an off/on toggle switch, you can flick the lights off and on rapidly for "lightning" effects. Keep all control switches within easy reach. The bridgerail is a good place for all switches, even though you may run out of hands and need to operate them with an elbow, if an assistant isn't available.

For more elaborate lighting, the 100-watt household bulbs in the two lamps can be replaced by 100-watt PAR bulbs. These come in several colors and in floodlight or spotlight types. The flood covers a large stage area with a more intense white or tinted light than the household bulb provides. The spot concentrates a higher intensity into a smaller area, also in white or color. A spot and a flood or two spots can create highly theatrical results. With two cut-off switches, you can test varying effects when these lamps are used singly or together.

If you find the spotlight is too intense, try a 75-watt PAR spotlight bulb instead.

A small household dimmer, which can be bought inexpensively in most variety or hardware stores, can be connected to one of the lamps. On cue, you can dim down the power on the flood so that only the spot remains. The spot should be preset to illuminate the magic table. To establish an eerie scene for Kandu, you might have a pink flood on the dimmer and a green spot in the other lamp. When the pink fades out, a spooky green remains.

If you can't find PAR bulbs of the color you want, it's possible to get clamp-on filters in a wide variety of tints. In no circumstances use colored paper to make a light filter. Paper is highly combustible, and a dangerous fire could ensue. When you have an audience that might include children, elderly people, or shut-ins, you owe it to them to make your production safe in every respect.

KANDU'S MUSIC AND
SOUND EFFECTS

All forms of theater make an appeal to the senses and the emotions as well as to the mind. Even though puppetry is primarily a visual art, no subsidiary appeal that could support the dramatic aspects of Kandu's performance should be ignored. Music, particularly, can be used to heighten suspense, build excitement, enhance a mood, and tighten the unity of a production.

By far the best type of musical background for Kandu is a recording on a small cassette. There are many exciting types of music you can use for Kandu's presentation. The following selections are suggested:

Saint-Saëns' *Danse Macabre* is eerie and descriptive, as well as tense and gripping.

Mussorgsky's *Night on Bald Mountain* gives an anticipation of weird events.

Gounod's *Faust*, when Mephistopheles appears, is suspense-building.

Decide what music you would like with each of Kandu's tricks, then make your cassette accordingly.

To make a preliminary rehearsal tape, play your selections on a turntable and hook in the cassette to your amplifier to record only the passages you want. These segmented selections will have to be tested during rehearsal. If the mood is wrong, or the duration of the music doesn't fit the stage action, they'll have to be retaped.

If you want to have bird twitterings and "raspberries" or other non-musical sound effects, as called for by the script, they ought to be added to the tape at the appropriate place.

After Kandu (and Ruff) have been rehearsed to where the performance is smooth and tight, you're ready to time it. You want to know to the second how long each section of the act takes. Once you've made up a schedule, you can elaborate on it by indicating the musical selection that will open the performance and its sound level. You can determine whether you want silence—and for how long—while Kandu is speaking, or whether you want additional music played softly as a background for his spiel. If you want music to punctuate the completion of each trick like an exclamation point, indicate on your schedule which selection starts when, its duration, and its volume. The music can come up full between tricks while Kandu is acknowledging the plaudits of the multitude. And allow time for applause at strategic moments.

The most exciting music should be saved for the most exciting trick, when Kandu makes himself disappear.

When you're satisfied with the timing of the performance and the integrated musical selections, you're ready to make a master tape. To do this, you must have all the musical selections prepared—and you may need a stop watch to achieve a high degree of accuracy. Some tape decks have a meter, which eliminates the necessity of a stop watch. Since you'll be using your voice "live" with the taped music in the background, it's best to make a full tape that has dead space between the musical selections. This does away with reliance on an assistant to turn the music on and off on cue.

Properly selected and recorded, music can give Kandu's performance an exciting new dimension.

SECTION 3

PUTTING ON THE SHOW

All your work—which has been fun in itself—has now added up to a show that, with rehearsals, is ready to go on. You've created your actors, costumed them, and taught them how to perform. You've built a stage, curtained, and set it, selected your musical background, and been scenic designer, carpenter, etc. Now you become director of the production in which Kandu will star, with or without Ruff.

In the script that follows, all music, lighting, and technical cues are supplied, but bear in mind that these are aids to help you start off in your marionette theater, not muzzles for your own ideas. Feel free to depart from this script and to improve on it to emphasize your particular abilities that can be transmitted to Kandu and Ruff.

"KANDU THE MAGNIFICENT AND HIS TALKING WONDER DOG RUFF"

Stage is set as shown in Figure 40.

Darken the room as much as possible by drawing curtains or blinds, if necessary, or turning off the lights. For an audience of young children, don't darken the house completely.

Start the recording. The music begins softly; comes up full for not more than thirty seconds.

Music fades and spot and floodlights come on half-power, revealing stage.

Taped voice of master of ceremonies (you?): **Ladies and Gentlemen, Boys and Girls, Children of all Ages! Introducing for your edification and entertainment the greatest master magician of all time, the one and only, the unique, Kandu the Magnificent! The management has spared no expense to bring to this fair community an attraction that will hold you spellbound! Ladies and Gentlemen, Boys and Girls, we give you Kandu the Magnificent!**

Music: Full fanfare!

Music fades as Kandu enters stage left, lights on full. He bows to all parts of the audience, arms outstretched in a sweeping gesture.

Thank you! Ladies and Gentlemen, one and all! Thank you, thank you for your gracious reception. It is a pleasure to appear before you. *He bows again.* **I hope to amaze and befuddle—I mean ENTERTAIN—you with demonstrations of the science and art of magic I have acquired through long years of arduous study in the mystic Orient. Please watch care-**

Kandu and Ruff performing together. Notice rabbit in hat and also magic hand. *Photo: Bob Daly*

fully everything I do. *He waves his hands in the air.* Please note that my fingers never leave my hand. *Wait for the laugh.* The crowned heads of Europe and Asia have nodded in recognition of my skill in the occult arts. In fact, after my last performance it was advisable for me to disappear for a while, so I did. Disappearing is an old habit of mine, acquired from an ancient yogi in the Himalayas, and old habits are hard to break. I keep disappearing and reappearing all the time—whichever comes first! But I must apologize to you good people for coming before you not at my best. I've just returned from a long and exhausting

journey and I'm a little tired. I trust you'll bear with me if I sit down for a moment or two before I commence with my astounding exposition of wizardry. Ah, here's a box just the right size to relax on for a minute. *He turns, looks at box, backs over to it, and sits down with a sigh of relief. He immediately jumps up.* What's going on? *He stands stage left of the box in profile and looks at the box. The box lid opens (pull lid string with your left hand) and flaps at him. He backs away a step or two. The box makes a "wah wah" sound. Kandu cocks his head to listen.* Oh, is that so? *He turns to face the audience.* Well,

56

Ladies and Gentlemen, it wasn't much of a rest, but it was all I needed.

Kandu walks back to the table, stands alongside it, facing the audience. Now, my friends, at this time I wish to call to your attention that upon my magic table are several interesting items. Please note particularly this blue flower in the pink pot. *(Or whatever colors your flower and pot happen to be.)* At first glance it would seem to be just an ordinary blossom in an ordinary container *(he gestures with a hand toward them)*, but to one whose eyes have been opened by profound studies of the occult, the truth is revealed. This plant comes from the depths of the darkest forests of Afghanistan, where it was tended by a green witch in a pot of black lentils. I shall disclose to you its secrets, which will confound you. *Kandu steps in front of the table and turns his back to the audience, concealing the table. Turn him around so: Continuing to hold the controller in your right hand, raise his left leg string with your left hand; keeping his right foot firmly on the ground, with your left hand pull the left leg string around so that Kandu pivots on his right foot 180°. When he faces the backdrop, release the left leg and with your left hand raise both hand strings so that the cape opens up Dracula-fashion. Your right thumb and forefinger will keep the arms raised, releasing your left hand to pull the string for the flower pot change-over. While his back is to the audience, with the cape concealing the table, Kandu says the magic words:* Alcatraz, Kandula, Homo Sapiens, Veranis Komodiensis! *(Or your own formula)* Voilà! *After Kandu says the magic words, drop his hand strings, lift his left leg with your left hand, and pivot him on his right foot to face the audience. He points to the plant as he says "Voilà" and bows to acknowledge the* applause. Thank you, Ladies and Gentlemen. From my heart, I thank you. You're such a wonderful audience I'll change the flower back for you. You do want it the way it was before, don't you? Did someone say no? Yes? No? Very well, your wish is my command. *He turns around, as before, repeats the magic words,* Alcatraz, Kandula, Homo Sapiens, Veranis Komodiensis, *and goes through the routine again. There! While he's bowing, the flower reverses itself in full view of the audience. Kandu hears the audience reaction, cuts his bow short, looks around, and sees the plant changing back and forth. He is somewhat flustered and expresses it by clearing his throat,* Ahem. *He faces the plant and says to it sternly,* Control yourself. Did you hear the magic words this time? Behave yourself or I'll summon up the green witch, and you know what she can do. *The plant slowly rocks to a reluctant finish. Kandu bows to the audience.* Magic is an exhausting business, Ladies and Gentlemen, and after this feat I have to get off these feet for a moment. *He walks over to the box and turns around to sit on it. While he is dropping his rump onto the box, the box slides away from under him. Kandu sits down hard on the stage floor and says,* Oof! *He turns his head to look at the box (turn the controller) and says,* My! You weren't brought up very well, were you? Don't you know that's not a nice thing to do? And it's dangerous, besides. *He picks himself up by lifting one foot first, then bringing up the rest of his body. He turns slightly to look at the box, which opens its lid and gives a Bronx cheer and closes. Kandu says,* I think there's more than one magician here. *He turns back to the table and goes toward it.* And now, Ladies and Gentlemen, Boys and Girls! A display of powers that will leave you bewildered, be-mused, and be-guiled. Why? Because here on my magic table lies a miracle of the ages. *He points. The pink flood fades. Turn the pink dimmer with your left hand, leaving only the eerie green light on full. At this point your pretaped cassette music,* Night on Bald Mountain, *perhaps, comes on softly as background.* See before you the severed hand of the mighty Fung Gum Bo, stolen centuries ago from his tomb in the fabled mountains of Tibet. Although this hand is more than a thousand years old—a thousand and one, to be precise—it has never lost the skill with which Fung Gum Bo, long dead chief sorcerer to the emperors of China, endowed it. No, it has never lost its touch with humanity. *Kandu is facing the audience during this spiel, gesturing to the table. While he speaks, the hand floats off the table (accomplish this with your left hand) and touches Kandu's shoulder at "touch with humanity." Kandu is unaware of this.* It is a most touching hand *(hand touches Kandu's hat, fondling it)* and it seems to have a life of its own. *The hand rocks in agreement and floats back to rest on the table. Kandu looks at the hand, not realizing it has ever moved.* Now, hand of the legendary Fung Gum Bo, from out of the past, we ask you to give us a message for today and tomorrow. *He raises his arms in incantation.* Alcatraz, Kandula, Homo Sapiens, Veranis Komodiensis! I command you by virtue of the sacred words, give us a message for the people of Brooklyn (or The girls and boys at Tommy's birthday party or PS 24 or 217 Main Street, or whatever) Give us, mystic hand, your message from Fung Gum Bo!

The hand floats across the stage to the backdrop, where, after some false starts, it pushes aside the concealing drapery and reveals your message: Peace!; Happy Birthday, Tommy; Merry Christmas; Congratulations, Team; *or*

whatever. *You do this by holding the magic hand's controller with your left hand. As you hold the controller against the bridgerail the magic hand appears to be writing, while your fingers push the draperies away from the prepared sign. Kandu has the option of spelling out the letters one at a time as they are revealed or of waiting until the entire message shows and then delivering the whole thing:* Happy birthday! Thank you, magic hand! Thank you, Fung Gum Bo! *The hand waggles in acknowledgment and floats off stage left. Suspend the hand offstage. Then turn the pink dimmer up with your left hand, while the background music fades. Kandu bows to the audience. A real ham.* Ladies and Gentlemen, thank you, thank you!

Kandu forgets about his troubles with the box and starts to sit on it. He remembers when halfway down and freezes. He thinks about it for a few seconds and decides not to sit. He backs away and looks at the box, which raises its lid somewhat and razzes him. Kandu says, This is *my* act, you, and if you don't watch your manners I'll make you disappear. *Box razzes him again. Kandu ignores it and turns to the audience.* Thank you, Ladies and Gentlemen, for your kind indudgence.

Change Kandu's controller to your left hand, take the hat controller in your right. (If you aren't ready to manipulate the hat, don't have Kandu wear it. Set the stage with the hat already on the table and eliminate part of the monologue.) You know every magician has a magic hat, and you have noticed, I'm sure, that mine is an especially splendid one. Observe: Alcatraz, Kandula, Homo Sapiens, Veranis Komodiensis! *The hat leaves his head and floats to the table, alighting on it upside down.* Please note that there is nothing in this hat. Magic hat—show the audience! *Tilt the hat controller.* **Absolutely nothing. Empty as my pocketbook** (*or gas tank* or *the treasury, or anything that can be related to a current situation*). *Hat sits back.* **Now, once again the magic words. Say them with me this time: Alcatraz, Kandula, Homo Sapiens, Veranis Komodiensis! No, please—this magic needs your full cooperation—louder this time. Alcatraz, Kandula, Homo Sapiens, Veranis Komodiensis! Voilà!** *The rabbit slowly emerges from the hat. While you are holding the hat controller with your right hand, hook your middle finger through the ring on the controller and pull it until the rabbit is exposed. Two inches should do.* (*See Figures 17 and 40 for a detailed explanation.*) **Thank you, one and all. I knew you were waiting to see if I could pull a rabbit out of a hat and I couldn't disappoint you.** *Drop the rabbit back into the hat and suspend the controller, as diagramed. Kandu milks his applause. Put his controller back into your right hand again.* **Now, my friends, no magician is worthy of the name unless he has a card trick or two. Behold!** *He lifts his cape with both hands and nothing shows but the lining.* **Nothing!** *He drops his arms and the cape. With your left hand, pull a Queen from its pocket in the left side of the closed cape. He raises his left arm.* **Lo and behold, Ladies and Gentlemen! The Queen of Hearts. With a wave of my hand** (*he waves his left hand*) **I shall transfer it to the other side of my cape.** *Drop the left hand string and raise the right arm, revealing the cape lining. Nothing happens.* **I'm sorry, Ladies and Gentlemen, we forgot the magic chant.** *He drops the right side and raises the left again, showing the original Queen of Hearts. He drops the left arm.* **Now, please say it with me: Alcatraz, Kandula, Homo Sapiens, Veranis Komodiensis!** *With your*

left hand, pull out the right-side Queen of Hearts, and then, still with your left hand, raise Kandu's right arm. **See, there it is. The Queen of Hearts. The card went from the left to the right, as you see. And that's right. If it wasn't right, it would be left. It wouldn't be right for it to be left, so it's not left, it's right. Right? Right!** *Drop Kandu's right arm.* **Did I hear someone say there are two different cards the same? Or two cards the same that are different? Do you believe I would do a thing like that to you?** *With your left hand, drop the right Queen back into its pocket and reveal the left Queen and the Queenless right side by opening both sides of the cape simultaneously. Close the cape by dropping the arms and with your left hand put the left Queen back in its pocket.* (*This gag can be continued with variations for two or three more times.*) **See—***open cape wide***—the Queen is gone. Perhaps her feelings were hurt by your suspicions. She is a very shy lady and won't appear again, but let me thank you on her behalf!** *He bows elaborately.*

Kandu is center stage, about to commence his next speech, when the box (left hand) sidles up to him. Kandu ignores it. **You are certainly a most generous audience, Ladies and Gentlemen.** *The box nudges Kandu's leg. Kandu pays no attention.* **I hope you will be as pleased by my next presentation.** *The box bumps Kandu hard. Kandu kicks at box, looks down, and says,* **Go away, boy, you bother me.** *Box goes back, flaps its lid once or twice, and subsides.*

May I direct your attention to the beautiful birdcage suspended on my right? Its sweet singer of songs has long since flown and it awaits a new resident. Please join me in the magic words that will conjure a new bird to its home. *With your left hand, turn the pink* *dimmer down half.* **All together now: Al-catraz, Kandula, Homo Sapiens, Veranis Komodiensis!** *With your left hand, raise his left arm and simultaneously, quickly pull the hidden bird from the cape lining. Then drop Kandu's arm string. With your left hand, fly the bird around and around the stage to the bird twitterings on your tape. If you can make bird sounds with your mouth or a whistle, it might be easier to do this than to have the tape timing be so accurate. After a few turns around the stage, fly the bird off and hang its controller offstage.* **Please, absolute silence, everyone. I want to have the bird return to its cage where it will be safe, properly fed, and cared for with loving kindness.** *Kandu turns his back to the audience, standing directly below the cage. In a quick motion, with your right hand snap his arms up over his head as far as they'll go. The cape will fly up and briefly obscure the cage; then drop the arm strings. During that interval, with your left hand pull the bird from the false bottom of the cage and then release the bird's string. The bird twitters for a few seconds. Kandu spins around to face the audience, points to the cage, and with your left hand you bring the pink light up full.* **Voilà!** *and Kandu bows.* **Ladies and Gentlemen, your reception has been so warm and welcoming, I am going to take the liberty of bringing on a friend of mine. He is my very best friend, and I hope he'll be your friend too and that you will be his. He's not an ordinary friend. He has been at my side through thick and thin, through good times and bad. He has shared my bed and board and has worked his heart out to help me in every way he could. Please give him a great big hand.** *Kandu stretches out his right hand and points to right. Fanfare. Ruff enters stage left, managed by your left hand.*

Kandu: **Oh! Ladies and Gentlemen, the talking wonder dog!** *Ruff stands there, wagging his tail.* **This is no ordinary animal. He can understand human speech, speak, calculate mathematical equations, and perform such incredible feats as to make him the marvel of scientists the world around. No ordinary canine, indeed, there are literally no intellectual concepts he is not capable of comprehending or demonstrating.** *To dog:* **I can see that our friends are somewhat skeptical, old friend, so we'll have to give them proof. Bow to the Ladies and Gentlemen.** *Ruff stands on his hind legs and bows.* **Now sit.** *Ruff sits in begging position.* **Very good. Now, tell us your name.**

Ruff: **Ruff.**

Kandu: **Ruff, is it? How do you do, Ruff. Tell us, how was your plane ride to this beautiful city?**

Ruff: **Ruff.**

Kandu: **I'm sorry to hear it was rough. But you arrived in time for a game of golf before you came here. How was your game?**

Ruff: **Ruff.**

Kandu: **Well, we all have good days and bad. You probably need practice. You should go out more instead of watching so much TV. You're always looking at westerns. And how are the bad guys?**

Ruff: **Ruff.**

Kandu: **Of course they're rough. How did you like that trail through the Rocky Mountains?**

Ruff: **Ruff.**

Kandu: **It was rough, all right. A picture like that makes you glad you have a place to come home to. And what does that have over your head?**

Ruff: **Ruff.**

Kandu: **That's right, my friend, a roof. And when we get back to our own home, I know you'll head straight for your own bed and**

your own sheets. Do you like silky sheets?
Ruff: **Ruff.**

Kandu: I like them rough too. I don't care for sheets that are too soft.

Kandu gets down on one knee and faces Ruff. You seem to have had a hard time lately, old friend. Don't worry. Things are bound to improve. *Kandu rises and faces the audience. While Kandu is delivering the following remarks, Ruff goes over to the box and sniffs it. The box opens lid and snaps it shut. Ruff backs away. Ruff's movements and the lid of the box are worked with the same left hand. The left thumb flips up the lid string and releases it. Kandu addresses the audience:* My friends, didn't I tell you Ruff was a most remarkable canine? Would you have believed any dog could be so intelligent? There are so many other demonstrations of his perspicacity, prowess, and peculiar propensities he could perform, but I shall not weary him or you with all of them. But because he is a marvelous mathematician—and he's good at adding, too—even subtracting—you should be treated to the thrilling spectacle of some of his astounding abilities. **Ruff!** *But Ruff is busy being suspicious of the box, nose down and tail end up.* **Ruff!** *Ruff hears and comes over.*

Kandu: **Ruff,** we're going to prove how good you are in arithmetic. Old friend, don't let me down. I'd like you to add one and one. *Silence.* One and one. Now, **Ruff,** you can do it. No coaching from the audience. One and one. *Ruff listens with ears up. Thinks with head cocked.*

Ruff: Finally answers: **Ruff, ruff.**

Kandu: **Good Boy!** Now, how much is two times one?

Ruff: **Ruff, ruff.**

Kandu: **Wonderful.** Isn't he wonderful, Ladies and Gentlemen? Now, how much is this, and this is a hard one, so listen carefully. How much is three from five?

Ruff: **Ruff, ruff.**

Kandu: **My** friends, is he or isn't he a genius? Did you ever know another dog that could do what this scientific curiosity could accomplish? But there's something else you should know about my best friend Ruff. It isn't just that he can do what ordinary canines couldn't begin to comprehend. No, he can do anything any ordinary dog can do—and do it better. **Ruff! Here, Ruff!** *But after the last mathematical demonstration, Ruff has gone sniffing back to the box. While Kandu is talking, Ruff comes alongside the box and lifts his near hind leg. The box is alarmed and jerks away.*

Kandu: **Ruff!** *Ruff drops his leg and goes to Kandu.* **Sit up, Ruff. Lie down. Jump over the box.** *Ruff sits up, lies down, and goes toward the box. The box backs away as it sees Ruff coming, but Ruff gives a huge leap and jumps over the box. The box and Ruff are managed with the same hand.* **Wonderful. Wonderful. Give him a big hand. Thank you, my friends.** *Ruff is on his hind legs, acknowledging the applause. He's a ham too.* **Ruff,** because you've given the folks in the audience such a fine performance, I have a present for you. Back in the dressing room there's a lovely surprise that's all for you. Take one more bow, and go get your reward. *Ruff bows three times.* That's enough, **Ruff.** Remember, it's Kandu the **Magnificent** who's the star of this show.

Ruff: **Ruff**—*and runs off stage left.*

Kandu: **He's** my best friend, and I love him, but after something like that I have a bone to pick with him. My friends, you have been very kind to me and I wish I could give a present to each and every one in the audience. That is impossible even for me, so the best I can do is create one bouquet for all of you.

All I have is this little boutonniere, but they don't call me Kandu the Magnificent for nothing. One more time, everybody: Alcatraz, Kandula, Homo Sapiens, Veranis Komodiensis! Presto! *Pull the flower string with your left hand and snap the bouquet from Kandu's lapel.* Ladies and Gentlemen, thank you, thank you, thank you. *Bows deeply.* And for my final and most stupendous tour de force: Before your very eyes, my dear friends, I shall make myself disappear. Say with me this last time: Alcatraz, Kandula, Homo Sapiens, Veranis Komodiensis! One, two, three! *With your left hand, black out both lights suddenly and briefly. With your right hand, remove Kandu to the right. When the lights are restored, the stage is bare. Kandu re-enters from the right and bows. He calls,* Ruff, here, Ruff! Come take a bow. *Ruff enters stage left with a bone in his mouth, which you have released from the controller.* Thank you, thank you, thank you, thank you.

Stage lights out. Clear the stage. House lights up. The end.

REHEARSALS

Several times in Part One we've referred to the necessity for rehearsals, but we are going to mention it just once more. Sometimes the major difference between a smooth, professionally presented puppet show and an amateurish-looking one is only that the former is rehearsed and rehearsed and rehearsed, until every movement is perfect, the timing is impeccable, and all the stage business goes off without a hitch. We know you want to present your show quickly and share your pride and pleasure with others, but don't damage that pride and stint the pleasure by offering less than your best. And achieving your best may

be only a few more hours of polishing the production—so rehearse!

TOURING KANDU

After Kandu has performed for your friends and relatives, he may be ready for church, community center, hospital, and school audiences. If you have a trunk stage, touring will be simple. If you depend on a table-and-desk stage, check on the ceiling height beforehand and make sure the right kind of furniture will be available to you. If you'll need a microphone to amplify your voice or your cassette tape, make arrangements for this beforehand as well.

Always let the people where you'll be playing know how much time you'll need to set up onstage. Compute how much time each step will take and, particularly if touring is new to you, double your estimate.

One of the most important matters to learn is the care of your marionettes. Kandu and Ruff should be packed separately, feet first, in a bag with the strings of each outside, as discussed. Establish a set routine, always wrapping in the same direction. This way, the strings won't become tangled and the marionettes will be ready for their next appearance onstage when you unwrap the strings and hang Kandu and Ruff on the bridgerail by their controllers.

If your lights are on a telescoped stand, they'll store compactly and provide the proper angle of throw of the mounted mini-spots. The small cassette with your taped music can be packed away easily. Your trunk will also hold the curtains and props, plus the uprights needed for the bridgerail.

If you are to move from home to hospital, etc., transportation facilities must be provided. The trunk can fit into the rear of a sedan or station wagon, or on a bus or train. If it's heavy, roll it on its wheels until you arrive at the transportation facility.

If you want to be invited back to perform on another occasion, remember your show is only one of the factors by which you'll be judged. Create a positive personal image by being reasonable in your demands for equipment and facilities and pleasant in your relationships. Show up on time. A treat—even a free one—loses its charm for those who may become frantic wondering whether it will arrive.

Above all, make sure your production is safe. Be sure your electrical equipment is in good condition and that you're using nothing combustible around your lights. Your cloth throw must be heavy enough so that you cause no damage to the furniture tops. Your "C" clamps for the bridge mustn't damage the legs of your borrowed table. No rough or splintered surfaces should present a hazard to a curious, exploring child. And your trunk should be provided with glides to keep it from marring floors or carpets.

Finally, when you have packed up and are ready to leave, police the area to make sure it's at least no worse than when you arrived. Half-filled paper coffee cups and cigarette butts left behind will influence the impression *you* leave behind. A professional-looking show, even if unpretentious and small-scale, supported by professional conduct on your part, will produce a climate of good will that can make future presentations possible.

PART TWO

BECOMING
A PUPPETEER

INTRODUCTION

Now that Part One, "The New Marionette," is behind you, if you've gone along with us you understand the essentials of stringed puppet construction and manipulation. Part Two will take you farther along, and when you have explored this part also we trust you'll be proficient in every aspect of marionette production.

The basic human and animal figures you've learned to make will continue to be the foundation of your expanded knowledge. We'll show you how to modify their designs to make variations of them, still built on the combination of frontal and profile views. Since there are some conditions when this simple construction won't make the best marionette for a particular purpose, we'll suggest other ways to make marionettes that can supplement your cardboard modular puppets.

A variety of stages will be presented to you so that you may select those that will answer the increased requirements of your greater technical ability and ambitions. We'll show you how to build sets and scenery for your stages and go into detail about two aspects of advanced puppetry rarely discussed: lighting and music. A how-to section on advanced puppetry under "Marionette Magic" will reveal the secrets of professional puppeteers, and "Putting on the Show" goes into practicalities not covered in other books.

Two more sections are worthy of your particular consideration: "Playscripts" and "Direction." They may give you insights into material for puppetry, dramatic structure, and reactions of audiences that could be very helpful.

While "Becoming a Puppeteer" will give you a strong base of comprehension and technique, to be a great puppeteer you'll use it as a point of departure, from which you'll develop new methods, new ideas of your own. Each new step in your progress will bring you increasing satisfaction, and the discipline every art form requires will enable you to reconstruct your triumphs for other audiences.

Having come this far, you must be presumed to be taking marionettes seriously, whether as a hobby or as a potential career. Accordingly, we suppose you understand a certain investment is called for so that you'll be able to put on the best show possible. As a hobby, puppetry is no more extravagant than other hobbies, and as a profession it can pay its own way. It's possible for you to make at little expense much equipment that would be costly indeed to buy. Throughout this part we have suggested alternative equipment or ways of construction wherever possible for you to avail yourself of the option to do it yourself and save. You can spend a fortune or virtually nothing. As you make the most of your resources, you'll be more and more pleased with your capabilities.

Part Two tells you everything you need to know to put on a show, but the business end of the operation is covered in Part Three. As you plan a production with the knowledge gained from Part Two and before you solidify your ideas, turn to Part Three to the section dealing with financial or legal aspects of the various areas of production. These two parts supplement each other.

Good luck!

PLAYSCRIPTS

A concept is necessary to launch any project, and in theater the concept is the script. The script embodies the idea for your presentation. It doesn't have to be in written form. It can be a clearly thought-through basis for improvisation, the framework for a plotless skit or revue, or a carefully detailed play complete with elaborate production cues. It's a plan to enable your marionettes to express your point in dramatic, forward-moving form. It must have meaning for you—be what is important for you to do.

The importance of a good script can't be overemphasized. As in the live theater, the marionette script is often the weakest part of the production. Superlatively staged and performed Broadway shows have frequently bombed because the playwright's material was inadequate. There are always relatively few so-called creative artists—authors, composers, and choreographers—to the large number of equally skilled "performing" artists—actors, musicians, and dancers. We can't promise that your careful study of this material on playscripts will enable you to turn out an instant masterpiece, but it will at least call to your attention some pitfalls to be avoided and some ideas of a positive nature you can incorporate into your writing.

If you don't feel capable of writing a script yourself—and admitting this is no disgrace—there are any number of published plays you may draw on and adapt for marionettes, since, unfortunately, there aren't many plays written for marionette production. However, bear in mind that in some circumstances royalty payments may be involved.

STRUCTURE

Regardless of whether your entertainment has a plot, it must be structured. Even a little vaudeville routine has to build to a climax of suspense, excitement, or laughter and a smash finish.

With or without a story line, there should be a focus on a main character with whom the audience can identify. Even in a series of skits, it helps hold the audience's attention if there is an "M.C." who reappears from time to time to introduce the acts.

In a play, begin the action by establishing

FIGURE 41 In developing the initial concept, start with a rough sketch to indicate the general mood and costumes and the relationship between the marionettes, sets, and props.

conflict, as opposed to activity or talk, early in the comedy or drama. Move the plot along briskly, but remember there must be quiet moments for the audience to appreciate your sub-climaxes and for you to build to the next. The writing should allow for different levels of dramatic intensity. If one speaks at a shout normally, there's no way to indicate emphasis when one needs it.

To write in a song or a dance when the plot or the characterizations call for it can give an added dimension of beauty or fun to your play, but using a song or dance merely to fill up time, provide another effect, or drag the audience's wandering attention back to the stage doesn't work. In the latter case, the song or dance becomes merely a cheap trick that only slows down the story.

To be successful, any play must have a unity of style, and this unity begins with the script. It is unity as much as anything else that permits the audience to believe in your little people and to be willing to enter their world. Belief, credibility, is what every artist in the theater is looking for. The author has to believe in his creation. If he doesn't, why should anyone else?

Consistency in characterization and dialogue is one expression of unity. In a story of Robin Hood, which would be set in Sherwood Forest in the days of Kings Richard and John, as an

70

example, you would develop situations and vocabulary appropriate to the time and place. This doesn't mean you have to use archaic language sprinkled with thee's and thou's. Rather, you should use a kind of timeless standard English free of sharply contemporary slang that insistently reminds the audience of today. It means you should avoid anachronistic references to things that didn't exist then or of which the characters couldn't have known: peanut-butter sandwiches, the subway system, the Arctic Circle, or kangaroos. It means you can't put your marionettes into positions where they have to perform actions foreign to their society. No page would kick King John in the seat of his pants—not when that King is absolutely sovereign, with the power of life and death over his subjects. Violating any of these canons is frequently good for a laugh—but that laugh is at the cost of irreparable rupture of the unity and belief in your play.

Of course, you may not be concerned with creating the illusion of reality. You may prefer to do a campy version of the story in which your virtuosity with the marionettes is the real star, not Robin Hood. This is legitimate entertainment, provided your audience has come expecting a travesty and not an affectionate retelling of a beloved story. More on this when we discuss *humor*.

PLAY STRUCTURE FOR THE MARIONETTE THEATER

In writing for marionettes, think of them as being like actors of the early cinema, where movements were exaggerated for better communication. Although we look back at the early motion pictures and smile a little, we appreciate that, as we are drawn into a film, we more and more accept the conventions the form imposed on its vast public. This learning to accept is necessary for any medium to which we're unaccustomed. Our first opera can be a confusing experience until we accept its form, or our first viewing of the Japanese Bunraku, where the puppeteers, dressed like black Klansmen, work the elaborately jointed puppets in full view of the audience. So the audience accepts the marionette theater and loses consciousness of its artificialities.

Any author who writes for the marionette theater must be aware of the full potential of the medium. Besides a general knowledge of theater writing, the puppet playwright must know everything a marionette is able to do. Marionette people can balance incredible objects, contort themselves into fantastic positions, and play on musical instruments with astounding properties (a trumpet can blow up a balloon; a piano keyboard can come apart and join together; a cello can play itself with its own bow; a drum can breathe in and out, etc.). Trees can walk, rocks divide, flowers fly. Nothing is impossible, and the playwright needn't be restricted to reality. However, except in a vaudeville routine, tricks have to be motivated. And beware the trap of falling in love with an effect that contributes little or nothing to the characterizations or the situations and slows down the story.

But the nature of marionettes sets some limitations, and a good puppet script allows for them. Marionettes can't show nuances of facial or finger movements, even though it's possible to construct various moving parts—eyes, brows, noses, mouths, fingers, etc. These movements can be expressed in broad form by a skillful puppeteer. Some marionettes can move their jaws; some can't. Even if *your* figures can, it's not always easy for the audience to locate the speaker. Distracting movements from the other puppets must be kept to a minimum; only the speaker should attract attention. Long speeches need some kind of visual interest to hold an audience, but speeches shouldn't be so short they are over with before the audience can locate the speaker.

A puppeteer can't manipulate more marionettes than he has hands for. If more than one puppeteer is required by the script, it should avoid action requiring one marionette to cross the stage behind another, to keep the puppeteers from getting in each other's way.

Along with awareness of the restrictions the marionettes demand, the puppeteer should be aware of his own limitations and not use material that asks more of him than he is ready for.

Because puppeteers have difficulty in finding scripts that recognize these limitations as well as because they wish to avoid payment of royalties, most write their own plays, tailoring them to operate within the restrictions and also to take advantage of special talents they may have. If you have particular abilities, create a logical reason for incorporating their expression into your script. If you are an adept dancer or mime, transfer your abilities to your marionettes. Many great puppeteers were originally trained as actors, mimes, and dancers for the live theater, but when they became unable to perform in direct person, they transformed themselves into superb artists in the world of the marionettes.

HUMOR

Humor is a frequently misunderstood element in the puppet theater. Although almost all audiences take for granted that puppets are *ipso facto* comic figures and come to a show prepared to laugh, this is not necessarily the case. A marionette is an actor, a tool for delivering the playwright's ideas. As any actor is, he is as capable of being tragic, tender, or troubled, farcical, superficial, or lighthearted, and his role depends on the script.

What many playwrights, including those writing for Broadway, tend to forget is that humor is welcome when it enhances a situation. A gag can be inserted at a highly emotional moment. But—is it in keeping with the characters, the time, and the place? Does it lighten the scene briefly so that the intensity of the underlying drama is emphasized, or does it shatter the mood by demolishing the credibility of the story or people?

If Cinderella's wicked stepsisters are amusingly clumsy, the audience will laugh without sympathy, and this will strengthen the play. If Cinderella is equally gauche, she may lose the concern of the audience. Therefore, Cinderella's humor must not be at the expense of our involvement in her problems and subsequent sharing of her triumph.

Everyone loves to laugh, and humor can be created in many ways by marionettes. Basically funny situations or stories, of course—but much more. Word plays—puns and such—can evoke good audience response, but best are those laughs that come from the puppetry medium. The charm of your marionettes, the unexpected stage business that they spring on an unprepared audience—these are what puppetry is all about—and if these are amusing and in keeping with the rest of your production, your audience can have a merry time indeed. Humor for children will be discussed under "Puppetry for Children."

ANIMALS AND BIRDS

Animals and birds make particularly delightful marionettes, so the playwright would be well advised to find some way of working their appearance into a puppet script.

These creatures can be given as much personality and individuality as the people marionettes of your troupe, and, like them, what your script may demand of the animals and birds doesn't have to be limited by what they can perform in real life. Donkeys can fly, parrots can swim. Dragons can do both and breathe flames as well if your script requires it. Whether your animals are warm and cuddly or menacingly ferocious, they attract a special kind of attention from the audience. A lonely child might identify with a dog or cat more than with a human puppet. An adult might be amused with the concept you have for a four-legged wolf who acts like a two-legged variety. A rabbit might be wistful, a vulture philosophical, a fox not so smart as he should be, or an elephant one that always forgets. Don't just have an animal in your script for the sake of having one. Create a situation where one or more can have a legitimate place in the action. In a meadow or forest scene, on the other hand, you might have several little friendly birds and animals peep around trees or boulders as part of your "atmosphere."

How your characters relate to these assorted animals tells a great deal about the kind of people they are. Are they kind? Wicked? Greedy? Generous? Animals make it possible for the audience to like the protagonist by the way he treats them. The villain establishes his meanness at once by his opposite treatment.

Whether for their own sake or the way other characters react to them, animals are an important part of the writer's resources.

PUPPETRY FOR ADULTS

Most members of the public presume that puppetry is an art primarily for children. This is not so today, nor has it ever been. All the

way back to the beginning of history, puppetry has been a family entertainment in the days when all members of a family participated in virtually everything together. The way contemporary Western society is structured, there seems to be a sharp line in many instances, separating material for adults from that for children. Puppetry is experiencing a rise in nightclub and college circuit bookings because those audiences find puppets hilarious when performing political satire or scatological comment on the passing scene. Moreover, even those who would be resentful or embarrassed if they accepted the material as coming from the puppeteer are hugely entertained when it comes from his creatures.

73

Scene from the marionette opera *The Impresario* by Mozart. Joe Ayers, Endwell, N.Y.

Topical revues can be very successful, but it's because they *are* topical. They must be updated constantly so that all the jokes and situations are as fresh as the latest headlines.

As mentioned briefly in the Foreword of *Marionettes Onstage!*, many great writers have written for the puppet theater, for adult or family audiences. Almost the whole body of worldwide literature is available for adaptation to puppetry, and some of the productions of today's marionette masters have been as dramatic or as funny, as moving or as exciting, as anything on the legitimate stage. If you don't feel inclined to work for children, this is an area for which you might develop plays.

Here is an outstanding example of marionette communication. The gestures are built in and the facial expression is direct and the movements are strongly developed in true characterization. David Syrotiak marionette.

Two politicians speak to the people under the guidance of the father of our country..."George Washington" from a Suib Marionette Production.

PUPPETRY FOR CHILDREN

Because so much puppetry is performed for children, we're going to consider at some length playscripts for them.

To begin with, "children" is a broad category and all of them below the age of thirteen can't be lumped together where entertainment is concerned. Obviously, what would amuse a four-year-old could be an affront to someone who is ten. The adventures that would have eleven-year-olds on the edge of their seats could induce nightmares in pre-schoolers. Therefore, unless you have material that will span the age ranges you might want to consider separate or modified scripts for pre-schoolers, for those children in kindergarten through the third grade, and for those who are older.

Some factors are the same for children of all ages. An identification figure will hold the children's attention and involve them in the onstage happenings. It helps if the protagonist is younger than most, if not all, of the other characters, but this is by no means a hard and fast rule. A grandmotherly, warm Mother Goose is effective, or a Circus Ringmaster with human frailties like a child's own. The identification figure should possess qualities that are socially acceptable and worthy of emulation.

For very young children, it's wise to stick to simple stories they're already familiar with. If you want to go farther afield for material, simple legends or folk tales with uncomplicated story lines and clearly differentiated characters can be effective entertainment. However, it's important to remember that young children don't crave the novelty of variety. On the contrary, they look forward to a dramatization of a story they know and they prefer it to be told straight—just the way they have it read to them at bedtime. They find security in seeing enacted just what they expect, and if they are pleased, they would as soon come back again and see the performance over without one change as see a different show. For these children, keep the characterizations black and white, without complexities.

Children in the next group, those up through the third grade, like dramatizations of tales by the Brothers Grimm, Andersen, and Perrault and such classics as *Pinocchio* and *Heidi*. Older children go for *Treasure Island* and *Tom Sawyer*, which younger children also enjoy, particularly if they've already seen them adapted for television or films. The older ones like original stories too, particularly if there is a situation they can relate to their own experience.

In this connection, there's an important point for the novice puppeteer to consider when selecting a script, especially a puppeteer who hopes to attract a paying public. Small boys and girls don't go to the theater on their own. Unless a production comes to a school and is presented on assembly time—and there the children are a captive audience—little ones receive their ticket money from their parents and usually are accompanied by them to the performance. Parents have a tendency to spend their money on productions that remind them of their own childhood. If the fairy tale or classic is one they loved, they don't mind sending the children or even going along.

Cinderella, Rumpelstiltskin, Little Red Riding Hood, Peter Pan—names like these will always fetch them. But do a less well-known fairy tale, or give it another title, or present an original contemporary story, and resistance to buying tickets can be phenomenal. This is not said to scare you off from presenting the "now" stories children need as much as the old standbys. It's to warn you you may have trouble marketing them until you've grown experienced and reputable enough for adults to be willing to take a chance on *you*, trusting that your unknown title will be up to the standard set by your familiar stories.

Characters are more believable to older

children if the marionettes have something of the same mixture of good and bad as the rest of us.

The climax should always be strong and definite in its resolution, but stay away from material where toning down an ending for small boys and girls will destroy the story. In *Hansel and Gretel*, the witch *must* go into the oven. In *Jack and the Beanstalk*, the Giant *must* fall down and be killed. Everybody knows that. If you can't show them properly without frightening the little children, then resist the temptation to dramatize them for that age.

While we're on the subject of excitement, we must face up to "violence." Many writers in the area of theater for children, including puppeteers, have dealt with the problem by avoiding it. They write the Ogre out of *Puss in Boots*, convert Jack's Giant to a misunderstood oaf who is bad only because he has no friends, and so on, destroying all the excitement, the blood and guts that have made these stories popular with children over the centuries. This approach is fallacious on several scores. To begin with, in their emasculated versions, stories that should fascinate older children in their unbowdlerized form bore them and everyone else except the very youngest. Next, these tales become dramatically weak. If Jack's Giant is in truth merely a big, overgrown, lovable puppy underneath, then Jack has never really been in conflict with evil, his victory is a sham, and there is no emotional reward for the audience to participate in. More, the child who goes to the theater expecting the story to be just as he knows it is disappointed. And adding campy gags or otherwise hamming up the performance to compensate may make the children laugh, but it doesn't keep them from feeling cheated all the same.

The result of this misguided effort to pre-

tend violence doesn't exist is that many children over eight have been virtually driven from theater for children. They turn to television and films for excitement in entertainment. If the nines through twelves are to return to theater for children, and the marionette theater as part of it, they'll have to be wooed with the kind of material that has at its heart the conflict between good and evil children have always loved. Scripts will have to be honest. While violence may be called for in the resolution of the conflict, it needn't be relished or dwelt on to the point where it becomes sadism. It wouldn't do to have a princess-heroine thrust into an oven, but no older child minds when a witch who has thoroughly demonstrated her hatefulness meets such a deserved fate. If it's necessary to kill off a giant or an evil brother because logic and justice demand it, don't revel in it. Avoid gratuitous brutality, get it over with speedily, and go on to something else. Only if we remember that a hero and heroine are heroic in proportion to the perils they overcome can we give older children protagonists they can identify with, respect, accompany into danger, and exult with in the end.

For *all* children, sex should be handled with the same sensitivity that violence requires.

Many playwrights for children feel that because a fairy tale or a classic is old hat to them it's dull to children and has to be brought up to date to be "relevant." They miss the point, already discussed here, that children like stories to be dramatized as they know them. But there's another obvious factor they overlook: A story is always new and exciting to a child who has never seen it before. To do a travesty or burlesque of *Goldilocks and the Three Bears* for a five-year-old could be a disaster. To do the same travesty for a ten-year-old could be successful, because the older child has outgrown the story and feels superior to the little ones who still take it seriously. To burlesque *Snow White and the Seven Dwarfs* for ten-year-olds could be equally catastrophic—*Snow White* still has an emotional grip on them and they are threatened by seeing a story they love distorted.

Children love to laugh. Sight gags, word jokes, grotesque situations—these can literally double kids up. But watch for those that may shatter the children's illusions.

There are several areas in which a show for children differs from one for adults. For the littlest children with short attention spans, thirty to forty-five minutes may be all they can take of sitting still. Older children can go for an hour or longer, but marionette shows for them seldom run over sixty minutes. For adults, a show can run as long as a Shakespearean tragedy.

Some playwrights like to do pieces for children that reflect their own nostalgia for their own childhood. Children miss the point of the emotion. They haven't lived long enough to be nostalgic about anything.

Although the subject matter of a play for children must be within their sphere of interest, and its treatment lie within their comprehension, it may be surprising to some how broad this sphere can be when handled intelligently and how fascinating it can be to adults.

This is something to bear in mind, because it may help avoid another common error of playwrights who are aware that in many instances children are accompanied to the theater by adults. In their eagerness to provide entertainment for the grownups, they write into the script gags intended for the adults' consumption only. The children may laugh as loudly as the adults, even at comedy they don't understand, but this sort of thing is unfair to them. It's condescending, for one thing, implying that what's good enough for kids won't do for anyone else, and overlooking the fact that good theater is good theater for anyone. If the production is good, the adult should enjoy it on his own level, he should enjoy it remembering his own childhood, and he should enjoy the pleasure of the child he has brought to the theater. If playwrights truly respect their audiences, they will be respectful of all elements of the show they place before them—beginning with the script.

It goes without saying that no one should write a script or adapt a play or story unless you have affection for it and it means something to you that you want to pass along. This is particularly true for children's material, but for all ages your belief in and understanding of the

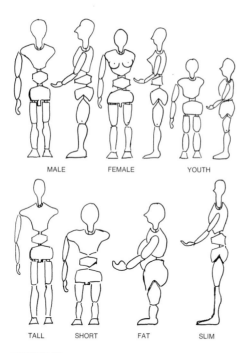

MALE   FEMALE   YOUTH

TALL   SHORT   FAT   SLIM

FIGURE 42

source material or original story are your first asset.

SOURCES OF SCRIPT
MATERIAL OR IDEAS

Where can you go for ideas and inspiration —for the motivation your stringed figures will require if they are to give a convincing illusion of life? If you want to adapt an existing story, there are the myths, folk, and fairy tales handed down to children and adults alike, generation to generation. And there are the classics of children's literature—some of which, like *Alice in Wonderland* and *Heidi*, were written for children in the first place, and some, like *Huckleberry Finn* or *Oliver Twist*, originally intended for adults but taken over by young people. For a mature audience, the entire fiction and historical sections of the library are at your disposal.

The Bible is a fertile source of ideas, particularly if you are interested in playing to religious organizations.

But you aren't confined to oral or written literature. The other arts may contribute ideas. Plays, of course, and also ballets, music, paintings, the circus . . .

Life itself may suggest material to you: your own experiences, the news, personalities, causes. Whatever interests you to a degree that you want to use it on your marionette stage to convey an effect, a feeling, or a viewpoint.

For home performances you may use whatever you find, either ready-made or modified by you; for performances with outside audiences, you may have to pay a royalty. (See Part Three.) With scripts developed from material in the public domain or entirely from your own head, this is never a problem.

EXPANDING THE CAST OF
PLAYERS

If you've followed all the suggestions in "The New Marionette," you'll have constructed Kandu the Magnificent and his Talking Wonder Dog Ruff. You now understand by doing how combining modular cutouts based on frontal and side silhouettes gives you plans for three-dimensional marionettes. In making Kandu and Ruff you have done more than develop two puppets; you have learned how to make two basic figures, prototypes of virtually all the human and animal marionettes you may ever need. You know how to make a tall, thin man (Kandu), so now you have to adapt his designs to turn them into a short, fat man, or a woman, or a child. You've made an animal (Ruff), but you may want to make a different kind of dog, or a horse, or a rabbit, or a cat, or a dragon. As with Kandu's patterns, modifications in the scale and proportions will give you

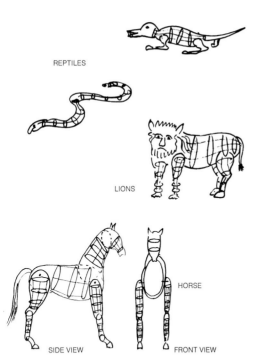

REPTILES

LIONS

HORSE

SIDE VIEW   FRONT VIEW

FIGURE 43

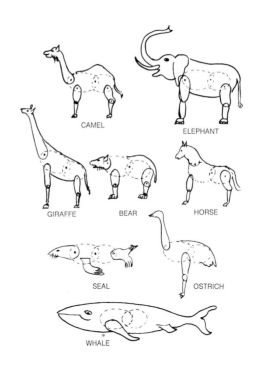

CAMEL   ELEPHANT

GIRAFFE   BEAR   HORSE

SEAL   OSTRICH

WHALE

MAKING ANIMALS OUT OF RUFF'S BASIC FRAME

FIGURE 44

whatever kind of four-footed creature your script calls for. Figures 42, 43, 44, and 45 give you suggested plans for different types and also ideas for how to develop your own plans for constructing original marionettes according to this method.

If this were a Hollywood film you were planning instead of a marionette production, when you were ready for casting, your casting director would search through his files and his memory to find performers for the several roles the script calls for. The marionette master must cast his play, but his job is at once easier and more difficult—easier because he can create precisely the character he has in mind, and harder because he won't be so lucky as to find exactly the right actor to step into a role. Many puppeteers build a specific puppet for each role once the play has been selected. On the other hand, there are those who have built up a kind of stock company of basic types that can be

adapted with minor changes to fit a variety of parts.

People come in all sizes, shapes, colors, and physical idiosyncrasies. Puppets come even more so, and a wide range of contrasts adds interest. If you have a "stock company" of basic puppets, your preconstructed actors can be fattened by cotton wadding, aged or made younger by make-up, and a completely new appearance created by a change of mustache, beard, hairdo, and clothing. If you build a new puppet for a specific part, you build in its physical peculiarities so that its movement will fit the characterization. A human actor may have to submit to torturous facial make-up and body alterations to be convincing in a role. The marionette created for a part, or modified for it, has no such problems. We can accept oddity in puppets, even abnormality, however extreme. What you must always remember is that if your marionette is to demonstrate any

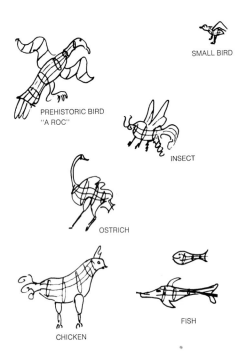

SMALL BIRD

PREHISTORIC BIRD
"A ROC"

INSECT

OSTRICH

CHICKEN

FISH

USING CARDBOARD DISCS TO GIVE DIMENSION

FIGURE 45

particular foible—a blinking eye, a heaving bosom, or a wiggling derriere—the effect requires special construction and special stringing (Figure 80). Sometimes altering a puppet for a special effect can be more onerous than starting from scratch.

Occasionally there is a call for one character so unique it can't be prepared in "blank" but must be designed and built specially. For example, if a play calls for an actor with two heads and feet like a chicken's, obviously you won't have one with just those particular attributes who has been waiting patiently, hoping that some year or other his time would come.

If you have a complete cast for a production, it's not a good idea to throw its actors into a pool, unless you know for certain you'll never be mounting that production at some future time. If there's any possibility of this, put its cast away carefully so that your revival can go

on with a minimum of reconstruction on your part—possibly only a touch-up with a paintbrush and cleaned and pressed costumes.

SCALE

A scale that governs an entire marionette presentation consistently is essential if an audience is to involve itself with it, trust it, and suspend belief in the world outside the theater. We suggest using a scale that's one third life-size. A smaller figure can't be seen easily in many theaters you may play, and a larger one makes for problems in transporting a show. With this one-third scale, a marionette requires only about 10 percent of the space a "live" show needs, even with the "actors" packed away as well. Your puppets must fit into this one-to-three ratio. The normal man of five feet ten, or seventy inches, reduces to twenty-three inches; the woman of sixty-six inches becomes twenty-two inches; and a child of forty-five inches becomes fifteen inches. The mathematical increase or decrease applies to giants and dwarfs. Our eyes accept Jack as "normal"; therefore a figure half again as tall is truly gigantic. David appears "normal" until he is dwarfed alongside Goliath, physically and dramatically. The Miller's Daughter is "normal"; when Rumpelstiltskin stands no higher than her waist, he is a convincingly little man. In each instance, the visual contrast is reinforced by the playscript and the props.

HEADS AND HANDS

The most important parts of any marionette, aside from you, are the head and hands. The other segments are by no means lifeless, but the head and hands have the major burden of communication, and it's essential to give extra care and attention to them.

HEADS

You know how to make heads based on the new, simplified method used for Kandu, but you may want to know some of the conventional procedures as well. Some of these conventional methods will be useful to you if you want to construct a head with movable eyes or mouth, which Kandu's head is not ideally suited for.

A knowledge of anatomy helps.

The two oldest basic methods of making heads are building up (modeling) and cutting away (sculpting).

Modeling. In modeling, a head is shaped on an armature (framework—Figure 46—that supports the outer shell) out of an oil-based softish clay that doesn't harden or dry out. One pound is more than enough for a one-third-scale marionette.

Working on a stand that allows you to see the three-dimensional head from all sides, you apply clay to the armature, building up the features. The clay is pliable, easy to work. When you are satisfied with your creation, there are two ways of developing a puppet head from it. In one case, a thin layer of papier-mâché (Papier-mâché is nothing but paper soaked in water to which glue or paste has been added. The paper is applied to an area as a strip or wad which, when dry, keeps its shape and adheres to the surface) is laid over the clay head in overlapping inch-wide strips. Five or six layers, depending on the thickness of the paper, will dry to a durable shell. For a head of accurate size, making your clay head slightly smaller than the finished result should allow for the thickness of the papier-mâché. After it

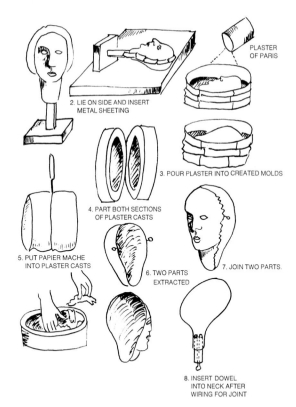

2. LIE ON SIDE AND INSERT METAL SHEETING

PLASTER OF PARIS

3. POUR PLASTER INTO CREATED MOLDS

4. PART BOTH SECTIONS OF PLASTER CASTS

5. PUT PAPIER MACHE INTO PLASTER CASTS

6. TWO PARTS EXTRACTED

7. JOIN TWO PARTS.

8. INSERT DOWEL INTO NECK AFTER WIRING FOR JOINT

FIGURE 46

has thoroughly hardened around the clay, with a sharp knife cut the papier-mâché into two sections, where the cuts won't destroy the details of the head. Remove the shell from the clay and repack the clay to save for future use. The two halves of the shell can be joined together with more strips of papier-mâché if all you want is an immobile face. However, if you want movable eyes, cut holes in the eye sockets and insert balls in them (Figure 80). For a mouth that will open and close, cut the lower jaw off the face (Figure 80) and hinge it as shown. If the character is to have his mouth open a great deal, you may wish to insert cardboard teeth behind his lips. When all the mechanisms are in place for operating the movable eyes, nose, mouth, etc., and the two parts of the head have been rejoined, the neck will have to be closed. For this, take a dowel about an inch long and the width of the neck opening, Fasten a wire loop through it (Figure 46). Plug the neck with the dowel, loop down, and secure it in position with glue and small nails or carpet tacks. When everything is together, the head can be painted or detailed. As with Kandu's head, heavy tempera paint or gesso can be used for filling in hollows or smoothing out rough areas. You can make your own gesso by mixing whiting with white glue and a little water. Use this as thickly as possible, filling in all cracks, cuts, and small holes. When bone dry, the head should be sanded and shellacked before it's painted.

Another modeling process requires the making of a plaster cast. For this, turn the clay head so that it faces you. Take little strips of brass sheeting (about two inches long each) or strips cut from a tin can, very thin, and divide the head in half by inserting them into the clay—close together or even overlapping slightly —all around the head: at the brow hairline, in front of the ears, down the sides of the neck, and across the bottom. The metal should protrude from the clay at least one inch. (Figure 46). Then, on a board, lay the head on its back and with extra clay make a "well" around the head at the edges of the metal (Figure 46). The well should be at least as high as the top of the face plus one inch. Mix plaster of paris by filling a vessel (A pound coffee can is the right size and can be discarded later.) about two thirds full of water and sifting the plaster (about a cup and a half) into it. (Never stir the plaster. This will create air bubbles that can spoil your mold.) When the mixture has the consistency of thick cream and there is no clear water on top, the plaster is ready to be spooned carefully over the clay face. Be sure

the plaster fills in all the space between the face and the well and is never less than three fourths of an inch thick at any point. Discard any leftover plaster immediately, before it hardens in your can. When your mold has completely hardened (about a half hour), you are ready to do the other side. From the board, remove the plaster, well, and head carefully and invert them. If the clay sticks to the board, separate them with a putty knife or spatula. Remove the metal strips from the clay. You may have to open the well to do so. Put the embedded head back on the board clay side up and coat the upper surface of the plaster with shellac. After the shellac dries, cover the plaster with a parting agent (petroleum jelly, salad oil, or any other substance that prevents sticking) in a thin layer. Replace the well, if necessary (Figure 46). Make up a fresh batch of plaster and cover the back of the head with it. When it sets, remove the well and separate the two halves of the mold. The clay of the head and the well can be combined and packed away for future use. If you model your clay head from the beginning with the intention of making a plaster-of-paris mold from it, avoid modeling undercuts into the head that will allow the plaster to fill in in such a way that it locks into the head and cannot be separated from it.

The mold is your negative form. Once again, coat the inside of both halves with a parting agent. To make two positive halves, line the mold with papier-mâché strips, pressing them against the sides to cover the curves without losing any of the shape you modeled (Figure 46). Leave the papier-mâché in the mold until it's dry; then you can remove the shell safely. Save your cast for making duplicate heads at a later date, if you wish. From this point, you can proceed with this papier-mâché head just the same way you would the head described in the previous process.

The plaster cast can be used with materials other than papier-mâché—plastic wood and Celastic, for instance. Both use acetone and aren't easy for those without experience, but practice will develop expertise. Proper ventilation is a must when using acetone. Celastic comes in sheets in three weights. We suggest the medium weight, which is as light as papier-mâché and stronger when finished. One layer is all you need for a puppet that won't be subjected to much wear and tear, but for heavy duty at least one more layer is recommended. Cut the Celastic into inch strips on the diagonal, dip them into acetone to soften them, and line the mold with them, pressing firmly against the form. Celastic gives a somewhat smoother surface than papier-mâché, but its cost is higher.

Plastic wood comes in one-pound cans and is a soft, puttylike compound. Roll it out in a baking pan until it's about a quarter of an inch thick. It should feel like pizza dough. If the "dough" is too hard or dry, dissolve in a little acetone. Sprinkle on a little talcum powder if it sticks to your hands. Dip your hands into water frequently to keep from getting gooked up, and work quickly. Apply the "dough" in one or more pieces to the greased inside of your mold halves as fast as you can. Collect all the plastic wood you don't use, replace it in its can, and seal the can tightly. After the plastic wood lining has dried in the mold, remove it and continue as with the other processes.

If you lined your mold with papier-mâché, you use papier-mâché to put your head pieces together, as described above. If you used Celastic, join the sections with a strip of Celastic, and if you used plastic wood, use the same material for joining.

Sculpting. The other method, dating back to antiquity, is carving or sculpting the head. Wood is the most frequently used medium, and the results can be magnificent when a great master like Basil Milovsoroff of Vermont is the artist. Wooden heads can be made with movable parts. However, except for balsa, wooden heads shouldn't be given to our new cardboard marionettes. Wood is too heavy and throws off the otherwise perfect balance. Plastic foam is catching on because it's inexpensive and very light, but it's difficult to carve fine detail and to correct mistakes. If subtlety isn't necessary and if broad features are shaped, plastic foam is an excellent material for a head without movable parts.

Other Techniques. Modeling and carving aren't the only ways a head can be made. Wire can be twisted into a recognizable head and left without "skin"—possibly with small lights set inside; tongue-depressor sticks can be soaked in water until they are soft, then bent and glued into a permanent position to form a head; a ball (plastic foam, cork, rubber, or even balled-up newspaper dipped in glue and then modeled) with buttons and flaps glued on for facial features and ears can be fun. Any number of materials and techniques your own ingenuity can devise are possible. Just take care that any head you make is light enough to keep the puppet's balance intact.

HAIR

After your head has been shaped and painted, you may find you want to carry your effect further—either to make it more lifelike or more of a caricature. The most obvious feature to encourage individuality is the hair. Figure 47 suggests some of the materials you have at your disposal for scalp hair, eyebrows, beards, and mustaches.

85

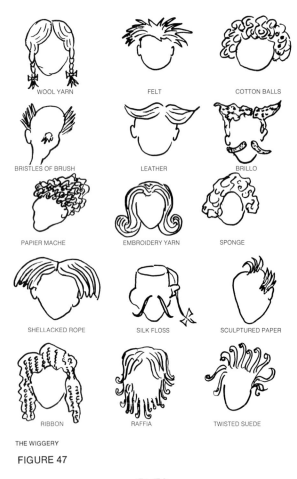

WOOL YARN · FELT · COTTON BALLS

BRISTLES OF BRUSH · LEATHER · BRILLO

PAPIER MACHE · EMBROIDERY YARN · SPONGE

SHELLACKED ROPE · SILK FLOSS · SCULPTURED PAPER

RIBBON · RAFFIA · TWISTED SUEDE

THE WIGGERY

FIGURE 47

EYES

In Part One we spoke of adding sparkle to Kandu's eyes by applying a touch of varnish. Buttons with facets that reflect light can create similiar effects. Small metallic spangles glued to the eyeballs may work in some instances, or small bits of colored glass. Inserting pins in the very center of the eyes, so that the pinheads catch the light, helps to bring about a lifelike expression.

HANDS

Hands can also be modeled, sculpted, or shaped from wire, just as with the heads. One simple way is to make a pattern or jig with finishing (headless) nails hammered into a block of wood. The nails should be set at the sides of the wrist, the fingertips, and where the fingers join the hand. Weave a flexible wire around the nails, in and out and back and forth, to form a hand (Figure 48). Slip the wire frame off the nails and shape it into the position you want for the hand onstage: with the index finger pointing, with the fingers separated to "pick up" a prop, with the fingers curled to fit around a sword hilt, or with the fingers clenched in a fist. After the position is set, cover the hand with cloth, papier-mâché, Celastic, or plastic wood. Be sure to keep the hand light so that it doesn't affect the balance of the marionette.

Carving hands from wood with movable fingers (attached to leather strips fastened to the palm) is possible for skilled craftsmen, but again, unless the wood is balsa, they will be too heavy for our new marionette. Hands can be modeled in clay, and just as the heads were made, use the same process in the medium of your choice (Figure 48).

COSTUMING

Importance of *Costumes.* Probably one of the most overlooked areas in puppet production is that of costuming. In every culture, people wear some kind of bodily covering—to conform to local notions of modesty, for decoration, or to indicate status in a clan or society or profession. Marionettes are costumed for all these reasons and more.

One of the main functions of a marionette costume is to cover the joints. There may be occasions when the puppet must appear nude, or virtually so (Tarzan, Lady Godiva, Hercules, swimming children, etc.), and then one has the choice of letting the joints show or devising ingenious methods to conceal them (e.g., a half-

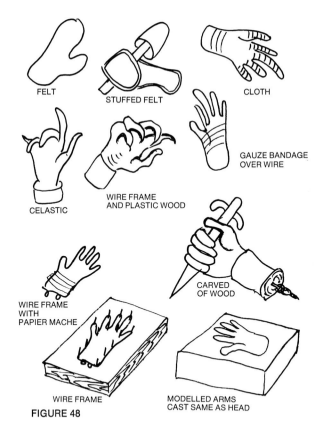

FELT   STUFFED FELT   CLOTH

GAUZE BANDAGE OVER WIRE

CELASTIC   WIRE FRAME AND PLASTIC WOOD

CARVED OF WOOD

WIRE FRAME WITH PAPIER MACHE

WIRE FRAME   MODELLED ARMS CAST SAME AS HEAD

FIGURE 48

naked gnome partly covered with leaves could have small leaves over his elbows and knees). Covering for illusion's sake is more important than for modesty's, because audiences don't apply the same standard to marionettes they do to human beings and are tolerant, even for children's performances, of a larger area of puppet "skin" than of persons'.

An even more important function of costuming is to identify the characters and communicate instantly the impression the author and director want to convey about their age, station in life, personal habits and attributes, and the era in which they exist.

Costuming is an art in itself, but in the theater it is subservient to the over-all production. Its sculptural qualities can make the most

of the marionette's own three-dimensional aspects.

Always remember a marionette is a relatively small object. Your taste will govern whether he wears the costume or it wears him.

Research. In a period piece requiring research, you'll be on safer ground with your costumes if you actually do the research instead of "faking" it. There are numerous books that go into as much detail as you'll need on every aspect of costume design, and some of them are listed in the Bibliography.

Art masterpieces of the era that concerns you can give you a feel for what your costumes should communicate so that you can give your several characters individual qualities without violating the atmosphere of belief.

Aside from obvious resources like libraries, there are other mines of information from which you may draw. Chambers of commerce, consulates, travel organizations, and air and shipping lines often can supply brochures illustrating native costumes. The *Smithsonian* and *National Geographic* magazines might be useful. And if you're investigating costumes of the last few generations, don't overlook your own family album.

Exaggeration and Verisimilitude. There's a difference between ordinary everyday clothing and theatrical costumes. In order to communicate on a stage, costumes have to exaggerate, be larger than life. Clothing indicative of poverty can be more ragged than in reality; of royalty, more sumptuous. This exaggeration must be contained within the style of the play and the context of the characterization if it is to be believed by the audience.

The most common error, particularly among new showmen, is to overdress, to overadorn the puppets. A poverty-stricken old peasant, for example, is shown in a velvet gown with satin

Costuming Goliath and King Saul from Suib Marionette Production of *David and Goliath*.

patches. She looks pretty, but no one believes in her. Even at the expense of making the characters less attractive, keep them credible by considering their economic status, time, and place.

Use "human" touches to reinforce the impression your costumes telegraph. For instance, in a *Hansel and Gretel* production a small plaid fabric used for Gretel's skirt was also the valance at the cottage window, suggesting that Mother was careful to waste nothing.

Color. Color is of prime concern. It can give the character's mood immediately, with gay, bright tones for happy or comic actors and subdued or somber tones for unhappy, retiring, or tragic ones. Bear in mind that no costume is an independent, isolated phenomenon.

Besides identifying and to some degree defining the actor wearing it, the costume comes in contact with those of the other actors and is seen against the backgrounds and set pieces of the stage. Therefore, the color of each costume has an aesthetic effect on the total production. If it "goes with" the other colors, the effect will be good.

Another factor not taken often enough into consideration is what happens to the costumes' colors when the stage lights are turned on them. Some colors will wash out under certain lights, or be altered subtly or drastically. When you select your colors, it's a good idea to test them with the filters you plan to use to verify the ultimate result. The subject of lights and colors is treated in substantially more detail in the section on "Lighting."

Fabric. The right fabric is as important as the right color. Available are wools, cottons, linens, silks, synthetics. Fur, toweling, canvas, felt, smooth leather, suede. Spangles, feathers, beads, mirrors. The list is endless, and virtually anything can make or trim a marionette costume. Expense is rarely a factor because the marionette requires such a small amount compared to what a live actor would need. The characterization of each puppet should determine your choice of the material to dress him. Hansel's starving peasant mother would wear a sturdy homespun type of skirt rather than a brocade. A beggar or Little Match Girl would be comfortable in the tatters no king or queen would deign to wear. Royalty would insist on velvet, perhaps ermine-trimmed.

The texture and weight of a fabric are to be considered. A fairy would have difficulty in flying wearing a heavy brocade, and she might be grotesque in a wool bouclé. She should be all silky gauze or chiffon. An earth-digging gnome would be absurd in organdy.

Unless you want to dazzle your audience or bewilder it, avoid glittering fabrics that catch the light, and remember that this also applies to sparkling ornamentation, and use it with restraint.

On a one-third-scale puppet, a print or woven pattern will appear three times as large as it really is. Accordingly, keep the figures on the cloth small, as well as using small decorative elements. Unless, of course, you are deliberately exaggerating for a special effect.

Finding patterns on fabrics tiny enough to meet the demands of scale may be difficult. One way to solve the problem is to start from scratch with a plain colored fabric, even unbleached muslin. Onto this material you can stencil or paint whatever designs you wish in your scale. Designs can be painted on velvets and other plushy fabrics too, sometimes with startlingly beautiful results.

In addition to a pattern, shadows and highlights can be painted on the fabric. Marking pens, tempera and spray paints, and tie-dyeing are only some of the coloring supplies or methods available. However, be careful that the paint you select is not too heavily glue-based. The amount of glue or sizing can affect the stiffness of the fabric.

Remember always the strings of your marionettes and avoid stiff fabrics, stiff painting, or stiff or projecting decorations that might catch them or hinder free joint movement.

Fabric Reserve Bank. Procuring fabrics for puppets is simple, since so little is needed and so many kinds are useful. Discarded clothing and attic trunks are possible sources of supply. Rummaging for remnants in yard-goods stores, theatrical costume houses, dressmaking establishments, and thrift shops can yield treasures at little cost.

We suggest you start to build a collection of odds and ends of fabrics and trimmings.

Have a box of velvets, brocades, fancy wools, silks, voiles, chiffons, nets, satins, taffetas, furs, and bejeweled and sequined materials that indicate a luxurious style of living.

Another box could hold more earthy fabrics: leathers, simulated animal skins, monk's cloth, burlaps, canvas, duck, felts, and coarse woolens.

A third box is for trimmings: tape, ribbons, laces, metallic strips, theatrical specials (glittering fabrics), cording, beading, fancy buttons, feathers—all small scraps to adorn and embellish your costumes.

Line. As important as scale, color, and fabric is *line* to a costume. Whether a fabric falls stiffly or drapes softly, whether the elements are gently curved or angular, are convex or concave—all this influences the audience's reactions to the character wearing it. Stripes, pleats, folds, gathers—whether wide or narrow, vertical or horizontal, draped elegantly or bunched clumsily—make a statement about your puppet's character or place in the world.

FIGURE 49

Constructing Costumes—Technical Problems of Marionettes. Don't ever forget it's a marionette you're costuming, not a human being. Not only, as mentioned earlier, should you use fabrics that won't tangle the strings or curtail movement, but the costume itself must not interfere with mobility. It must be loose enough at the joints and, if a skirt, be full enough at the knees to allow the legs natural extension. Study a dancer's costume to appreciate the free-flowing qualities essential for full movement.

In many instances a puppet wears the same costume throughout the entire play, but it is sometimes required to make costume changes. Cinderella's slavey rags are magically transformed into a sumptuous court dress (Figure

50) or, more prosaically, a marionette may need to change from outdoor to indoor clothing, or from winter to summer wear. Changes can be made in view of the audience or offstage. One way to change clothing is to pull a costume off the marionette up the strings and keep it near the controller, or slide a new costume down the strings to cover what's being worn. Or a coat can be taken swiftly from a marionette if it has been slit in the right places (Figure 50) or is made with Velcro (Figure 50).

Costuming can even let your puppet serve double duty. If it has completed its stint onstage as one actor, its garb can be drawn up to reveal another outfit underneath—or a new costume can drop down over the old. A mask can change the puppet into another character or, less drastically, age him perceptibly between scenes.

Even though we've said a puppeteer wears many hats, it was never in reference to actual costuming. Now we're suggesting that the puppet can wear many hats—literally. Think of an actor who presents many faces to the audience, indicating each new characterization by changing his hat. If he begins by wearing a tiny beret, he can proceed by merely having another model dropped from the controller to cover the first. And so on. This is an instance where the capability of your marionette to perform a trick could influence the script to find an acceptable dramatic reason for doing it.

Dressing a puppet has at least one advantage over costuming a live actor. The marionette will give you indulgent cooperation regardless of how many fittings you require or how long you take. He will move into and hold any position you like.

You can shape his clothing by draping the

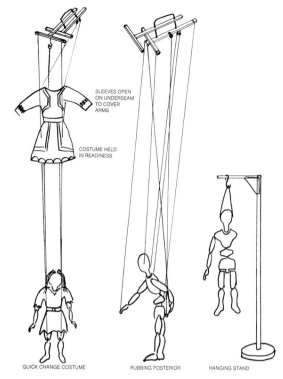

SLEEVES OPEN
ON UNDERSEAM
TO COVER
ARMS

COSTUME HELD
IN READINESS

QUICK CHANGE COSTUME   RUBBING POSTERIOR   HANGING STAND

FIGURE 50

fabric directly on the marionette's body and cutting the pieces in position, leaving a generous seam allowance. Or, if you prefer, you may first cut a pattern by draping thin paper, cutting it to style and fit, and then transferring it to the fabric. Before connecting the costume parts, tape them to the figure to see if the effect is right and if mobility is unencumbered.

In constructing costumes that in the ordinary course would require elaborate underpinnings—extra-wide shoulders, padded hips, and such—it's sometimes easier to build up the puppet than the costume. But be careful how you drape the fabric over these extensions. A poorly executed bustle skirt can look like a slipcover on a camel.

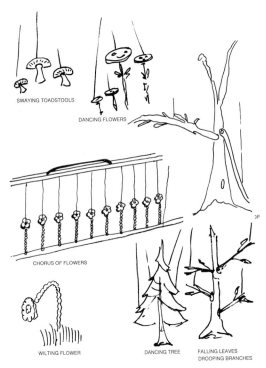

SWAYING TOADSTOOLS

DANCING FLOWERS

CHORUS OF FLOWERS

WILTING FLOWER

DANCING TREE

FALLING LEAVES
DROOPING BRANCHES

FIGURE 51

FLORA...

If your script calls for flowers, shrubs, or trees, you have to determine whether this vegetation is stationary and a prop or "does" something and is a puppet. If it does something, then we have to know the best way to do it. Let's take specific examples.

Jack's beanstalk has to grow before our eyes to the top of the stage. The stalk could be composed of a ladderlike series of green cardboard discs, larger at the bottom of the stalk than at the top, fastened to a heavy green line. If Jack's mother has thrown the magic beans into a pot or behind a wall, the number of leaf discs on the stalk can't be greater than the pot or the wall will conceal. It's better to build the stalk first so that you can make it look convincing, and then provide for its con-

cealment. When each leaf is connected by sturdy green twine in three places to those above and below it, the stalk won't twist or twirl as it is raised. The bottom disc is anchored to the bottom of the pot or rests, weighted, on the stage floor. The top disc is attached with black string to its own controller.

A chorus of smiling daisies can be made of stalks of lead beading (such as a dressmaker uses for hems). The lead beading comes in strips, which should be cut to your design and covered with greenery for stems. For an attractive three-dimensional look, glue on several layers of colored fabric petals and green felt leaves. Anchor the flowers to a wood strip and attach the heads to a controller. If the flowers are to act in unison, fasten them to a single long controller (Figure 51). These flowers can sway and dance and they can lie hidden under a blanket of snow (a brown cloth with "snowy" patches of absorbent cotton, overlaid by white cheesecloth) until spring comes. Then, raised by their controller, the flowers can push back the snow, burst into bloom, and grow before our eyes.

Trees can be adept performers and have diverse personalities. You can give them individual personalities in terms of their characteristics. A weeping willow might always be mournful; an oak, virile or gruff; a chestnut, comforting and bountiful. Branches can droop. Hinged into the trunk, they can be joined in two ways. Insert the branch into a slot and pin or wire it into position (Figure 51) or interlock two screw eyes, screwing one into a wood strip in the trunk and the other into the branch. The former method permits only an up-and-down movement; the latter, movement in all directions.

Trees can shed their leaves. When a wintry blast occurs, two or three leaves on individual

92

controllers can be lowered to the ground. Then the other leaves, which look as if they are fastened to the branches at different heights but are really attached to one long controller (Figure 51), fall to the ground and are "blown" about. It's a pretty touch to leave one leaf on the tree.

A tree can get up on its roots, use them as feet, and clump around. Or turn itself inside out to become something else.

In the section on "Props" there are other suggestions for how to construct trees and shrubbery. And the section on "Marionette Magic" and special effects will give you explanations of how to create a particular trick. Even though what you have in mind may not be spelled out, you will almost certainly find a special effect embodying a principle that can be adapted to your needs.

Remember that all animated flora are attached to controllers and must be hung in place. A hanging strap or hook must be included for each piece so that, after the tree or flower or whatever makes its last stage appearance, it can be hung offstage, freeing the puppeteer for other matters.

...AND FAUNA

No marionette theater is really complete without its complement of birds and beasts. Economics is only one of the factors precluding the live theater from competing in this area. Ask any circus manager what it costs to feed his collection.

Animals can't always be counted on to do what is hoped of them onstage. A marionette creature can be depended on not to exercise his individuality and independence at an inopportune moment of the performance.

A marionette can be taught to perform tricks impossible to living creatures and be completely at one with the world of your imagination. Birds, particularly, are at home in the marionette theater. They scarcely seem to need their wings to fly. Figure 45 gives several ideas for the simple construction of a variety of birds.

Adapting Basic Designs. Having made Ruff the Talking Wonder Dog, you know how to make an animal puppet. Figures 43 and 44 show you how to create additional animals for your menagerie by adapting his designs and using the basic principle of combining frontal and profile silhouettes. You can create any animal, from a giraffe to a whale, with cardboard modules.

Since many creatures may appear in your productions only briefly, or with only a portion of their anatomy being seen onstage, pages 80, 81, and 82 have diagrams of marionettes made even more simply than Kandu and Ruff. In some instances, these are made with only a few disks of cardboard held together by string (where flexibility is required) or by stiff wire (for rigidity) and then covered. These suggestions are intended to fire your imagination so that you can use the new theory of puppet construction for virtually any figure.

Scale. A problem may arise in the construction of these animals: the matter of scale. We've been using a one-to-three ratio in the height of our people puppets, but this may be impractical with other life forms. If a six-foot man is reduced to two feet, a butterfly would be virtually invisible at the same scale, and an elephant would burst the confines of your stage. Therefore, the scale would have to be distorted so that the butterfly would be considerably larger than its normal scale size and the elephant considerably smaller. A twelve-pound cat chasing a ladybug would normally be about four and a half or five inches high at the shoulder, but inasmuch as it would naturally be enormously larger than the insect, some liberties would have to be taken with its scale so that the actions of both are reasonable.

Adjustments in scale are influenced by factors such as visibility, theatrical effectiveness, and credibility.

PERFORMING

The puppet stage, like any other, is peopled with artists whose business is to perform in such a way that the audience will accept them as the characters they are portraying, as well as the make-believe world in which they exist.

As with scripts, so it is with acting: Belief is the first ingredient. If you believe in the reality of your characterzations and in the emotions motivating them, you can persuade the audience to believe in them also.

The actor communicates through a combination of body and vocal language. Along with all the other hats the puppeteer wears he has to don that of the actor and learn enough of the actor's craft to teach his marionettes all they need to know.

Many persons who would die of embarrassment if they had to address a meeting or appear onstage as themselves lose all their inhibitions when backstage anonymity allows them to speak through their puppets. Sometimes they are the most amazed of all at the conviction with which their little people perform.

BODY COMMUNICATION

You have learned basic manipulation of a human puppet and an animal in Part One, but the nuances of movement the marionette's body can convey through your hands are yet to be explored. Anger, fright, joy, amusement, anticipation, fatigue, drowsiness, shame, and rejection can all be expressed through manipulation. In many instances the basic strings will be enough, but there may be situations in which additional stringing is called for. Impatience, demonstrated by having the marionette tap his foot in exasperation, needs a special string to the toe. A wrathful woman with arms akimbo needs additional strings to bring her hands to her hips. But acting is more than special strings.

When you built the puppets you took into consideration what the script required of them in the way of physical appearance. Now you have to look at them again, to study the way their movement can develop their characterizations. You have to think with your muscles. What does it feel like to be an old man whose back hurts, who wants to sit in the sun but who has to walk six miles? What does it feel like to be a four-year-old just finding out that the world lies outside his door? What does it feel like to be a young mother who has skipped her breakfast so that her child could eat? Or a forty-year-old businessman late for an appointment?

In every case the marionette would walk differently. Is the old man fat or thin, and how does this change his gait? Is the mother going to a feast, or has she returned empty-handed from the market? Is the businessman expecting to clinch a big deal or to lose his shirt?

Their physical characteristics have been built into the marionettes, so now it's up to you to rehearse them in their roles until the audience can recognize each actor by the quality of his movement even without the costumes and make-up. When you manipulate each figure, if you think "Why am I doing this? How do I feel?" you'll discover that a whole range of manipulative techniques will occur to you. As a strong man, you won't just lift a thousand pounds casually from the floor. No, you'll tug at it tentatively, strain, settle your feet, stagger under the weight, and raise it triumphantly, if shakily, over your head. You can be Juliet, torn between fear and hope on her balcony, or Hamlet pondering his future, or the Emperor Jones in his madness. You can be a curious, ear-wagging rabbit, a recalcitrant mule, or a fighting bull.

Work on your characterizations until they say in mime all that can be conveyed without words or other sounds. Introduce the voices of your marionettes, adjust their body movements to the dialogue of the script, nodding heads or gesturing with hands to add naturalism to what they are called upon to say or listen to.

VOICE COMMUNICATION

The marionette's voice communicates in several ways. The most obvious is that it conveys the playwright's dialogue to the audience, but it also to a large extent defines the character and his emotional and physical state.

Because the voices will be coming from behind a curtain and because marionette faces are totally or partly immobile, it's not always easy to tell who is speaking. Therefore, it's necessary to do as much as possible to assure clarity. The first thing to bear in mind is that enunciation must be precise—sharper even than if the actors were live. Emphasize the verbs so that the essential meaning of a sentence comes across. Also stress the most important word remaining: "I shall *go* to the *store*." In an auditorium with bad acoustics or outside disturbances, this could make a significant difference.

Next, a variety of voices distinctly different from each other makes identification simpler. If you are adept in sending your voice from soprano to *basso profundo*, you won't need any help. You'll just have to learn how to make the transitions from one character's voice to another's without pausing as your actors talk to each other. If this is too much for you or you don't have the necessary range—and it's more than most puppeteers can manage without a sore throat—you might want to work with someone else. A woman with a high voice and a man with a low one are an ideal combination for a small show. The woman can play other women, children, small animals, fairies. The man can do some females too—usually comic in falsetto—but his specialty would be heroes, villains, large animals, and awesome characters like God in a Bible story. The stronger the vocal contrast the better.

There are many tricks to alter your voice. Putting cotton wads in your mouth, talking through your nose, bringing your voice up from your chest—all these affect your tones. Changing the shape of your mouth may also work. However, be careful not to achieve these different vocal qualities at the expense of enunciation. If what you have to say is unimportant or can be said adequately with body communication (a nod of the head, a wag of a tail), consult with your playwright self as to whether the dialogue might not be cut.

The voice should confirm other characteristics. A giant's voice could be booming, ominous. A witch might speak in a cackly falsetto. A young man's voice might be robust; a girl's, light; an old woman's, frail. Generally, small puppet, small voice: a sad little voice for a sad little mouse and a heavy snarl for a tiger. However, for comic effects, small puppet, large voice works well, and vice versa. Whether the character is open-handed or niggardly, compassionate or spiteful should be indicated as much by the voice as by the visual attributes of the marionette.

Likewise, although animal sounds must be related to the species giving vent to them, they should also reveal individual traits. Either in wordless sounds or dialogue, the voices should enhance whatever characteristic of loyalty, duplicity, slyness, or timidity the script asks for. Animal sounds don't necessarily have to be realistic, but if you want realism, there are recordings of animal noises that you can tape.

Voices should be differentiated by speech patterns. An overworked housewife might be shrill and brusque; a country bumpkin might be oafish and slow; a beggar, timid and pleading; a squirrel, rapid and chattering; a snail or a tortoise, lethargic or sleepy. A guttersnipe wouldn't sound like an Oxford don.

In the live theater, "topping" lines—that is, having one actor start his speech before another is quite finished—gives a performance a sense of actuality. In the marionette theater, where a puppeteer has to top himself in a different voice, this skill must be mastered to keep the production from dragging.

If you decide, instead of relying on your own voice with possibly an assistant's or partner's, to tape your show with a full complement of actors, please refer to pages 139–142 on taping the performance.

Always, the vocal utterances are coordinated with the visual movements.

Before putting the final stamp of approval on your marionettes' performance, test the body communication by itself and then the vocal. Studying each one separately, one as a pantomime and the other as if it were a radio program, can enable you to spot weaknesses and correct them before rejoining the two halves.

Care for Your Voice. Your voice is one of the tools of your craft, and, like other equipment, it must be cared for. Some exercises from an expert might help you to make the most of it. Don't overwork your voice, and give it opportunities to rest. Allow yourself plenty of time before a performance to set up your stage and marionettes and then to rest for a little while. Relax as much as you can, and then, when the lights go down and your curtain goes up, your voice will serve you as one element of a professionally smooth performance.

MARIONETTE STAGES

There are many kinds of stages in the live theater and many for the puppet theater as well. The kind of stage you decide on should be the one that will best suit the type of marionette production you'll be presenting. Whether your staff consists of you alone or whether you'll have the assistance of other puppeteers, whether you'll be set up in one location where your audiences come to you or whether you'll tour to go to them, and how elaborate your show will be—all these factors enter into your decision.

In Part One we dealt with makeshift or simply constructed stages. Now your more skillful puppetry requires more advanced technical facilities. We've devised four basic stages, one of which should be just right for you.

STAGE #1

This is a portable stage designed for a one-person operation, usually for a quick presentation where seating is unavailable (a shopping mall, a supermarket, a bank, etc.). It has the best features of the trunk stage suggested for

Kandu in Part One, but it has additional desirable qualities. This stage is super-compact and can contain *everything* you need to put on your show with—provided, of course, that your professional-quality production is relatively modest in scope.

The solitary unit is on casters. When disassembled for transportation it's easy to move around.

The height of the performing area is particularly good—thirty-six inches above the floor. This is a height passers-by can see without straining or pushing.

A minimum ceiling height of ten feet is necessary. There are no maskings to conceal the puppeteer. With this stage, you must be sure of what you're doing and perform smoothly, since there's nowhere to hide.

STAGE #2

Stage #2 is also designed for touring, and it can hold two or three operators. The units that hold all your equipment can be folded to a size that will fit into a station wagon or small van.

The bridge is simple and serviceable and will sustain the puppeteers' weight. The stage floor, however, is light and designed only for marionettes, scenery, and props.

Stage #2 sets up easily by two people and is reasonably light. It accommodates your lighting equipment and whatever other gear you need for a first-rate show.

If you have a production that needs greater facilities, a study of these plans will show you how to adapt them to special situations.

Notice that Figure 52 depicts a series of screens that frame in the center stage, which is exclusively for marionettes, and that a puppet booth is incorporated in each side of the arrangement. This is a modification of Stage #2 and it is justified only if you intend to use hand or rod puppets with your marionettes. These booths can be used to have puppets hold the attention of the audience while the marionettes' scenery is being changed, or to have the puppets comment on the main action of the marionettes. Remember, if you use hand or rod puppets you'll need at least a third puppeteer so that he can function while one or two operators reset the center stage.

STAGE #3

This stage is for a permanent or resident marionette theater. Because it is not intended to be moved from the premises, it can provide an unparalleled amount of storage. The supports for the bridge are two wardrobes each four by five feet—large enough to hold props, scenery, lights, tools, and puppets. The two units are joined by a spanner that makes a bridge twelve feet long by thirty inches wide and five feet off the ground. The bridgerail and backrail are also stored in these closets, which are on heavy-duty casters and can move freely when detached from each other.

The performing area is also a sturdy unit, made in two sections and with its own casters. The two vertical pieces secured to the stage (performing) area serve a double function: They support the forward bridgerail and house all the mini-spots for the lighting system.

In front of the forward bridge, velvet-covered masking units are attached, and these are the frame of a proscenium theater. A "traveling" curtain is placed along the forward bridgerail, which is the "act tableau" complete with draw facilities.

All parts that the puppeteers would walk on can be carpeted to cut down backstage noise, and the stage floor is canvas-covered.

All the way in the rear, past the backbridge, provisions are made for a rear-view projection screen, which serves also as a cyclorama.

When all the parts of Stage #3 are put together, it functions well. When taken apart, Stage #3 stores well.

STAGE #4

Stage #4 is a combination type, permitting use of marionettes center stage in conjunction with hand and rod puppets. This is different from the modification of Stage #2. In this, the hand and rod unit is downstage, with the marionette stage having its proscenium arch at the rear of the hand puppet stage. This is not an ideal set-up for touring.

First, to conceal the hand puppeteers, the frame must be built sufficiently high. We suggest that the puppeteers manipulate their actors from a sitting position, on a bench or chairs, rather than standing, to reduce the height required. They could squat, also, but this could result in physical discomfort and an impaired performance. Over-all depth requirements are a minimum of ten feet.

The marionette stage behind this frame would have to be at least four feet high. This is an advantage, since the high presentation level allows maximum visibility for the audience, regardless of whether the house seats are on a "raked" or sloping floor. You will need at least eleven feet of playing height, and if you'll be on a raised stage, add that height to the eleven feet and check whether the ceiling will accommodate it.

This stage allows for combined effects, where stringed and other puppets interrelate. Set

pieces in the forward (hand puppet) section give another dimension. As mentioned under Stage #2, the hand puppets can take over while changes are being made on the marionette stage.

MULTI-MEDIA STAGE

A combination of the features of the various stages can be used for multi-media (Figure 63). This composite stage is useful for allowing non-stop action, since attention can be focused in several areas simultaneously or successively.

CURTAINS

In the proscenium theater, marionette or otherwise, stage curtains are customary. What the audience sees is a room with the fourth wall removed, or a part of a forest or garden with trees and shrubbery cleared from the fourth side, so that one can look into a scene unimpeded by the technicality of complete enclosure. It's this fourth side that disappears when the curtain goes up.

Draw curtains, those which go from side to side, are the most common for the marionette stage. A simple up-and-down curtain, sometimes on a roller, is called a *roll-away*. Also used is the "tableau" curtain, where the curtain is parted vertically and each section is lifted diagonally to drape and frame the stage picture. The "contour" curtain is effective—the most famous is the Radio City Music Hall curtain—producing a scalloped effect as it rises.

You may do without a draw or other curtain, provided your sets are masked by the absence of light (a "blackout")—effective for certain types of production.

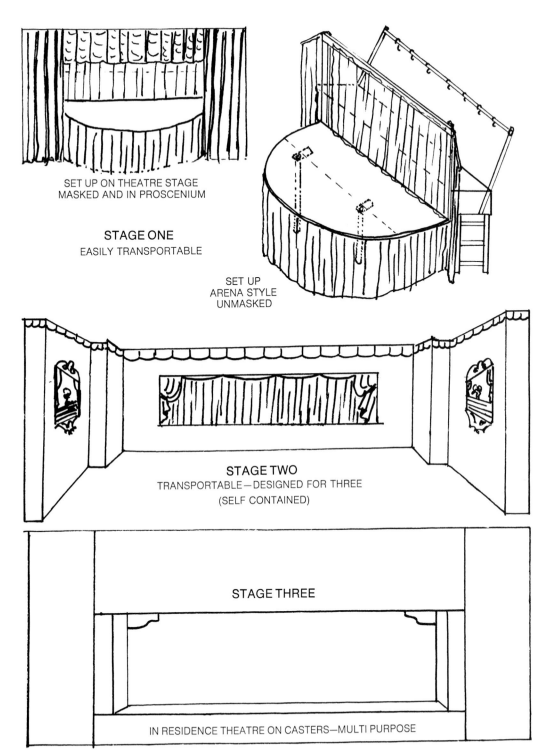

SET UP ON THEATRE STAGE
MASKED AND IN PROSCENIUM

STAGE ONE
EASILY TRANSPORTABLE

SET UP
ARENA STYLE
UNMASKED

STAGE TWO
TRANSPORTABLE—DESIGNED FOR THREE
(SELF CONTAINED)

STAGE THREE

IN RESIDENCE THEATRE ON CASTERS—MULTI PURPOSE

FIGURE 52

SPECIFICATIONS FOR STAGE ONE

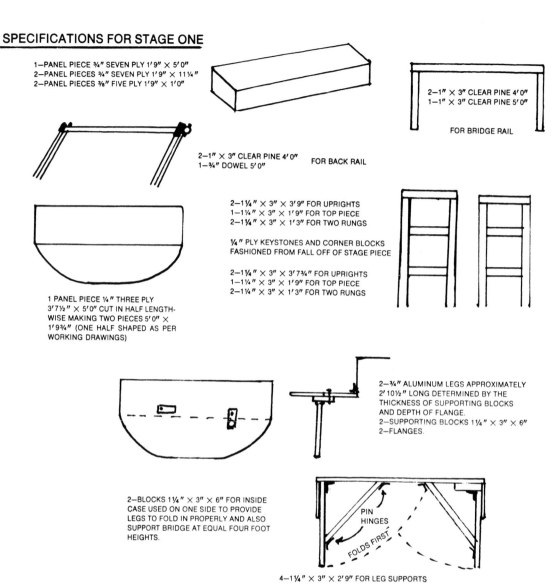

1—PANEL PIECE ¾" SEVEN PLY 1'9" × 5'0"
2—PANEL PIECES ¾" SEVEN PLY 1'9" × 11¼"
2—PANEL PIECES ⅜" FIVE PLY 1'9" × 1'0"

2—1" × 3" CLEAR PINE 4'0"
1—1" × 3" CLEAR PINE 5'0"

FOR BRIDGE RAIL

2—1" × 3" CLEAR PINE 4'0"   FOR BACK RAIL
1—¾" DOWEL 5'0"

2—1¼" × 3" × 3'9" FOR UPRIGHTS
1—1¼" × 3" × 1'9" FOR TOP PIECE
2—1¼" × 3" × 1'3" FOR TWO RUNGS

¼" PLY KEYSTONES AND CORNER BLOCKS
FASHIONED FROM FALL OFF OF STAGE PIECE

2—1¼" × 3" × 3'7¾" FOR UPRIGHTS
1—1¼" × 3" × 1'9" FOR TOP PIECE
2—1¼" × 3" × 1'3" FOR TWO RUNGS

1 PANEL PIECE ¼" THREE PLY
3'7½" × 5'0" CUT IN HALF LENGTH-
WISE MAKING TWO PIECES 5'0" ×
1'9¾" (ONE HALF SHAPED AS PER
WORKING DRAWINGS)

2—¾" ALUMINUM LEGS APPROXIMATELY
2'10½" LONG DETERMINED BY THE
THICKNESS OF SUPPORTING BLOCKS
AND DEPTH OF FLANGE.
2—SUPPORTING BLOCKS 1¼" × 3" × 6"
2—FLANGES.

2—BLOCKS 1¼" × 3" × 6" FOR INSIDE
CASE USED ON ONE SIDE TO PROVIDE
LEGS TO FOLD IN PROPERLY AND ALSO
SUPPORT BRIDGE AT EQUAL FOUR FOOT
HEIGHTS.

PIN
HINGES

FOLDS FIRST

4—1¼" × 3" × 2'9" FOR LEG SUPPORTS

AFTER REMOVING SUPPORTING LEGS (REMOVE PINS OF HINGES) MAIN LEGS FOLD

HARDWARE SPECIFICATIONS FOR STAGE ONE

6 butts hinges 3" x 1½" for stage floor.

4 butt hinges 1½" x 2" for legs attached from bottom of stage floor to the legs
(2 supports for each leg).

8 pin hinges for leg supports (detachable for storage)

1" rosin coated nails for all keystones and corner blocks ½ pound.

1 box # 1" screws for box unit.

1 pound 1½" rosin coated nails for box unit. Use both nails and screws to secure
this unit as it is the wear and tear for both use and storage that takes most abuse.

1 dozen carriage bolts ¼" x 2" for attaching bridge rail, back rail and supporting
legs.

4 heavy duty rubber casters for easy transport.

FIGURE 53

ONE MAN PORTABLE STAGE LIGHT AND TRANSPORTABLE

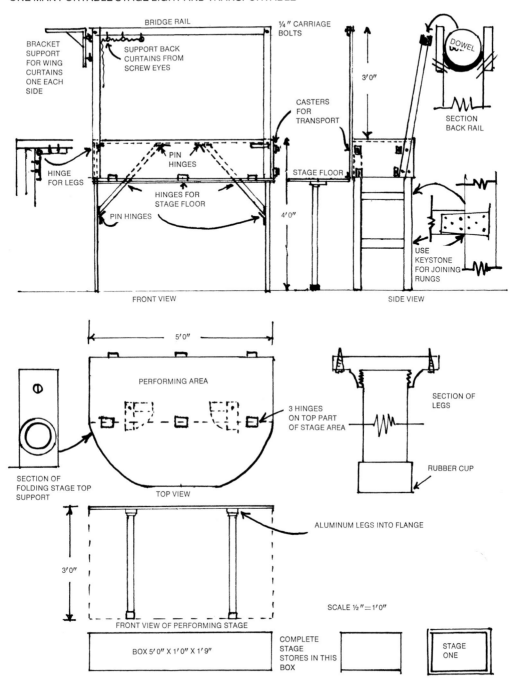

BRIDGE RAIL

¼" CARRIAGE BOLTS

BRACKET SUPPORT FOR WING CURTAINS ONE EACH SIDE

SUPPORT BACK CURTAINS FROM SCREW EYES

DOWEL

SECTION BACK RAIL

3'0"

CASTERS FOR TRANSPORT

PIN HINGES

HINGE FOR LEGS

STAGE FLOOR

HINGES FOR STAGE FLOOR

PIN HINGES

4'0"

USE KEYSTONE FOR JOINING RUNGS

FRONT VIEW

SIDE VIEW

5'0"

PERFORMING AREA

3 HINGES ON TOP PART OF STAGE AREA

SECTION OF LEGS

SECTION OF FOLDING STAGE TOP SUPPORT

TOP VIEW

RUBBER CUP

ALUMINUM LEGS INTO FLANGE

3'0"

SCALE ½" = 1'0"

FRONT VIEW OF PERFORMING STAGE

BOX 5'0" X 1'0" X 1'9"

COMPLETE STAGE STORES IN THIS BOX

STAGE ONE

ARENA TYPE MARIONETTE STAGE 5'0" x 3'6" x 3'0" H

FIGURE 54

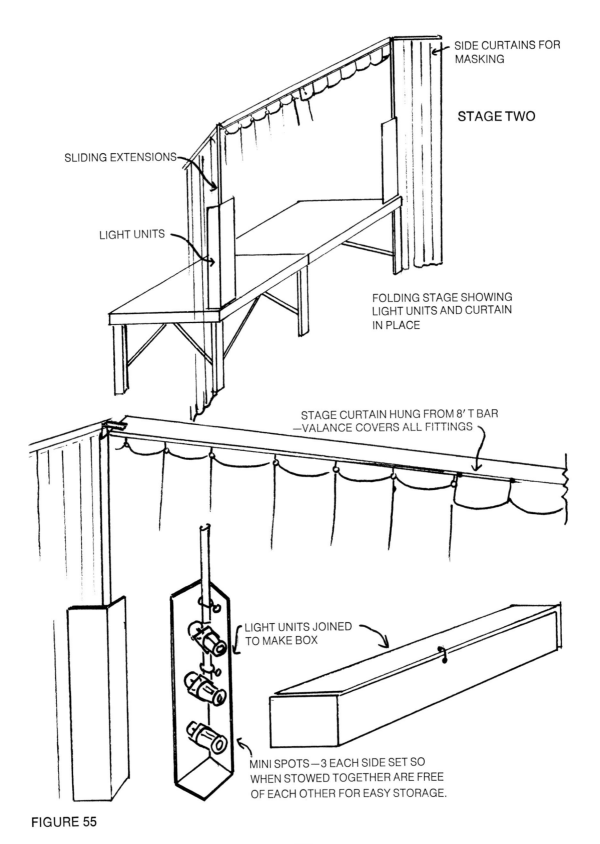

SIDE CURTAINS FOR MASKING

STAGE TWO

SLIDING EXTENSIONS

LIGHT UNITS

FOLDING STAGE SHOWING LIGHT UNITS AND CURTAIN IN PLACE

STAGE CURTAIN HUNG FROM 8' T BAR —VALANCE COVERS ALL FITTINGS

LIGHT UNITS JOINED TO MAKE BOX

MINI SPOTS—3 EACH SIDE SET SO WHEN STOWED TOGETHER ARE FREE OF EACH OTHER FOR EASY STORAGE.

FIGURE 55

102

SPECIFICATIONS FOR STAGE TWO

STAGE PERFORMING AREA REQUIRES:
2—¼" THREE PLY PANEL 2' 6" × 4' 0".
4—PIECES 1" × 2" × 4' 0" FOR FRAMING.
4—PIECES 1" × 2" × 2' 4½" FOR FRAMING.
6—PIECES 1" × 2" × 2' 4" FOR LEGS.
3—PIECES 1" × 2" × 2' 3" FOR LEGS.
(THIS FOR THREE SETS OF LEGS, IF
ADDITIONAL LEG IS DESIRED ADD PIECES.)
48 SCREWS ¾" #4 TO SECURE PANEL TO FRAMING.
(ALSO USE NAILS TO FILL IN)
8 PIECES 1" × 2" × 2' 3" FOR LEG SUPPORTS.
4 METAL STRAPS ¼" × 1" × 2' 3" FOR LEG BRACES.
2 METAL STRAPS ¼" × 1" × 1' 3" INSIDE LEG BRACE.
12—¼" × 1½" CARRIAGE BOLTS FOR BRACES.
8—¾" × 2" FIXED HINGES FOR LEGS.
24—¾" #6 SCREWS FOR HINGES.

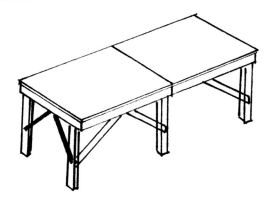

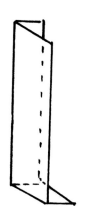

LIGHT BOXES FOR MINI-SPOTS AND
TO SUPPORT UPRIGHT FOR CURTAIN.
2—¾ SEVEN PLY 9" × 4' 0"
1—¾ SEVEN PLY 9" × 9¾" FOR END.
2 WING NUTS AND CARRIAGE BOLTS ¼" × 1¼"
FOR SECURING BOX TO STAGE FLOOR.
DUPLICATE SAME FOR ADDITIONAL BOX
(ONE FOR EACH SIDE.)

T BAR UNIT REQUIRES 1—1" × 4" × 8' 0".
1—1" × 2" × 8' 0" FOR CROSS BAR
THAT HOLDS CURTAIN AND VALANCE.
2—6" ANGLE BARS EACH END.
IF 8' UNIT IS TOO LONG FOR YOUR FACILITY
(I.E.: TRANSPORT) THEN SPLIT THIS UNIT IN
TWO AND MAKE ADEQUATE MIDDLE SUPPORT.
ANOTHER VARIANCE ON THIS UNIT CAN BE AN
ALUMINUM POLE JOINED IN CENTER BY
CONNECTOR PROPERLY THREADED FOR TWO
FOUR FOOT UNITS. S HOOKS PRESET IN THIS UNIT.

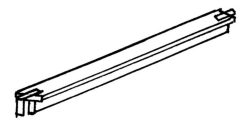

FIGURE 56

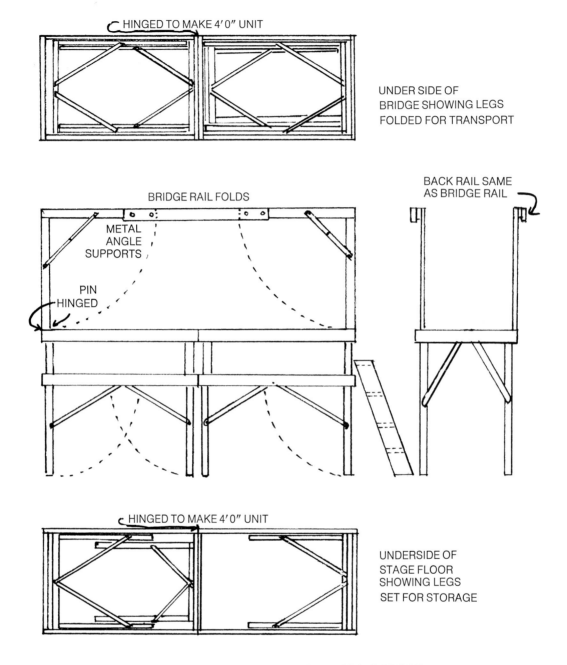

HINGED TO MAKE 4'0" UNIT

UNDER SIDE OF
BRIDGE SHOWING LEGS
FOLDED FOR TRANSPORT

BRIDGE RAIL FOLDS

BACK RAIL SAME
AS BRIDGE RAIL

METAL
ANGLE
SUPPORTS

PIN
HINGED

HINGED TO MAKE 4'0" UNIT

UNDERSIDE OF
STAGE FLOOR
SHOWING LEGS
SET FOR STORAGE

STAGE TWO SHOWING BOTH COMPONENTS: STAGE AND BRIDGE

FIGURE 57

SPECIFICATIONS FOR STAGE TWO

THE BRIDGE UNIT REQUIRES THE FOLLOWING:
2 PANELS ¾" SEVEN PLY 2' 6" × 4' 0"
4—1" × 3" × 4' 0" CLEAR PINE FOR FRAMING.
4—1" × 3" × 2' 4½" CLEAR PINE FOR FRAMING.
48—¾" #6 SCREWS FOR SECURING PANELS TO FRAMING.
8—1¼" × 3" × 4' 3" CLEAR PINE FOR LEGS.
4—1¼" × 3" × 2' 4½" CLEAR PINE FOR TOP OF LEGS.
8—METAL STRAPS ½" × 1" × 2' 0" FOR BRACES.
8—1" × 2" × 2' 6" CLEAR PINE FOR LEG SUPPORTS.
16—¼" CARRIAGE BOLTS 1½" LONG FOR LEG SUPPORTS.

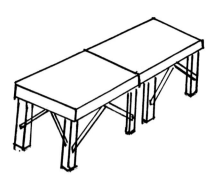

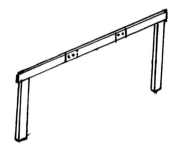

BRIDGE RAIL AND BACK RAIL REQUIRES:
4—PIECES 1" × 3" × 3' 0" FOR UPRIGHTS.
4—PIECES 1" × 3" × 3' 0" FOR RAILS.
2—PIECES 1" × 3" × 3' 0" FOR JOINING
BOTH PARTS OF BRIDGE AND BACK RAILS.
8—¾" × 2" HINGES.
24—¾" #6 SCREWS FOR HINGES.

ONE LADDER ESSENTIAL, IF TWO NEEDED
MAKE DUPLICATE.
2—1" × 6" × 3' 0" CLEAR PINE FOR ACCESS LADDER.
4—1" × 6" × 2' 0" CLEAR PINE FOR TREADS.
2—1" × 3" × 2' 9" FOR VERTICAL SUPPORT.
1—1" × 3" × 2' 0" FOR TOP OF SUPPORTS.
2 HINGES AND SCREWS FOR SAME.
A SMALL KITCHEN LADDER CAN SUBSTITUTE THIS
UNIT AND SERVE MOST ADEQUATELY IF PROPER
HEIGHT.

FIGURE 58

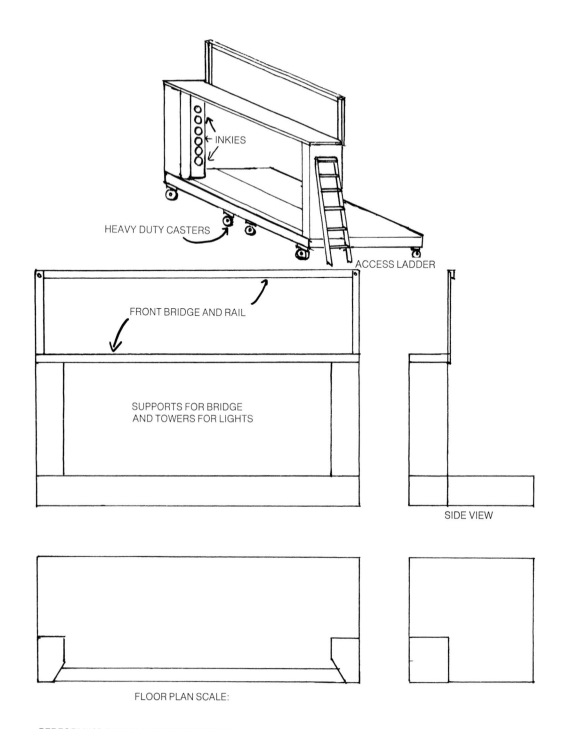

INKIES

HEAVY DUTY CASTERS

ACCESS LADDER

FRONT BRIDGE AND RAIL

SUPPORTS FOR BRIDGE
AND TOWERS FOR LIGHTS

SIDE VIEW

FLOOR PLAN SCALE:

PERFORMING STAGE AND FRONT BRIDGE

FIGURE 59

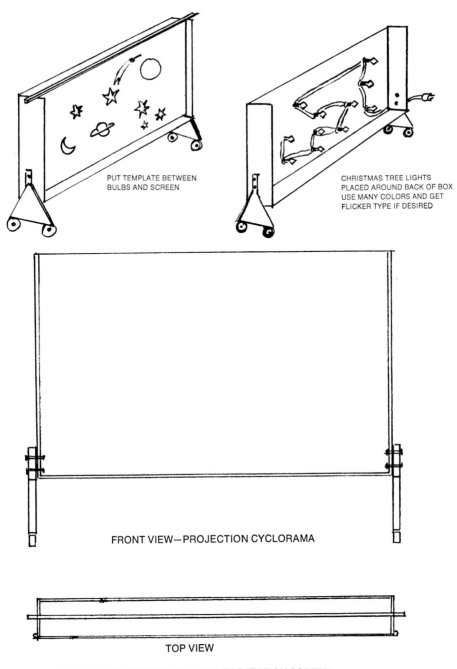

PUT TEMPLATE BETWEEN
BULBS AND SCREEN

CHRISTMAS TREE LIGHTS
PLACED AROUND BACK OF BOX
USE MANY COLORS AND GET
FLICKER TYPE IF DESIRED

FRONT VIEW—PROJECTION CYCLORAMA

TOP VIEW

COMBINATION CYCLORAMA AND PROJECTION SCREEN

FIGURE 60

107

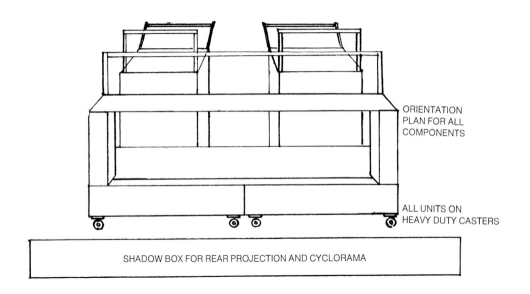

ORIENTATION PLAN FOR ALL COMPONENTS

ALL UNITS ON HEAVY DUTY CASTERS

SHADOW BOX FOR REAR PROJECTION AND CYCLORAMA

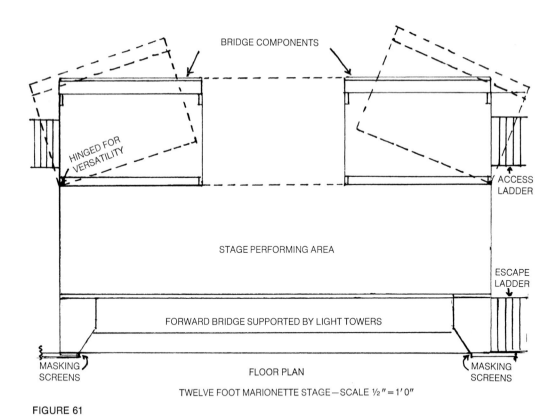

BRIDGE COMPONENTS

HINGED FOR VERSATILITY

ACCESS LADDER

STAGE PERFORMING AREA

ESCAPE LADDER

FORWARD BRIDGE SUPPORTED BY LIGHT TOWERS

MASKING SCREENS

MASKING SCREENS

FLOOR PLAN

TWELVE FOOT MARIONETTE STAGE—SCALE ½″=1′0″

FIGURE 61

108

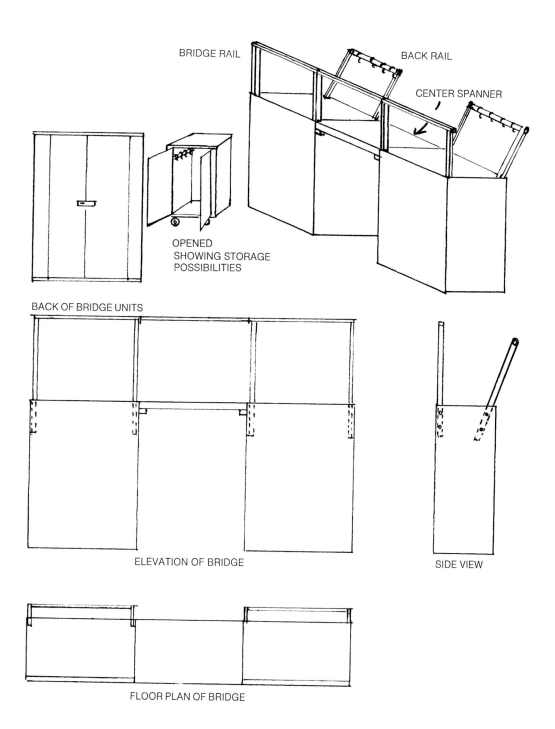

BRIDGE RAIL

BACK RAIL

CENTER SPANNER

OPENED
SHOWING STORAGE
POSSIBILITIES

BACK OF BRIDGE UNITS

ELEVATION OF BRIDGE

SIDE VIEW

FLOOR PLAN OF BRIDGE

FIGURE 62

109

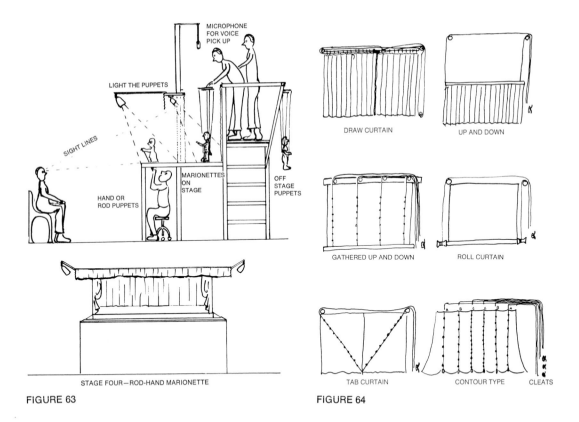

FIGURE 63

Labels in figure: MICROPHONE FOR VOICE PICK UP · LIGHT THE PUPPETS · SIGHT LINES · HAND OR ROD PUPPETS · MARIONETTES ON STAGE · OFF STAGE PUPPETS · STAGE FOUR—ROD-HAND MARIONETTE

FIGURE 64

Labels in figure: DRAW CURTAIN · UP AND DOWN · GATHERED UP AND DOWN · ROLL CURTAIN · TAB CURTAIN · CONTOUR TYPE · CLEATS

SCENERY
WHY SCENERY

Scenery for the marionette is based on the same principles as scenery for the "live" theater, but this is a point not always appreciated by the puppeteer. As in the "live" theater, there are occasions when dramatic considerations dictate that your actors play on a bare stage set only with light, but there are many other occasions—most of them, as a matter of fact, when some kind of scenery can be used to enhance your production.

What does scenery do? Most obviously, it decorates your stage. It also establishes an environment for your players. A sun or moon indicates the time of day; clouds, the weather; trees or rocks, whether outdoors or in; the architecture, whether a contemporary drama or a period piece. Scenery sets the style and mood of your play—whether it is fantasy or realism, stark tragedy or gay romp. And all this instant communication before the actors appear or say a word.

SCENERY AND MARIONETTES

Why do some puppeteers object to stage decor? It hampers the marionettes, they say. It snags the strings. It dominates the action. True, badly designed scenery does all this, but a scene designer who is competent in the live theater knows how to deal with these problems. A marionette scene designer has to be aware of the special requirements of the stringed puppet and adjust his plans accordingly.

110

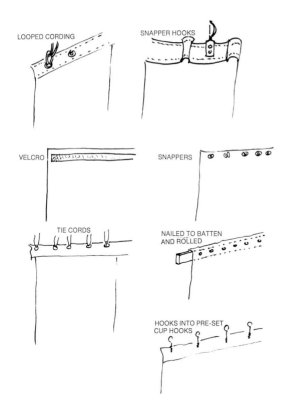

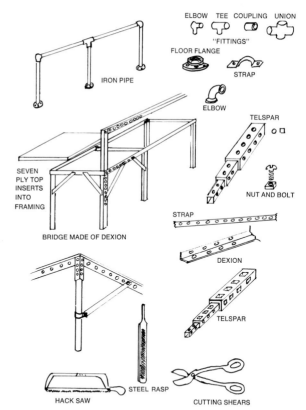

OTHER METHODS FOR CONSTRUCTING A MARIONETTE BRIDGE

FIGURE 65

FIGURE 66

Let's look at the question of scenery's inter-fering with the marionettes. With marionettes, we have to understand that most of the action takes place center stage (see Figure 38, Part One), with particularly important scenes down-stage. Therefore, these major playing areas should be free of encumbrances, except where specifically required by the script (e.g., a chair downstage center for a character to sit on). If bulky scenery or set pieces are concentrated upstage, and there is enough uncluttered space for a marionette to maneuver freely around smaller pieces in center stage, interference doesn't exist. Properly placed wing pieces allow the marionettes free entry to the stage or egress from it.

In the live theater, many "drops" are flown in and out. These are the only kinds of back-

drops that in themselves just don't work with a traveling marionette theater. The equipment to raise and lower these drops must be sus-pended, and it gets in the way of the touring puppeteer.

Only in one area do the strings of the puppet make special set design necessary. A marionette can't walk through an archway or a door be-cause the strings can't go through the solid wall in which the opening is cut or through the lintel over it. But the illusion of walking through can be created. One way is by break-ing the overhead archway, and by cleverly painting all the surrounding areas, erect an architectural structure that allows this action (Figure 67). Another way is to have the archway extend above the sightlines or out-side them—in effect, "faking" the entry. If a

111

A production in rehearsal showing the basic structural units. Tom Lloyd worked the forward bridge whereas Mary Ann Haas and Margo Nielsen worked the back bridge. Suib Marionette Production.

puppet is to enter a conventionally constructed doorway, its strings can be preset inside the door (Figure 68); on cue the character enters and goes about his business. However, reversing the procedure with the scene in progress presents other problems.

As for sets snagging the strings—for a string to snag, it has to catch on *something*. This doesn't mean no scenery. It means no projections in the playing area that could hook a string, and no rough or splintery edges on set pieces. Plastic foam, for example, which might

be used for a wall or a throne, should have all its cut edges sealed with papier-mâché and sanded and sharp corners rounded off. A wood table or flat should be sanded smooth.

When it comes to the set's dominating the production, controlling this is more of an artistic problem than a technical one, but a combination of artistry and proficiency can deal with it. To begin with, the set should not overwhelm the action by sheer physical bulk. Except to make a point through exaggeration, it should be in scale with the marionettes and not take up room needed as much for dramatic purposes as for logistical ones. An adage says the set should *repose*, never *im*pose on the production. Extraneous detail should be eliminated, necessary detail softened, so that busyness doesn't distract the spectator's eye from the action.

While the scenery should never obtrude, to say that it should go unnoticed is untrue. You must strike a balance between giving it its due weight for dramatic and aesthetic purposes and letting it take over.

Ways of emphasizing or minimizing the set will be dealt with when we discuss color and lighting.

Since puppetry is a three-dimensional visual medium, scenic effects that augment the impression of depth can help the spectator accept

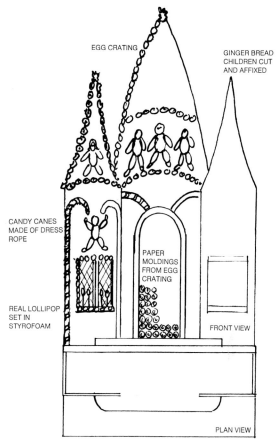

WORKING SKETCH FOR GINGERBREAD HOUSE

FIGURE 68

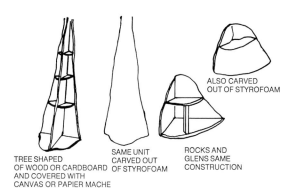

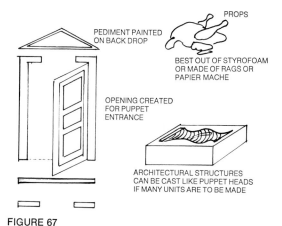

FIGURE 67

the marionettes' world by making it look real for the little people who dwell in it.

DESIGNING THE SET

Whether the script for your production is your own or the work of another playwright, keep in mind that the set is one of the factors

113

that contribute to the total expression of the author's ideas. The style you give your scenery can enrich the author's concept or demolish it. Can that concept be rendered visible to an audience by making the set realistic, or fanciful, or abstract? Or staged in the period for which it was actually written or changed to another time and place to develop fresh insights? Actually, this is a decision that should be made by the director, but since with most small companies the puppeteer is the director too, your director self will have to confer with your scene designer self before you draw up your plans.

There are practical considerations, aside from dramatic ones, that should affect your scenic designs.

If you intend to present your show in more than one place, remember that touring requires that your set be collapsible—not onstage, perish the thought!—for storage, setting up, and packing. Sometimes even a minor change that has virtually no effect on the visual aspects of the set can make an important difference in the compactness with which the set can be put away.

If a scene is to be short, you must weigh the dramatic importance of its set against the relative importance to the entire production. Unless the brief scene is to be climactic, it isn't practical to concentrate a major part of your resources in time, expense, or energy on its physical attributes. We aren't implying that a five-minute scene in an hour-long production should be shoddy or ill-considered. Not at all. We're suggesting instead you develop a set that performs its essential functions with a minimum of construction, consistent with the over-all style of your theater piece.

Consider, wherever possible, combining small units into large set pieces. The more complete

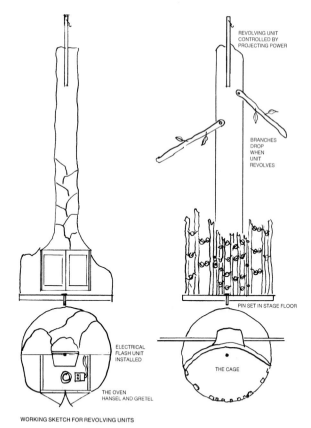

REVOLVING UNIT
CONTROLLED BY
PROJECTING POWER

BRANCHES
DROP
WHEN
UNIT
REVOLVES

PIN SET IN STAGE FLOOR

ELECTRICAL
FLASH UNIT
INSTALLED

THE CAGE

THE OVEN
HANSEL AND GRETEL

WORKING SKETCH FOR REVOLVING UNITS

FIGURE 69

your scenic units are, the fewer individual sections there are to handle, the more easily and quickly you can change sets. A landscape unit can come complete with foliage, cottage exterior, rocky glen, and stone wall. A palace interior can have its stairway, thrones, columns, and wall hangings all in one piece. A space station can include in its construction the lunar mountains and ravines in which it sits. A circus tent can hold as one unit the bleachers, animal cages, and center ring.

Take advantage, when your budget and skill permit, of the technology of the live theater. Rear screen projections can be used to supplement or replace physical sets (Figures 60 and 61). Revolving stages (such as turntables or lazy Susans) are cumbersome and unwieldy for a

The Witch and Gingerbread House and Hansel and Gretel from a Suib Marionette Production.

traveling show, but they can be an aid to exciting effects in a resident puppet theater.

Scenery is usually designed in "elevation"— that is, in scale drawings drafted accurately. From the paper elevation to the finished set is merely a matter of labor. Creative labor, and fun, but labor nonetheless.

Let's look at a stage from a designer's standpoint. All the way back, starting from the rear, many stages have a cyclorama. This is a drop that covers the entire back of the stage, from floor to ceiling sightlines. It's important that this be made of a seamless fabric so that any color or pattern projections on it will be clean and without blemish. It makes a sky background, is frequently pale blue, and can be given any number of pastel or brilliant colors by lighting effects. Coming forward toward the audience, we reach the middle area, where backdrops or scenic units can be suspended. In front of the middle area are the set pieces or prop units (Figure 38, Part One). Within the stage revolving units can be placed.

Many times a scrim comes between the actor (the marionette) and the audience. This scrim is a heavy, porous, cheesecloth kind of fabric that allows partial visibility when lights are directed at the performers behind it. As the lights behind the scrim fade and the lights in front of it go up, the scene disappears. A scrim is effective for dreams or "out of this world" sequences, but there's no point in having one unless it will be used to some purpose—as with all equipment.

CONSTRUCTION MATERIALS

Backdrops, if you choose not to have a plain muslin or velveteen back curtain, can be painted on canvas and hung from the bridge-rail. In the painting use a minimal amount of glue or the paint will crack when the curtain is rolled up. A rubber-based paint will have more elasticity than one with a glue base. A backdrop is always rolled with the painted side out.

Scenery can be made from virtually anything—plastics, wood, cardboard, papier-mâché, household rubbish. Because you are using a one-third scale, quantities that would be inadequate for life-size requirements can be generous for your marionettes. Accordingly, scenery can often be made from all kinds of boxes and packing materials readily obtainable from supermarket discards or from other local merchants.

Plastic foam, a packing material usually to be found in large pieces in the trash discarded by furniture and appliance stores, is rapidly becoming a mainstay for puppetry since it's light in weight and easy to store and cart around. In the unusual event that you can't find it free, it can be bought in eighteen-inch by thirty-six-inch blocks. It can be scored with a knife and broken or carved with a matte knife, a band saw, or even a blow torch into handsome sculptural forms for set pieces and props. Plastic

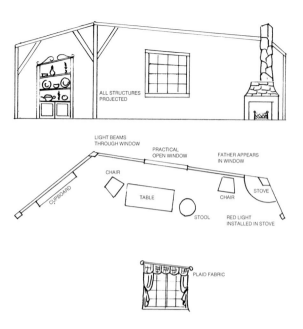

WORKING SKETCHES FOR BROOM MAKERS COTTAGE

FIGURE 70

foam takes paint beautifully—tempera and liquid dyes that give a more translucent, less reflecting finish that makes the scenery appear more recessive—a desirable quality in sets.

Plywood is heavy but otherwise excellent for architectural and structural pieces.

SET CONSTRUCTION

We said it before but we'll say it one more time: Beware of rough or splintery edges on your sets, or sharp projections on which your strings can snag. Round off corners so that strings can slide over them. If raw plastic foam or corrugated cardboard edges pose a threat to manipulation, finish them off with papier-mâché and sand them smooth.

As to the actual construction, keep in mind that set pieces have the purpose of enhancing your production. They are not intended to be

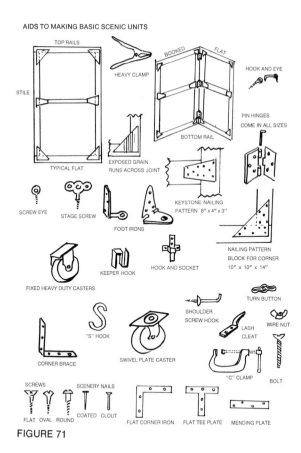

AIDS TO MAKING BASIC SCENIC UNITS

TOP RAILS

STILE

HEAVY CLAMP

BOOKED FLAT

HOOK AND EYE

PIN HINGES
COME IN ALL SIZES

BOTTOM RAIL

TYPICAL FLAT

EXPOSED GRAIN
RUNS ACROSS JOINT

SCREW EYE

STAGE SCREW

FOOT IRONS

KEYSTONE NAILING
PATTERN 8" x 4" x 3"

NAILING PATTERN
BLOCK FOR CORNER
10" x 10" x 14"

FIXED HEAVY DUTY CASTERS

KEEPER HOOK

HOOK AND SOCKET

TURN BUTTON

SHOULDER
SCREW HOOK

WIRE NUT

LASH
CLEAT

"S" HOOK

SWIVEL PLATE CASTER

CORNER BRACE

"C" CLAMP

BOLT

SCREWS

SCENERY NAILS

FLAT OVAL ROUND COATED CLOUT

FLAT CORNER IRON FLAT TEE PLATE MENDING PLATE

FIGURE 71

independent works of art to be examined closely from every angle. They are to be seen by the audience, and only what the audience sees must be finished in believable detail. What is seen from above or from backstage can be untrimmed, except as to being finished off so as not to catch the strings.

The sets must be constructed sturdily, particularly if they are to be much handled. Other factors will also influence the construction, particularly if the show is to tour: lightness, compactness, and collapsibility.

A set piece may have to look heavy, but build it so as to weigh as little as possible. The illusion of weight—for the side of a mountain, for instance—can be created by paint or other decoration.

Figures 70 and 71 give various methods of construction that allow for maximum compactness and suggests the kind of carpentry and hardware that will give you the desired results most simply. Each scenic piece should have its own packing case to keep it fresh and in good working order at all times.

Cardboard, beaver board, or masonite can be used to make traditional flats, but they must be reinforced.

Fabric or papier-mâché is used for scenic units, often over a framework of twisted wire, chicken-wire mesh, or shaped wood.

All manner of odds and ends can be used in scenery-making. Just for example—egg carton paper molds can be used to create an illusion of depth as the trim on a Victorian house. After a while, you'll find you've developed the habit of looking at everything around you with an eye to utilizing it on your puppet stage, and you'll think twice before you throw almost anything away. Keep your mind working and your eyes peeled. The world around you is a treasure trove for the puppeteer.

Collapsibility requires a little more work to achieve than the building of a permanently erect unit, but it's well worth it. Figure 72 demonstrates how minor adjustments in the construction enable you to take down the set piece for packing.

Flats, the mainstay of the live theater for box sets (a room with one wall removed), are frequently used in the marionette theater. Their reduced scale simplifies construction, but large units require proper support whenever rails (horizontal architectural bars) and styles (vertical architectural bars) are joined (Figure 70). Corners of cardboard, beaver board, or masonite must be braced to prevent warping (Figure 70).

When standing units must be joined to-

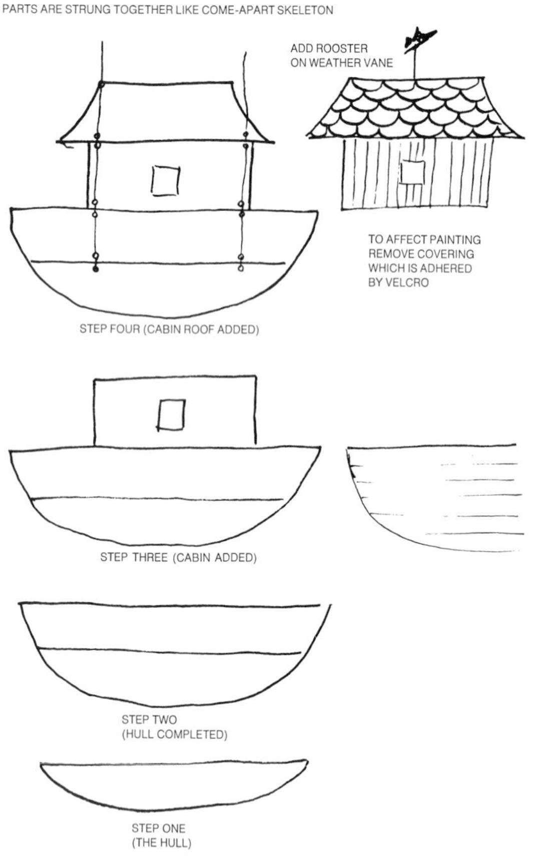

ADD ROOSTER
ON WEATHER VANE

TO AFFECT PAINTING
REMOVE COVERING
WHICH IS ADHERED
BY VELCRO

STEP FOUR (CABIN ROOF ADDED)

STEP THREE (CABIN ADDED)

STEP TWO
(HULL COMPLETED)

STEP ONE
(THE HULL)

BUILDING THE ARK ON STAGE AND
THEN PAINTING. ALL PIECES LIE FLAT ON STAGE.
THEN FALL INTO PLACE AFTER PULLING PROPER STRINGS.

FIGURE 72

gether, a hook and eye is a good method (Figure 71) and so is the use of pin hinges (Figure 71).

If a set piece is top-heavy or otherwise unbalanced with a tendency to fall over, counterbalance it by fastening a heavy "fisherman type" of lead sinker out of sight where it will hold the unit upright. These sinkers come in ounce sizes in any sporting-goods store.

Screws come in assorted sizes as to length and thickness. Instead of forcing a screw into the wood and possibly splitting the board, it often helps to use an awl or a drill to start a hole for the screw. When you screw two pieces of wood together, be sure the screw isn't too long, or when it is set flush in one board it will protrude through the back of the other.

For extra strength, before inserting the screw into the wood, dip it into glue. If you are using nails where additional security is necessary, rosin-coated nails are superior to ordinary nails.

With both screws and nails, the smaller the hardware number, the thinner the shafts.

SET COLOR AND PAINT

A coat of paint is one of the set designer's greatest assets. Paint covers up what you don't want to show—the materials the set is made of, details of construction, and even sometimes clues to how certain tricks are performed. Scenes can frequently be set more simply with painted decoration than by any other means— an interior of a cottage or the side of a mountain with rocks and flowers. With paint, the spectator's eye can be diverted to a specific part of the stage, or away from it.

The colors you select, together with the way you light them, are the most important single factor in creating a mood. The sunny yellow of buttercups in a field would be incongruous in the shadows of a haunted castle, where you might prefer black, burnt umber, and a bilious green.

Psychologists have written extensively on the effects of color on the emotions. Red suggests excitement, danger, and blood. Blue is cool, calm, simple, and sometimes chilly. Yellow is vigorous, warm, and youthful. These are the three primary colors. As to the secondaries, violet is traditionally the color of royalty, green can suggest spring and nature and is easy to live with, and orange is warm and comforting. Black can be mysterious, unearthly; white, serene, pure, or innocent.

The primaries and secondaries, when used in pure tones, can give a harsh appearance to a set. They are much more sensitive and interesting if they are blended with each other or with earth tones: raw and burnt umber, raw and burnt sienna, Indian red, etc. The addition of white or black to these blends can make for a variety the eye appreciates.

When selecting your colors, keep in mind that the background or backdrop color must not be so similar in color or intensity to that of the puppet performer that one fades and washes out the other, or so strong and detailed that it dominates the characters or distracts from them. Take into consideration the colors of the costumes and select a background color to set them off. And above all, think about the atmosphere you want to establish—an ambience of terror or gaiety, of a spooky midnight or a cloudless noon.

Before you start, you'll need a "palette" of basic colors—that is, a supply of the primary and secondary colors, with a selection of earth tones and black and white. If you don't have much surface to cover, tempera paint is fine. However, if you're planning extensive painting, it's less costly to buy "dry" colors from a paint store.

All paints are composed of three elements: a pigment, a solvent, and an adhesive. The dry paint, which is the pigment, needs the addition of water (the solvent) and glue (the adhesive) to become usable. Cold-water glues are advisable, and white glues of that type are easy to apply and give satisfactory results.

To prepare the paint, first mix your colors dry to blend just what you want. To concoct the sizing, put water into a vessel and then add the glue. When the mixture is tacky to the touch, add some of it to the dry color you've selected. The final mixture should be one third pigment and two thirds sizing.

If the surface to be painted is porous, you'll use less paint if you seal it first. If you intend to use tempera, you may use a coat of shellac. But if you're going to use the dry paint, a coat of the glue-and-water mixture you've already prepared without the pigment will seal the surface as well.

Paint can be sprayed on or applied with a brush or a sponge or a rag or a roller. It can be scumbled, spattered, glazed, dripped, grained, marbleized, stenciled. There are many arts-and-crafts books and pamphlets that give full directions for these and other techniques, and new products are always being introduced to the market that make other techniques possible.

Part of the beauty of puppetry lies in the unity with which one person can endow a production. Set design is one factor of that unity, and while it doesn't demand a high level of technical proficiency, it requires a substantial amount of judgment. If the puppeteer has an understanding of the factors that produce a harmony of style between the sets and the other aspects of the show—the script, the direction, the acting, the music, the costumes, the lighting, and the special effects—and a comprehension of the aesthetic qualities the audience has a right to expect, the scenery should be superb.

PROPS

Stage properties, commonly known as "props," exist in every form of theater, but they have special qualities in the theater of the marionette. Puppetry itself is a form where reality and fantasy frequently blur, and nowhere is this more in evidence than with props. On the live stage, a rose is a rose. On the marionette stage, who knows what a rose can be? Or do? Just as the audience adjusts its convictions of realism to the puppet protagonists, so does it

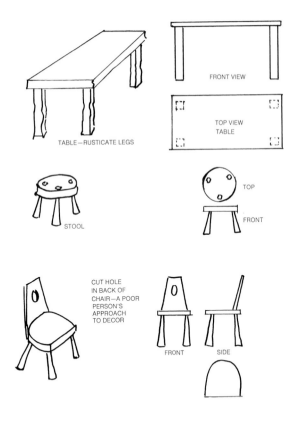

TABLE—RUSTICATE LEGS

FRONT VIEW

TOP VIEW
TABLE

STOOL

TOP

FRONT

CUT HOLE
IN BACK OF
CHAIR—A POOR
PERSON'S
APPROACH
TO DECOR

FRONT   SIDE

PROPS AND FURNITURE FOR BROOM MAKERS COTTAGE

FIGURE 73

their world. A dining-room table and chair seat would be, ordinarily, thirty inches and eighteen inches high. Therefore, in your marionettes' house, they would be ten and six inches high. A fifteen-inch sofa seat would be five inches. Once this is established as normal for the world of the marionette, then a three-foot-tall man entering a room equipped in this scale becomes, to the audience, truly a nine-foot-tall giant. When Alice grows and shrinks in *Wonderland*, there are two ways to create this illusion. One is by having Alice herself change size—and the props remaining the same emphasize the differences. The other is to keep Alice unchanged, making the props smaller to indicate her growth and larger when Alice becomes tiny.

Don't forget, if the upholstery fabric has a figure or a textured design, the pattern will look three times its size onstage. Accordingly, select a small figure or a smoothly woven fabric that will allow your furniture and draperies to stay in scale.

MATERIALS FOR PROPS

Marionette props can be made of virtually anything. Sometimes when the scale is close to the one-third, articles can be found that require little if anything to be done to be turned into props. Doll accessories, for instance: cups and saucers, baby bottles, little baskets, umbrellas, suitcases. Miniatures: liquor bottles, mirrors, picture frames, candlesticks.

As we suggested earlier, it's not always necessary to buy what you need. More often than not just what you need is precisely what someone has just happened to toss out and there it is, waiting for you. If you must buy, inexpensive toys, scraps of cloth, and miscellaneous gadgets are available in a wide variety of shops.

accept that puppet props are not necessarily what they appear to be and is not disturbed if a chair walks across a room or a broom curtsies. When a rock divides at "Open Sesame!" only Ali Baba is incredulous.

SCALE

The audience must believe as much in the props as it does in the marionettes. The most important element in this belief is the scale of the individual props. Unless you're dealing with giants or dwarfs, the one-third scale of your people marionettes must be applied to

CONSTRUCTION

Where you have to make something from scratch, the same techniques you've already learned in constructing marionettes, costumes, and sets can be applied and on the same materials: wood, wire, papier-mâché, plastic foam. Sometimes the simplest kind of shaping—chicken wire covered with a "skin"—can fool the eye once paint and possibly other decorations have been applied.

Whenever possible we suggest you use the same "knockdown" technique as for Kandu's table. Furniture and other props made with interlocking front and side-view patterns, rounded out with small modules if necessary, assembles quickly, packs flat, and requires minimal storage space.

When you build upholstered furniture, it's not necessary to make it soft and cushiony. Marionettes are insensitive to the comforts of home. As long as the furniture looks good to the audience and sounds right when a puppet drops into it, put it together in the most serviceable way.

STRINGING PROPS

If a prop is to "do" something—float through the air, fall apart or whatever—it should be strung to its own controller. Every prop that has strings needs at least two, strategically placed so that the prop won't twist or spin out of control while it's being manipulated.

LIGHTING
MARIONETTE LIGHTING

Every theatrical presentation demands to be seen, and whatever lights make this possible must also enhance its production values. Today in puppetry, many of even the best of puppeteers shy away from involvement with professional lighting of the kind and quality the live theater has been utilizing for years. Puppeteers seem to feel either that lighting is unimportant or, at the opposite extreme, that its complexities are too much for them. Some consider *any* stage lighting to be adequate and the absence of light to be mood-setting. Nothing is farther from the truth. Existing light is frequently insufficient to let the audience see the action, and onstage darkness should exist only when the script or director calls for it. Even where a script specifies total darkness, it's often wise, particularly with an audience of young children, to keep low-key lighting.

Think of your lighting as a component of a stage picture and of your puppets as three-dimensional figures requiring illumination. The problems of lighting a marionette show are essentially no different from those of any other stage presentation. However, the marionette theater imposes two restrictions. The light source must not be set so high that it will catch the puppeteers' hands and cast their shadows on the working stage. Ground lights must be set so that they don't interfere with stage action. Aside from these, everything that applies to the theater at large applies to marionettes. In placing lighting equipment, set the angles to light the puppets, not the scenery. Light the floor and the actors on it, not the backdrop. Shadows on anything other than the stage floor are taboo, except in special cases where a "follow spot" can spotlight a puppet as it moves around the stage.

Even though your scenery may be magnificent, don't get carried away and overlight the set and set pieces. The actors—the marionettes—should dominate the stage. Lighting should support them, not their setting. To avoid distracting from the marionettes, the puppeteer should be in inconspicuous black.

If you're doing a nightclub floor show or a "platform" show, the type of lighting usually provided is a single follow spot—an arc or zenon lamp—with color adaptors. It's the only source of light, and variations in color and intensity are all you can expect (Figure 74). If you want to reduce the intensity and there is no dimmer, the opening of the iris of the spotlight can be adjusted. On a professional follow spot it's possible to get an adaptor for a color wheel in a wide choice of colors. A strong Leko (see next section) with an iris and color frame can be rigged to serve where there is no follow spot. Make sure it illuminates the marionettes and not you, except when the light includes you as you take your bows.

The proscenium type of theater provides an arched frame for its stage. This theater allows the widest possible latitude in achieving effects because virtually any kind and quantity of lighting equipment can be mounted wherever needed.

Read the rest of the section on lighting carefully, and don't be intimidated. Taken bit by bit in understanding and built up piece by piece in equipment, lighting can be dealt with by any novice. But if you feel the electrical details are something you don't want to be involved in, by all means turn to a qualified stage technician or lighting designer to plan with you and determine the minimal equipment your production requires.

MOOD AND MOTIVATION—
AND EQUIPMENT

Two aspects of lighting must be called to your attention: *mood* and *motivation*. Mood is the total quality of the light and *motivation*

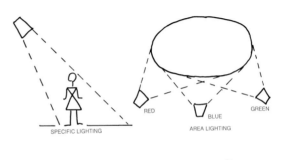

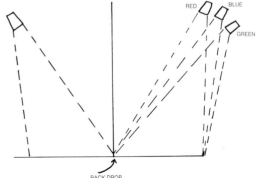

FIGURE 74

is its source (the sun, a lamp, a candle, etc.) and reason for being (morning, afternoon, etc.). In order to attain mood and motivation we need special equipment.

There are two primary instruments used for theater lighting. They're known as the *Fresnel* and the *Leko* (a plano/convex spotlight). The Fresnel gives soft-edge area lighting and the Leko sharply defined specific lighting. Although the live theater employs both of these, for the marionette theater we recommend a Fresnel mini-spot, commonly known as an "inkie," with

122

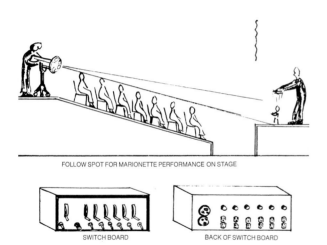

FOLLOW SPOT FOR MARIONETTE PERFORMANCE ON STAGE

SWITCH BOARD

BACK OF SWITCH BOARD

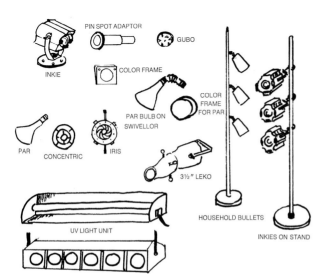

PIN SPOT ADAPTOR

GUBO

INKIE

COLOR FRAME

COLOR FRAME FOR PAR

PAR BULB ON SWIVELLOR

PAR

CONCENTRIC

IRIS

3½" LEKO

HOUSEHOLD BULLETS

INKIES ON STAND

UV LIGHT UNIT

STRIP LIGHT

FIGURE 75

a conversion unit (a pin-spot adaptor) that changes the characteristic of the area lighting instrument to a specific lighting unit. We make this suggestion because it's more economical and more flexible to buy Fresnels and adapt them than to buy single-purpose, more costly instruments. This adaptor with the double lens concentrates the light sharply into a directed area (Figure 75). The bulbs for the inkie are 100- and 150-watt bayonet type. For most shows at least twelve inkies would be called for, with three pin-spot adaptors plus

three dimmers. Dimmers are discussed below.

The cost for this equipment could run high if you were to buy it from the standard sources. Only the sky and your budget could set a limit to what fancy lighting units you might add. Making a good part of your basic lighting equipment yourself would slash your expenses drastically. Your real costs would be in your time, which only you can evaluate. If you give due heed to the safety factors involved, the same as for any electrical project, there's no reason why you should let the prospect of constructing your own lighting systems daunt you.

Much of your material can be purchased at little cost or salvaged from household discards. The housing, the metal part in which the bulb sits, can be made of stove or vent pipes, which are cylindrical and need only a bottom. This bottom could be a disc of wood fitted to the hollow of the pipe, with a standard socket attached to the inside, the wires coming out the back. With an electric drill you make a series of holes at the bottom end, through which go the screws that hold the wooden plate in place. Figure 76 shows this construction and variations for flood and spotlights. Be aware of the safety factors.

Housings can be made from large coffee cans, forty-six-ounce fruit-juice cans, aluminum mixing bowls, etc.

Lenses can be affixed to some of these units for increased efficiency in lighting (Figure 76). If you'll be using Cinemoid filters in front of any home-made units, allow for proper ventilation (Figure 76) by putting a series of pin holes through the filters. The holes won't affect the quality of the light and they'll let the heat escape. Otherwise you'll find that smoke from these units will upset your audiences—and you too.

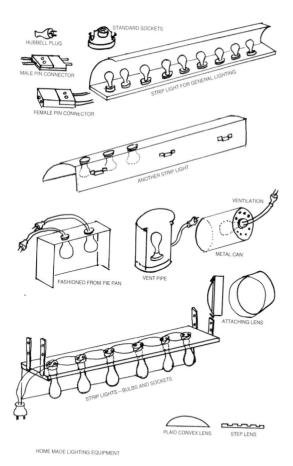

HOME MADE LIGHTING EQUIPMENT

FIGURE 76

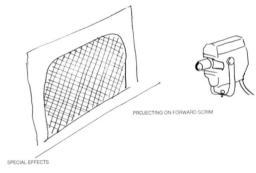

PROJECTING ON FORWARD SCRIM

SPECIAL EFFECTS

FIGURE 77

Strip lights are also used for general lighting and are great for lighting up the sky. You can make your own strip lights by attaching a series of standard electric sockets to a wood strip. Wire these in parallel (Figure 76) and use ordinary household colored or white bulbs with them. With twelve bulbs, 40 watts each should give enough light. For additional illumination, use bulbs with increased wattage or more sockets and more 40-watt bulbs. Bear in mind the total wattage this unit requires and check to be sure the fuses can carry the total load.

CONTROL—AND EQUIPMENT

Mood and motivation are affected by the intensity of the light. Control of the amount of light—the intensity—is exercised by dimmers. For a marionette stage these sell for a couple of dollars for a simple household gadget (as discussed in "Lighting Kandu") up to about $25 for a more advanced dimmer.

The same complete control we have over the marionettes must be extended to the lighting. A lighting control panel known as a switchboard is designed for this purpose. All lighting instruments are plugged into this switchboard,

All housings should be painted with lamp black. After they dry, allow the lamps to burn for an hour or so to burn off the paint. The units will smoke for a while until the black is well married to the metal of the housing, so be sure to season them *before* your performance.

So that each completed unit can be hung or otherwise attached, it will need a U-shaped strap arm of metal with three holes—two for the unit and one for the attachment (Figure 75). You can decide on the proper arm for suspension, wall attachment, or floor placement.

through the dimmer or through toggle switches (Figure 75). Six 1,200-watt dimmers should be able to handle the most elaborate production, but two dimmers should be adequate for most normal requirements. On a limited budget, you'll find that several household dimmers of the 300-watt capacity may be used to form your own switchboard when mounted properly.

FOCUS—AND EQUIPMENT

Focus is the direction of light to the desired area.

Your concern is that the playing area be illuminated clearly and well defined by the light. To this end, every lighting instrument should be focused properly. Moving the wing nut at the bottom of the instrument aligns the bulb with the reflector.

All lighting instruments should be within easy reach for a marionette stage, and you can adjust the position of a light with little effort.

Adding a pin-spot adaptor to the Fresnel mini-spot allows you to get a sharp focus and specific directional lighting. (This adaptor is a sliding double lens that magnifies the light and increases the intensity.) Contrary to popular impression, although this adaptor magnifies the illumination, it doesn't increase the area the light covers. If anything, it intensifies the light in a smaller area.

All Leko instruments (and the inkie with the pin-spot adaptor has been converted to a Leko) have shutters. These shutters are metal strips that are already in the instrument so as to allow for sharply defined framing of the light on the projected area. With this equipment you can very simply frame in a specific area with light. The shutters work in "opposites."

The top shutter cuts off the bottom line of light, the bottom shutter cuts off the top line, the right shutter cuts off the left line, and the left cuts off the right. With these shutters you can box in your light to cover one thing and nothing else.

To give a soft edge to the concentrated area of light, adjust the barrel of the pin-spot adaptor to the desired off-focus degree.

A basic rule of lighting a scene is to illuminate where the actor is or intends to be. If your equipment is limited and you can't move your light focus, then move your actor. You compensate for your stationary focus by lighting areas of the stage with varying degrees of intensity and different color tones. If an actor—in our case, a marionette—wishes to express an altered mood, he is directed to move to that part of the stage where the intensity and tone would convey the effect you're seeking.

COLOR—AND EQUIPMENT

In color, the entire spectrum of the rainbow is available to you. The primary colors of light are different from those of pigment. The light primaries are red, blue, and green, and these colors are obtained by using filters known as *gels* or *Cinemoid* in front of your instruments and projecting the light through them. For additional hues you can cross-mix colors between instruments or put two different colored gels in the same instrument. Putting a red filter and a green one in the same instrument will black it out. Don't! Each colored filter, when directed to an object of the same color onstage, will whiten it out. (Example: A red light on a red lipsticked mouth will "pale" it out.) Combining a red instrument with a green instrument will give an onstage color of amber or orange, depending on the relative intensity of each lamp. Combining red and blue will give magenta or violet, depending on intensities. Blue and green will give turquoise. And, of course, you have each primary color in its own intensity. To achieve a wide range of professional effects at minimal cost, use one dimmer. Hooking the dimmer into the reds only gives a cool blue-green, good for twilight or night scenes, among others. Tying the greens only to a toggle switch will enable you to use only your blue, giving a colder light for night or dream sequences. If the dimmer blocks out the green, the resultant purple gives a mysterious light. Resetting to dim out the blue gives a warm, sunny cast to your light. Neither red nor green alone is pleasant over a long period, but for a short span green can be eerie, and red, passionate and vibrant.

As the colors of light affect each other and the mood of the production, so too they affect the colors of the scenery and the costumes. Therefore, before making your final decision as to the paint for your set or the fabric for your costumes, test them under your filtered lights to check that they don't pale out, muddy, or otherwise alter their character.

In the lighting design, the entire stage must be included. It's a good policy to have a red, blue, and green instrument in each area, and their focus should be "soft-edge." If you have more than twelve instruments, you may not have to be so economical in your selectivity. With more leeway you could add straw, surprise pink, and "bastard amber." Turquoise, magenta, and pink are additional serviceable colors. However, bear in mind that if you're using the same light set-up on tour, every instrument must serve at maximum capacity, and every bit of excess equipment is additional weight and handling.

SPECIAL LIGHTING EFFECTS—AND EQUIPMENT

To throw a pattern of light, either as a shadow or a design in color, onto the floor of the stage or the backdrop, an accessory to the Leko with its pin-spot adaptor is used. It's called a *Gobo*. Gobos are pattern cutouts or templates constructed from tin or aluminum foil. These templates are inserted at the focal point of the Leko, in the pin-spot adaptor where the light rays cross (Figure 75). The patterns can be projected into specific areas and can replace scenery. They're simple and inexpensive to make yourself from the thin metal of disposable pie plates or frozen-food dishes. To add color to the pattern, attach gels across the pierced openings of the template. Just wet your finger, dampen the gel, and press it into position.

For a flickering, staccato effect, the strobe light gives results of a quality unmatched in other theater lighting. It's ideal to use to give an effect of early cinema, bodies in motion, or space travel. However, a less expensive way of approximating this effect is a simple on/off switch. It's hard on the hand but easier on the pocketbook.

For weird and wonderful "black light" effects possible no other way, the U.V. (ultraviolet) light is used. With this U.V. light, no other stage lights are used, and eliminating all other light aids the illusions. The puppets and props specifically painted to react under the U.V. light will be the only visible objects. When these effects are done artistically, they can be theatrically overwhelming. But fascinating as the U.V. is, remember that basically it's a gimmick, and any gimmick can be overworked. Professional U.V. lights are available from

126

theatrical lighting supply houses, but inexpensive U.V. bulbs that screw into ordinary sockets can be found in psychedelic "head" shops. The U.V. paint is available from any art-supply store.

Lighting for multi-media productions is discussed under that heading.

LIGHTING CAPACITY AND SAFETY

The power your lights draw can be computed on the simple rule of ten amperes to every one thousand watts. In other words, using twelve 100-watt instruments adds up to twelve hundred watts or twelve amps. This amperage can be used on most household outlets without blowing a fuse, but check your fuses to verify that they have this capacity. Also look into what other electrical equipment may already be on the same circuit. If you plan your show with equipment exceeding this load, you must split your electrical equipment so that part can be hooked into one circuit and the rest into another equal to the fuse limitations.

Whatever equipment you use must be safe. The wires must be in good condition, well insulated, and of the correct capacity. The fuses must be able to carry your load.

Even though the levels of intensity you set may be satisfactory in your own theater, you may find that on tour the lights seem different. This can be due to variations in voltage. At certain times of the day utility companies may adjust the flow of current because an excess of power may be surging through their lines. Watch for this, and if you find that your lights are affected, modify your control to compensate.

As a good puppeteer, you will have to be prepared to deal with emergencies. If you should be playing out of doors where electrical power fails or is otherwise not available, don't hesitate to harness the headlights of cars. If you're playing indoors and there is a power failure, high-powered flashlights and auxiliary beam spots may save the day.

LIGHTING PROCEDURE

After all the lights are put into position and focused, add the gels for color. The levels of intensity of the several instruments must be set. If you have a refined switchboard with several dimmers, what you can do with your lights may be a revelation to you. Now is when your artistic judgment is called into play. Each area of the stage will require a gradation of intensity, and this, with the colors you've selected, establishes the mood. Most dials or potentiometers (levers) used for dimmer control have a numeral indication. Accordingly, your light cues are indicated to direct specific lights up to a designated number. These levels of intensity should be discussed with the director (your other self) and the determination made on dramatic and aesthetic grounds.

As you see, it's essential that a lighting plan be devised from the first rehearsal, or even sooner, in the planning preliminary stages of production. This plan is usually developed by the lighting designer, who, with the director, analyzes the emotional, dramatic, and aesthetic requirements of the script. The plan specifies the kind and amount of equipment needed, the angles and intensity of light, the positioning of the equipment, and the colors to be used. The plan covers the opening visual effect, and indications on a "spec sheet" notify the lighting engineer when to modify the lighting for subsequent changes in mood or action until the final curtain.

MUSIC AND SOUND EFFECTS

Although puppetry is primarily a visual medium, like other theatrical arts it's at its best when it draws on related arts to expand its dimensions. Marionettes may be effective when performing in silence, but background or incidental music can enhance a production enormously, and the right kind of sound effects is a necessity.

If you are capable of composing and playing your own music, you can add two more hats to the collection you're acquiring as master puppeteer. However, if you wish merely to be musical director, the recorded music for every mood is an unlimited resource.

APPROPRIATE MUSIC

To support your marionettes emotionally and convey the mood of a scene, few factors are as effective as music. And nothing can be so destructive as badly selected music that quarrels with the unity of your production by insisting the play is happening at one time and place when the dialogue, costumes, and set state that it's occurring elsewhere. As we mentioned under "Playscripts," consistency is an expression of unity.

We don't need actual ancient Egyptian music if we're doing a folk tale of old Egypt. No one today can be sure what Egyptian music of four thousand years ago was like. And we don't need to reproduce literally the twelfth-century music of King John's court for Robin Hood. What we want for backgrounds or between scenes is music that doesn't remind us strongly of *another* time and place and that carries the flavor of the play's period in scale, harmonics, or rhythms.

If the marionette sings or dances, the appropriate music is even more important in sup-porting your play or demolishing belief in it. Unless you are deliberately "camping," Pharaoh wouldn't waltz and Robin Hood and Maid Marian wouldn't tango. An understanding on your part of the kind of music sung or danced to in the era of your presentation goes far toward giving your production an integrity all too few possess. These pages are a guide to some of the possibilities available to you and how to use them to best advantage. In a period play, the music and the costumes will suggest the kind of dance movement your marionettes should have.

PUPPET DOMINATION

Remember that your marionettes are *little* people, and their music should reinforce the quality of fantasy that is their forte. They should be the focus of attention, not the music any more than the set or lights. Puppeteers commonly choose instruments with a light tinkly quality: a xylophone or marimba, a harpsichord, a celesta, a mandolin, a zither; electronic sounds such as a synthesizer makes, or an electric organ; bells, whistles, kazoos, or children's musical toys. Any instrument can be used, just as long as it doesn't dominate the action. However, if there is a dramatic situation where you want the marionettes to be overwhelmed—e.g., Noah's flood—then the music is a tool to express the elements' domination over the helpless populace.

ABSTRACT QUALITIES

Music is perhaps the most abstract of the arts. Except in a few instances when it includes a bird call we know is a cuckoo's or a sound we can tell is an automobile horn, music isn't literal in its subject matter. True, a piece like

Pictures from an Exhibition might have been inspired by Mussorgsky's reaction, but in expressing a visual reaction in terms of sound, we have an abstract non-pictorial musical design that doesn't necessarily make the listener think of an exhibition of paintings. Indeed, it would be surprising if the unprepared listener would think of paintings at all. What a composer might mean to convey as the sighing of wind through pine trees might put one listener in mind of a calm ocean, another of butterflies in a garden, and another of sleeping children. If we recognize a piece of music by its title, this suggests a specific meaning, but those of us who don't know the name are free to interpret what we hear as subjectively as we please. Par-

ticularly with children, the music must stand on its own feet, without literary allusions that are meaningless to the ear.

Listed are some categories for music which, at least according to the composers' intentions, imply a variety of moods or conditions. They may impart something else to you. What we've set down as a love theme or a melody suggesting autumn may impress you as being more indicative of serenity. The best idea we can offer is to listen to a great deal of music. Listening, and keeping your marionette production in mind, you'll become aware of unexpected measures very different from other passages of the same work, which could be just what you want.

MUSIC FOR SITUATIONS

WEDDINGS

A. Glazounov	"Wedding Procession March" (Op. 21)
K. Goldmark	*Rustic Wedding* symphony (Op. 26)
E. Grieg	"Wedding March" from *Peer Gynt Suite*
R. de Koven	"O Promise Me"
F. Mendelssohn	"Wedding March" from A *Midsummer Night's Dream* (Op. 21/61)
R. Wagner	"Wedding March" from *Lohengrin*

CHILDREN, TOYS, PUPPETS

J. Bratton	"Teddy Bears' Picnic"
E. Coates	*Cinderella*
E. Coates	*The Three Bears*
C. Debussy	*Children's Corner Suite*
L. Delibes	*Coppélia* ballet
E. Elgar	*Dream Children* (Op. 43)
E. Elgar	*Nursery Suite*
E. Elgar	*Wand of Youth*, Suites 1 and 2 (Op. 1)
M. Falla	*Master Peter's Puppet Show*
V. Herbert	"March of the Toys" from *Babes in Toyland*

E. Humperdinck	*Hansel and Gretel*
L. Jessel	"Parade of the Wooden Soldiers"
D. Kabalevsky	*7 Nursery Rhymes*
G. Kleinsinger	"Tubby the Tuba"
G. Kleinsinger	"Peewee the Piccolo"
A. Liadov	"Musical Snuff-Box" (Op. 32)
L. Mozart	Toy Symphony (Movements 3, 4, 7 from *Cassation for Orchestra and Toys in G*)
G. Pierné	"March of the Little Lead Soldiers"
S. Prokofiev	*Cinderella* (Op. 87)
S. Prokofiev	*Love for Three Oranges* (Op. 33)
S. Prokofiev	*Peter and the Wolf* (Op. 67)
M. Ravel	*L'Enfant et les Sortilèges*
G. Rossini	*La Cenerentola*
E. Satie	*MHS 1475/6*

LULLABIES

J. Brahms	*Lullaby*
B. Godard	"Berceuse" from *Jocelyn*
E. Grieg	"Berceuse" (Op. 38, No. 1)
E. Grieg	"Cradle Song from *Peer Gynt Suite*
A. Khatchaturian	"Lullaby" from *Gayne* ballet

ANIMALS, BIRDS, INSECTS

A. Dvořák	"Legend No. 7"
E. Grieg	"Little Bird" (Op. 43, No. 4)
E. Grieg	"Papillon" (Butterfly) (Op. 43, No. 1)
O. Respighi	*The Birds*
N. Rimsky-Korsakov	"Flight of the Bumble Bee"
G. Rossini	"Cat Duet" (vocal)
C. Saint-Saëns	*Carnival of the Animals*
R. Schumann	*Papillons* (Op. 2)
I. Stravinsky	*The Rite of Spring (Le Sacre du Printemps)*.
I. Stravinsky	*Firebird Suite*
P. White	"Mosquito Dance"

ACTIVITY

L. Beethoven	Last movement from "Sonata" (Op. 10, No. 2)
G. Bizet	Marche and Impromptu, *Jeux d'Enfants* (Op. 22)

G. Gershwin	*An American in Paris*
F. Mendelssohn	"Rondo Capriccioso"
F. Mendelssohn	"Scherzo"
F. Mendelssohn	"Song Without Words" (Tarantella) (Op. 102, No. 3)
N. Paganini	"Perpetual Motion" (Op. 11)
S. Prokofiev	Last movement from Classical Symphony No. 1 in D (Op. 25)
N. Rimsky-Korsakov	"Flight of the Bumble Bee"
J. Strauss, Jr.	"Thunder and Lightning, Galop" (Op. 324)
R. Wagner	"Spinning Song" from *The Flying Dutchman*

VIOLENCE, BATTLE

L. Beethoven	Allegro di Molto e Con Brio, 1st movement from "Sonata" (Op. 13)
L. Beethoven	Presto Agitato, *Moonlight Sonata*, 3rd movement (Op. 27, No. 2)
M. Falla	"Ritual Fire Dance" and "Dance of Terror" from *Amor Brujo* ballet
G. Holst	*The Planets: Mars* (Op. 32)
A. Khatchaturian	"Saber Dance" from *Gayne* ballet
S. Prokofiev	Selected passages, *Scythian Suite* (Op. 20)
D. Shostakovich	Last movement, 5th Symphony (Op. 47)
P. Tchaikovsky	*Marche Slave* (Op. 31)
P. Tchaikovsky	Selected passages, 4th Symphony (Op. 36)

MILITARY BAND MUSIC

E. Elgar	*Pomp and Circumstance* marches (Op. 39)
J. Sousa	Any marches
F. Suppé	*Light Cavalry Overture*
P. Tchaikovsky	*1812 Overture*

BUGLE CALLS

A. Tomlinson	Adjutant's Call
"	Assembly
"	General's March
"	Reveille
"	Taps
"	To the Colors

SEASONS, NIGHT AND DAY, WEATHER

L. Beethoven	*Moonlight Sonata* (Op. 27, No. 2)
L. Beethoven	*Pastoral* Symphony No. 6
L. Beethoven	Sonata for Violin and Piano No. 5, Op. 24 ("Spring Sonata")
A. Bliss	"Dance of Summer" (from *Adam Zero* ballet)
C. Debussy	*Clair de Lune*
F. Delius	*On Hearing the First Cuckoo in Spring*
F. Delius	*Summer Night on the River*
A. Glazounov	*The Seasons* (Op. 67)
E. Grieg	*Morning Mood* (Op. 46, No. 1)
E. Grieg	"To the Spring" from *Lyric Pieces* (Op. 43)
F. Grofé	*Grand Canyon Suite*
F. Mendelssohn	*Andante tranquillo con Variazioni* (Op. 83A)
F. Mendelssohn	"Melody in F" ("Spring Song") (Op. 62, No. 6)
S. Prokofiev	*In Autumn*
S. Prokofiev	*Summer Day Suite*
S. Prokofiev	*Winter Bonfire* (Op. 122)
M. Ravel	*Daphnis and Chloe*
G. Rossini	"The Storm" from the *William Tell Overture*
R. Sibelius	*Night Ride and Sunrise* (Op. 55)
L. Sowerby	*Comes Autumn Time*
A. Vivaldi	*The Seasons*

WATER: SEA, RIVER, LAKE, FOUNTAIN

B. Britten	"4 Sea Interludes" from *Peter Grimes*
C. Debussy	*La Mer (The Sea)*
F. Delius	*Summer Night on the River*
A. Liadov	*The Enchanted Lake* (Op. 62)
F. Mendelssohn	*Fingal's Cave Overture* (Op. 26)
O. Respighi	*The Fountains of Rome*
B. Smetana	*The Moldau* (from *My Fatherland*)
J. Strauss, Jr.	*Blue Danube* waltz (Op. 314)
V. Thomson	*The River Suite*

MOOD MUSIC PEACE, SERENITY, INNOCENCE

J. S. Bach	*Sheep May Safely Graze* (Cantata No. 147)
S. Barber	*Adagio for Strings* (from *Quartet*, Op. 11)
G. Bizet	*Adagio* (3rd movement, *l'Arlésienne Suite*)
C. Debussy	*Afternoon of a Faun*

F. Delius	*North Country Sketches*
F. Delius	*Walk to Paradise Garden*
E. Elgar	*Introduction and Allegro for Strings* (Op. 47)
F. Mendelssohn	*Song Without Words* (Op. 102, No. 6)
F. Schubert	Trout Quintet in A Major (Op. 114)
R. Schumann	*Träumerei* (Op. 15, No. 7)

LIGHTNESS, GRACE, CHARM

G. Bizet	*L'Arlésienne Suite*
W. Boyce	Eight symphonies
F. Mendelssohn	*A Midsummer Night's Dream* (Op. 21/61)
G. Pierné	*Entrance of the Little Fauns*
M. Ravel	*Mother Goose Suite*
P. Tchaikovsky	*The Nutcracker* (Op. 71)
P. Tchaikovsky	*The Sleeping Beauty* (Op. 66)
P. Tchaikovsky	*Swan Lake* (Op. 20)
A. Vivaldi	Concerto in F (Pincherle No. 278)

HUMOR, WIT, WHIMSY

A. Arensky	"The Cuckoo" (Op. 34, No. 2)
F. Couperin	*Pièces de Clavecin*
E. Grieg	Amusing Dance (Op. 17, No. 18)
E. Grieg	Humoresque (Op. 6, No. 3)
L. Mozart	Toy Symphony (Movements 3, 4, 7 from *Cassation for Orchestra and Toys in G*)
A. Ponchielli	"Dance of the Hours" (from *Gioconda*)
E. Satie	*Trois Gymnopédies*
E. Satie	*Trois Morceaux en Forme de Poire*
R. Strauss	*Till Eulenspiegel* (Op. 28)
P. Tchaikovsky	Humoresque (Op. 10, No. 2)

LOVE

L. Beethoven	Piano Sonata No. 23 (*Appassionata*)
J. Brahms	*Valse*
F. Liszt	*Liebestraum*
F. Mendelssohn	*Song Without Words* (Op. 38, No. 2)
F. Mendelssohn	*Song Without Words* (Op. 102, No. 1)
I. Paderewski	*Love Song* (Op. 10, No. 2)
A. Rubinstein	"Melody" (Op. 3, No. 1)
P. Tchaikovsky	*Romeo and Juliet* overture
P. Tchaikovsky	Selected passages from Fifth Symphony
R. Wagner	*Tristan and Isolde* theme

HAPPINESS, JOY

A. Dvořák	Slavonic Dances (Op. 46, 72)
E. Grieg	Piano Concerto (Op. 16)
W. Mozart	*Eine Kleine Nachtmusik* (Serenade in G) (K. 525)
W. Mozart	1st movement of G Minor Symphony, No. 40 (K. 550)
O. Nicolai	*Merry Wives of Windsor* overture
J. Offenbach	*Gaité Parisienne*
G. Rossini	*La Boutique Fantasque*
D. Scarlatti	Harpsichord sonatas
R. Schumann	*Carnaval* (Op. 9)
G. Telemann	*Don Quixote*

EERINESS,   MYSTERY, and IMPENDING DOOM

L. Beethoven	*Coriolanus* overture
P. Dukas	*The Sorcerer's Apprentice*
E. Grieg	*Abduction of the Bride* (2d *Peer Gynt Suite,* Op. 55)
E. Grieg	*March of the Dwarfs* (Op. 54, No. 3)
F. Liszt	*Mephisto Waltz*
F. Liszt	*Todtentanz* for Piano and Orchestra
J. Massenet	*Andante Molto Sostenuto* (from *Phèdre* overture)
M. Mussorgsky	*A Night on Bald Mountain*
M. Mussorgsky	*Songs and Dances of Death*
C. Saint-Saëns	*Danse Macabre*
F. Schubert	*The Erl-King*
J. Sibelius	*The Swan of Tuonela*
R. Strauss	*Death and Transfiguration* (Op. 24)

SADNESS, GRIEF, DEATH

L. Beethoven	*Moonlight Sonata,* 1st movement (Op. 27, No. 2)
H. Berlioz	Excerpts from *Symphonie Fantastique* (Op. 14)
F. Chopin	"Funeral March" (from Sonata Op. 35)
F. Chopin	"Prelude" (Op. 28, No. 4)
F. Chopin	"Prelude" (Op. 28, No. 20)
E. Grieg	"Ase's Death" (1st *Peer Gynt Suite*)
E. Grieg	"Elegy" from *Lyric Pieces* (Op. 47)
E. Grieg	"Funeral March"
E. Grieg	*Heart Wounds* (Op. 34, No. 1)

E. Grieg	"Melancholy" from *Lyric Pieces* (Op. 47)
J. Massenet	*Elegie* (Op. 10)
F. Mendelssohn	"Funeral March" (Op. 62, No. 3)
S. Rachmaninoff	*Isle of the Dead* (Op. 29)
M. Ravel	*Pavane for a Dead Princess*
A. Rubinstein	"Romance" (Op. 44, No. 1)
R. Schumann	*Andante Pathétique* No. 1
J. Sibelius	"Valse Triste" (from *Kuolema*)
P. Tchaikovsky	*Chanson Triste* (Op. 40, No. 2)

RELATED SITUATIONS AND MOODS

It would be manifestly impossible to list every theatrical situation or every mood that music can cover, nor are we attempting to do this. You can find music in the categories we've supplied that has a quality in common with an unlisted specific need. As examples: For witches or giants, see if "Eeriness" will serve. For fairies, try "Lightness." For hatred or rage, how about "Violence" or storms in the "Seasons" section? Or the "Children" for elves or pixies, or "Activity" for conversation, racing, swinging?

Of course, you can also use this list to ferret out other works by the same composers or by their contemporaries you may prefer.

MINIMUM RECORDING LIBRARY

Recordings without number are available from shops and libraries, and your selection will wind up by being a combination of what you need and what you like.

Three records that have been generally useful are particularly recommended:

Columbia MS 7165, with the New York Philharmonic and Leonard Bernstein: *The Sorcerer's Apprentice, Night on Bald Mountain, Till Eulenspiegel,* and *Danse Macabre.*

RCA Victor LM 2177, with the London Symphony and Pierre Monteux: Excerpts from Tchaikovsky's *Sleeping Beauty*, Opus 66.

London SP 44095: Eighteen selections of circus music from Ringling Brothers and Barnum & Bailey—fanfare, jungle music, marches, etc.

These three cover such a variety of moods they can serve as the nucleus of a music library, and while you'll want to supplement them eventually, they may satisfy your immediate basic requirements.

MUSICAL UNITY

For one production, a puppeteer will often choose passages from several sources. His "spooky" music could be drawn from Mussorgsky's *Night on Bald Mountain*, Grieg's *Hall of the Mountain King*, and Saint-Saëns's *Danse Macabre*, while a playful scene could be backed up by Couperin. This may work or it may not.

To achieve a unity in your music that will be part and parcel of the over-all unity of your production, you might try culling all the incidental music for a show from the same work or the same composer. There are many major compositions of such richness and variety that the possibilities are unrestricted. Stravinsky's

Rite of Spring and *Petrouchka*; Ravel's *Daphnis and Chloë* and *Trio in A*; Rimsky-Korsakov's *Scheherazade*; Tchaikovsky's Third, Fourth, Fifth, or Sixth Symphonies; any of Brahms's four symphonies; any of Bruckner's symphonies; or Berlioz's or Wagner's orchestral passages. Much of Bach, Mozart, Haydn, and Handel can be adapted to puppetry. The list is endless.

READILY AVAILABLE RECORDED COLLECTIONS

We're not listing suggestions for holidays such as Christmas because there are so many record and tape albums of holiday music that the most cursory search unearths an enormous body of appropriate material. In the same vein, whether you want concert music on a particular country (Prokofiev's *Overture on Hebrew Themes*, Brahms's *Hungarian Dances*, Offenbach's very French *Can-Can*, Ippolitov-Ivanov's *Caucasian Sketches*, Albeniz's *Iberia* . . . Ketelby's *In a Persian Market* and *In a Chinese Temple Garden* are standards for the Near East and China, and Kreisler's *Tambourin Chinois* and *Caprice Viennois* are popular for China and romantic Vienna) or authentic ethnic music of a culture, there is a wealth of it. In the latter area, we recommend the Nonesuch Explorer Series of recordings that give beautiful performances from virtually every region of the globe. Collections of patriotic music, college medleys, Civil War songs, spirituals, music of the Gay Nineties, and a wide range of other themes are available in every record shop and library.

PERIOD MUSIC

You may want to set a production in a specific time in the past, for which the music we have suggested so far is not just right. So that you'll know what to look for in European music from the Renaissance on, we're including a brief mention of musical eras and a few of the leading composers for each. (You'll notice they overlap. There is no hard and fast cut-off date for any of them.) To check on dances of the periods, you can refer to any comprehensive record catalogue and you'll find that most of the composers contributed a considerable output to the popular dances of their day.

ERAS OF EUROPEAN MUSIC

Renaissance 1400–1600
William Byrd
Giovanni Gabrieli
Heinrich Isaac
Claudio Monteverdi
Giovanni Palestrina
Thomas Tallis
Tomas Luis de Victoria

Baroque 1575–1750
Johann Sebastian Bach
Arcangelo Corelli
Girolamo Frescobaldi
George Frederick Handel
Henry Purcell
Alessandro Scarlatti
Heinrich Schütz
Antonio Vivaldi

Rococo 1700–1800
Carl Phillipp Emanuel Bach
Johann Christian Bach
William Boyce

Classic 1750–1850
Luigi Boccherini
Christoph Willibald Gluck
(Franz) Josef Haydn
Wolfgang Amadeus Mozart

Romantic 1800–1900

Hector Berlioz

Frederic Chopin

Felix Mendelssohn

Niccolo Paganini

Franz Schubert

Robert Schumann

Impressionistic 1875–1925

Claude Debussy

Frederick Delius

Charles Tomlinson Griffes

Maurice Ravel

JAZZ, ROCK

You'll note that the foregoing lists don't include jazz, rock, or other popular tunes of the day. We haven't omitted them because we're snobs on the subject or because we feel they'd be out of place. Not at all. In a production set in a contemporary situation, nothing could be more fitting than current music, and children especially respond to the music of today. But except for a handful of tunes that become "standards," most popular songs last at best only a season or two, and few things "date" a show so quickly as last year's dead music. Therefore, when you use popular music, make your selection as timely as possible and be prepared to retape the music if it becomes stale.

Among that of others, the music of George Gershwin and Kurt Weill has already stood the test of time. Their music fits the puppet stage because marionettes move beautifully to their beat and tempo.

CATALOGUES

Any library with a music collection or any store selling recordings will make available to you publications listing selections generally available. One such catalogue is the *Schwann-2 Record and Tape Guide* (W. Schwann, Inc., 137 Newberry Street, Boston, Massachusetts 02116).

The legal aspects of using music composed, arranged, or performed by others will be dealt with in Part Three.

SOUND EFFECTS

In the days of early radio there were tricks for every sound need, many borrowed from the legitimate theater. Some sounds can be made very simply as they occur in your play, or they can be recorded along with the rest of your performance for the ear.

A block of wood rapped sharply against a hard surface (your back bridgerail is convenient) can be a gunshot or a door slam. Two half coconut shells can sound like galloping hoofs. In the "Special Effects" section under "Thunder and Lightning" we speak of making thunder with a thunder sheet or a radiator cover.

Successful as these techniques can be, they are being replaced by sounds that have been recorded on tapes or records. A collection of related sounds is packaged in one unit that can run for thirty to forty-five minutes. These tapes or records are usually packaged in albums, but it is possible in many instances to buy only the one you want. One record might cost about $6. However, if you want only two seconds of a particular sound, you still have to buy the complete unit. If you have access to a good public or university library, it's often possible to borrow a sound record or tape, and in that case you need only duplicate on your own equipment the parts you have use for. The *Schwann-2 Record and Tape Guide* lists available sound effects, the manufacturers or distributors, and whether they come in cartridge or cassette tapes or records. Additional sources of information are the catalogues of record or electronic supply stores or of theatrical supply houses.

For special sound effects of an individualistic nature, you may have to depend on your own ingenuity. If an awesome voice—that of God, for example—has dialogue to read, you may need an echo chamber. Echo chambers may be rented from sound recording studios. Many music departments of universities have echo chambers, and these may often be borrowed or rented. A university may also have a sound laboratory consultant whose services might be helpful to you for special sound effects.

SOUND AMPLIFICATION

For puppets to communicate with an audience, they must be audible. The best show in the world is a flop if it can't be heard.

In the good old days when puppetry was one of the few forms of mass entertainment, traveling showmen would go from town to town, setting up elaborate stages or simple booths in the streets, in fairgrounds, on the commons. They worked almost always in the open air and developed either booming voices or shrill, penetrating ones to reach to the limits of the crowds they would attract. When they were in situations where their voices couldn't carry—before huge fairground mobs or in large theaters—performances were primarily in pantomime and communication was essentially non-verbal, with stress on action holding the audience.

When a puppet show is given today, the problems are the same, only now we have devices that make it easier for us to be heard. Of course, in a basement playroom or intimate theater the voice of the puppeteer can be heard distinctly. In a large house the puppeteer has to depend on a sound amplification system, his own or what comes with the school auditorium, church meeting hall, etc. Out of doors, depending on the size of the crowd you draw, your distance from the audience, the amount of street noise, and so on, an amplification system may or may not be necessary.

SOUND SYSTEMS

To tape your show yourself with professional quality, a reel to reel tape recorder is recommended, preferably portable. There may be instances when two recorders are better: for playing background music on one while dialogue is recorded over the background on the second and to record a duplicate tape without splices on one from a patched-together original tape. The speakers should be in phase and compatible with the rest of the equipment or the resultant sound will be fuzzy or inaudible.

Live sound can be recorded through the mikes, which are plugged into the tape deck. Phonograph or radio sound can be recorded on your own tape-deck reel through extension cords, without picking up interference from outside noises.

Try not to use tape longer than 1,800 feet, since longer tapes will be too narrow. Polyester or Mylar-based tapes are preferred.

Sound amplification and playback systems have three components: the microphone, the amplifier, and the speaker (two speakers are essential for stereo recordings), plus the recording-playback device. These may be the same as the recording equipment. If the show is taped, the microphone isn't necessary unless you use it for your introduction and occasional spontaneous remarks interjected into the performance.

Some halls have good public-address amplifiers, but many don't. Since you must be self-contained and independent in your operations, it would be better for you to be prepared with your own amplifiers.

Accessories for sound equipment would include a tape splicer, splicing tape, and a cord to convert stereo to mono where necessary. A supply of assorted jacks and conversion plugs is a good idea.

There are many competing brands on the market with all kinds of technical jargon describing them. How do you choose? First, determine what your requirements are. For a large hall you need more powerful equipment with better fidelity than for an intimate studio. When you're ready to buy, we suggest that you consult a good sound technician or the latest pertinent issue of *Consumer Reports* (a publication of Consumers Union of the United States, Inc.) for comment on quality and prices.

A word of advice: Sound equipment, particularly good sound equipment, is tempting to thieves. *Never* leave it around unguarded or you may be virtually assured you won't have it long.

TAPING THE PERFORMANCE

If the marionettes' voices or sound effects are a problem for you, one way out is to tape your sound. You can bring in all the live actors you need for the taping and record the auditory parts of your show.

Taping the sound track of a production has become a commonplace with puppeteers, from amateur to the most professional. A good tape is invaluable, so it shouldn't be made hastily. Plan it as for a live stage show. Get the best voices you can, with a good variety of tonal qualities and, if possible, a director who can deliver a tight performance, synchronized with the action. In rehearsal, run through the marionette business for the live actors and mark the scripts with the pauses and time to be allowed for the puppetry action. Allow everyone involved enough rehearsal time so that the performance can be blocked, then staged, and run through live without tape before attempting the actual recording.

We suggest recording at the 7½ speed, which gives optimum fidelity. With this 7½ speed, a 1,200-foot tape will give you thirty minutes to each side of a two-track tape. If your act is within that time or you can turn it over without interrupting your operations to obtain the second thirty minutes by running the tape the opposite way, you have no problem. Otherwise you have to find longer tape or record at 3¾ speed, which doubles your time.

In addition to the master tape, it's a good idea to make a duplicate that you'll use for rehearsals and performances, so you'll always know the master is safe and available in emergencies. Many puppeteers make a cassette recording as well, to be used for rehearsals and back-up. If the master and duplicate tapes fail, the cassette recording can be amplified, using a microphone at its speaker. Some fidelity will be lost, but the cassette will be usable in an emergency and may save the day. The cartridge of a battery-driven cassette will give you the additional opportunity to perform in areas where electrical power is not available—say, at an outdoors picnic or garden party.

Taping the entire show—voices, sound effects, and music—has obvious advantages. However, there are disadvantages which may not be evident at first glance. A kind of spontaneity is lost, which is only realizable with live performers. If there's an interruption from

All characters should be costumed according to the role, never to be treated as dolls. Notice Gretel's plaid skirt made of same fabric as on curtains.

The family is together, Hansel making brooms, the mother laments, Gretel tends to her goose and the father takes to drink.

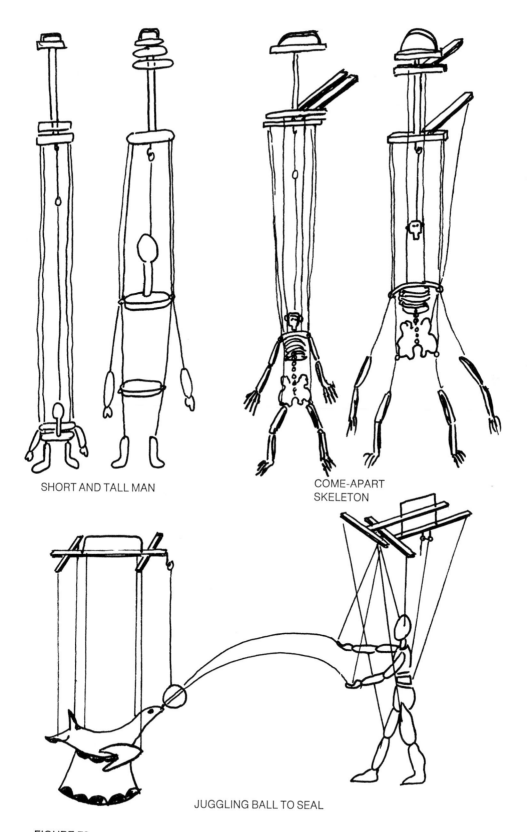

SHORT AND TALL MAN

COME-APART
SKELETON

JUGGLING BALL TO SEAL

FIGURE 78

the audience—a child makes a remark the puppeteer would like to respond to—the tape permits no deviation from its inflexible routine. If anything goes wrong onstage to throw the timing of the production off, the tape nevertheless runs its predetermined course on its original schedule, unless an alert stage manager makes the difficult adjustment immediately.

Some puppeteers have worked out a happy compromise of a half-and-half taping. Musical backgrounds, sound effects, special effects, or synthesized accompaniment are taped. These can be started and stopped at will and integrated into a production using live voices.

In most instances it's not a good idea to use taped voices in some sections and live voices in others unless the taped voices are meant to produce a special effect (ghosts, dream sequences, the voice of God, etc.).

For a small one-man show, such as Kandu's, where no more than two marionettes are onstage at one time, no elaborate taping is necessary. A background recording of appropriate music is all you need on a simple cassette you can run single-handed. But for a more complex production, you will need to follow more complex procedures with, perhaps, more elaborate equipment.

MARIONETTE MAGIC

We've spoken of marionettes as being the elite of puppetry, as indeed they are. The illusions they can create are numberless. These illusions are part of the magic that marionettes can bring to an audience. They enhance a production, sometimes brilliantly, but some puppeteers develop them until the illusions become gadgetry and take over the show. The mechanics become more important than the end result. Carried to the ultimate in gadgetry, there are

marionette shows today that run without any assistance except from the operator who turns switches on and off. A trick for the trick's sake has no value. It must be integrated into the story to punctuate it with surprise, shock, or amusement, contributing to the plot and the dramatic structure.

Throughout the centuries puppet masters have developed ingenious methods to startle, amaze, and amuse their audiences. Many of their acts were headliners in vaudeville. Although they've seldom been successful on television, where the audience credits the camera rather than the puppeteer with the magic, today's puppeteer can use the old techniques as triumphantly as ever.

The simplest trick won't work unless you rehearse it to perfection. Elaborate illusions need even more practice. The rewards come from the ohs and ahs of the audience, but there's another return you may value even more highly—the respect of your fellow puppeteers. They know how you create your effects, but they can admire the theatrical professionalism of a colleague.

Your opportunities for fun and games with your marionettes and special effects are endless. The most absurd situations are possible if you can work them into a production where they have credibility. This is your challenge.

SPECIAL STRINGING FOR SPECIAL EFFECTS

Many "normal" movements that are relatively simple for hand and rod puppets require a little thought to work for marionettes. Frequently special stringing enables them to perform with conviction and deceptive artlessness.

Passing an item from one marionette to an-

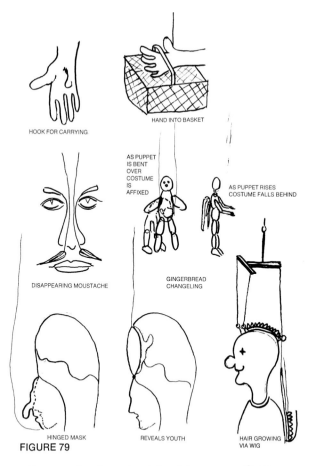

HOOK FOR CARRYING

HAND INTO BASKET

AS PUPPET IS BENT OVER COSTUME IS AFFIXED

AS PUPPET RISES COSTUME FALLS BEHIND

DISAPPEARING MOUSTACHE

GINGERBREAD CHANGELING

HINGED MASK

REVEALS YOUTH

HAIR GROWING VIA WIG

FIGURE 79

other way around. Other objects would be "picked up" similarly. Some puppeteers have experimented with magnets, and it is possible to pick objects up with them in certain circumstances. The weight of the magnet must not upset the marionette's balance; the magnet must be strong; the object must be light enough to be affected; and nothing else can be on the stage to be disturbed by the magnet or influence it.

To remove a dagger or sword from a marionette's scabbard, attach a string from the hilt to the controller. The hand has been shaped to fit around the hilt and is placed on the dagger. The dagger's string is then pulled through the grasping hand, and it looks as if the weapon has been pulled free of the scabbard to be ready for battle.

A puppet that is to smoke has a special string that goes from the cigar, cigarette, pipe, or hookah through the mouth and out through the top of the head to the controller. When this string is pulled it brings the cigar or whatever to the mouth. In the section on "Weather and Smoke" we tell you how to develop this effect further.

In a Suib Marionette production of *Hansel and Gretel,* one of the show stoppers was the witch's ride on her broomstick, not only over the stage but out above the audience on prepared wires. To do this, mount the stage witch on a prop broom that has its own controller. The broom strings are at the ends of the broom, as far apart as possible to give the witch room to mount between them without tangling. To have the witch fly over the audience you have to have two more identical witches designed in fixed flying positions. One of them flies to the back of the house or the balcony, to disappear behind a prepared black curtain. The other, who has been waiting on the oppo-

other can be done in at least two ways. Setting the hand string of two puppets nearer the wrist allows them to exchange a basket or other article that has a handle. Another method is to imbed a cup hook in the palm of the hand of the puppet who is to receive the article, which allows the marionette to grasp the handle (Figure 79).

Picking something up must be done with realism. Suppose a loaf of bread is lying on a table. The loaf would have a string running to the bridgerail. The marionette's hand must be open with the fingers parted, and the hand is placed over the loaf so that the string passes through the separated fingers. Pulling the string of the loaf creates the impression that the hand is lifting the bread, although it is actually the

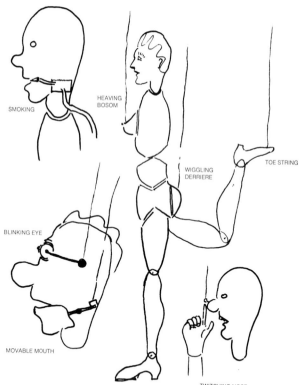

SMOKING

HEAVING
BOSOM

WIGGLING
DERRIERE

TOE STRING

BLINKING EYE

MOVABLE MOUTH

TWITCHING NOSE

FIGURE 80

site side of the house, then rides her broom back to the stage. The extra witches are suspended from a rigging similar to that used for a household clothes line and pulley but employing thin, strong cord. Strobe lighting effects add to the dramatic impact, and this is discussed in the section on "Lighting."

A juggling puppet needs special strings: two through each ball or club to the hands. Shifting the pull on the strings from one hand to another, you make it appear that the puppet is performing a great feat. Put a bit of lead buckshot into each ball or club for additional weight to snap them sharply into the juggler's hands. The juggled items could be decorated to represent the earth and the moon, pollution and survival. Figure 78 shows a juggling act between a man and a seal—the very zenith of showmanship.

If a puppet is to rub its posterior, tap its foot, holds its arms akimbo, scratch its nose or thumb it, all these special gestures need special strings (Figure 80).

There may be times when you'll want a "chorus" line—a row of horses marching abreast in unison, flowers stretching to welcome the sun, ballet dancers kneeling to the Swan Queen. A *tandem* control is the best way of handling this. It's actually a multi-control to which the members of the chorus line are attached in such a way that they move as a unit (Figure 81). Just for fun, you might want to have one individual of the chorus off the tandem control and doing its own unregimented thing.

SPECIAL MARIONETTES FOR SPECIAL EFFECTS

Sometimes special strings are not enough to have the marionette perform according to your wishes, and in that event what is needed is a marionette whose basic construction permits that effect.

The "tallest man in the world" enters as a midget and grows before our eyes. This is a simple illusion to create. The puppet consists of a head, lower legs and feet, and forearms and hands, with two horizontal strips of wood making up the entire torso. All the parts are attached by strings to a two-section controller (Figure 78). Manipulating one section or the other, you make the midget grow or the tallest man shrink. The real trick is the shirring of the costume to conceal the inner workings of the figure. When Alice of *Alice in Wonderland* shrinks and grows, the same principles are applied.

One of the most commonplace and necessary puppets in "show biz" is the come-apart skeleton. The arms and legs join the torso by strings

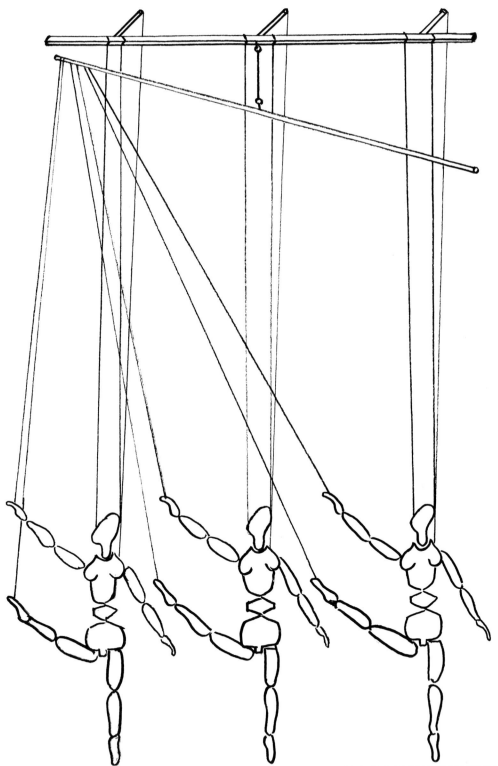

A TANDEM CONTROL FOR CHORUS LINE BUT ALL MUST DO SAME MOVEMENT

FIGURE 81

that go through small screw eyes. When the strings are released, the arms and legs separate from the body. The head too is on a separate string to let it come away from the rest of the marionette, with two guide strings to direct the head to its shoulders again (Figure 79). Rumpelstiltskin, Humpty Dumpty, or a figure representing "Society" can be made this way, to break apart and come together again. So can a trombone player who literally blows his head off. David is able to decapitate Goliath when a pin through the giant's neck, holding his head to his body, is released.

It's an easy matter to open a mouth, blink an eye, twitch a nose, or heave a bosom—provided those parts have been constructed to be movable (Figure 79).

Changelings or *transformations* are a delight. Classical transformations consist of a hoop-skirted woman who changes into a balloon with a gondola full of children, or a Turk with full trousers, turban, and flowing sleeves who becomes a set of wives and children. Newer versions could be a clown who becomes a troupe of performing poodles or a fat politician who changes into enough voters to swing an election. Transformations are simple in concept but laborious to execute because so many parts have to be built. The approach to their construction is to work backward from the final effect (Figure 82).

A combination of transformation and tandem control can produce theatrical results. Again, using an effect from *Hansel and Gretel*, a row of gingerbread cookies (puppets doubled over covered by cookies) turns into children (the puppets stand straight, shedding the cookies and revealing themselves) and then dance together.

If a lovely princess is to change into a hag, a hinged mask can fall over her head and a costume, held in readiness up at the controller,

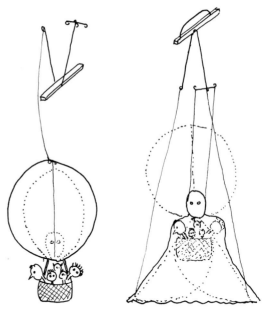

TRANSFORMATIONS—FROM OLD WOMAN TO BALLOON WITH CHILDREN

FIGURE 82

can be dropped into place over her (Figure 79).

A less drastic alteration is the disappearing mustache, constructed to be pulled up into a hollow nose. Contrariwise, hair can be grown on a bald head by concealing a wig in a knapsack arrangement between the shoulders where the costume can blend with it and conceal it; presto!—and the wig is pulled into place on the scalp (Figure 79).

A fish can eat a smaller fish and in turn be eaten by a larger one. For this you need three fish, the larger ones with a mouth large enough to eat the next smaller (Figure 83). A pianist hits a wrong note and discovers a cat in the piano's harp. A clarinetist blows in vain until a balloon inflates from the other end. (This needs rubber tubing going through the hollow of the prop instrument through the marionette, with a balloon preset in the clarinet and an assistant offstage pumping air into his end of the tube.)

Tubes can be built into puppets for various effects. In *Alice in Wonderland*'s caterpillar, the smoke tube runs from the hookah, down through its body, out at the mushroom, and down the side away from the audience and then offstage. An old man smoking in a rocking chair can have the tube go through his body and out through his hip to the far side of the chair and then offstage. To make these marionettes portable, we suggest a connection piece between the body tube and the rest of it so that the puppets can be disconnected.

A "computerized man" special puppet was made by twisting wires into the shape of a human robot and worked by very thin electrical wires that were hooked up to tiny Christmas-tree lights woven into his body. At his heart was his "computer bank" connected to a dimmer. Other pinpoint lights in his body were controlled by individual switches. Some of the units were controlled by flashers so that the lights pulsated. (See "Lighting" to manage this.) All equipment for operating the "computerized man" was located in the controller.

SPECIAL DEVICES FOR SPECIAL EFFECTS

Magical marionettes live in the enchanted world of the theater. Never before in the history of man's ingenuity in creating special theatrical effects has so much been available to draw on. Light, sound, chemicals and plastics, and electrical and mechanical equipment to utilize them have been developed to a degree where no special effect is impossible of achievement— one way or another. This equipment has rendered obsolete many of the theatrical effects of yesterday, but there are many old devices as useful as ever to the puppeteer.

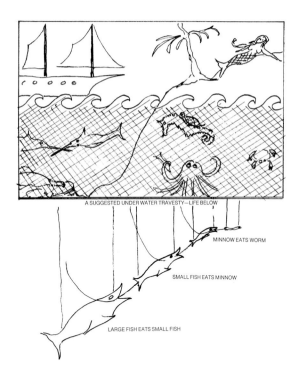

A SUGGESTED UNDER WATER TRAVESTY—LIFE BELOW

MINNOW EATS WORM

SMALL FISH EATS MINNOW

LARGE FISH EATS SMALL FISH

ECOLOGY AT WORK

FIGURE 83

We shall explore enough basic special effects to cover virtually any situation you want to create.

WEATHER

Mist, Fog, and Smoke. Mist, fog, and smoke are combined for discussion because all three are produced identically, the only difference among them being that of density. There are many ways of making all of them.

One of the easiest methods to create an effect for a small area of the stage is to blow talcum powder out by squeezing the large rubber bulb into which you have previously put it. This can be messy to clean up.

Smoke or steam can appear to be issuing from a cauldron if you put dry ice into it and sprinkle water on the ice just before the curtain rises.

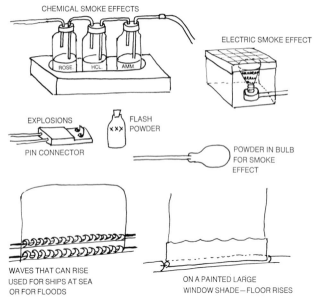

CHEMICAL SMOKE EFFECTS

ELECTRIC SMOKE EFFECT

ROSE. HCL. AMM.

EXPLOSIONS

PIN CONNECTOR

FLASH POWDER

x x x

POWDER IN BULB FOR SMOKE EFFECT

WAVES THAT CAN RISE USED FOR SHIPS AT SEA OR FOR FLOODS

ON A PAINTED LARGE WINDOW SHADE—FLOOR RISES

FIGURE 84

A fire extinguisher with CO_2 (carbon dioxide) emits a dense mist that can cover a wide area.

There are small pellets sold as accessories to make smoke for toy electric trains. These can be placed in a heating cone (Figure 84), and they will give off smoke when the cone is plugged into an electrical outlet. It's possible to buy a ready-made smoke box, which is a heating cone in a metal container covered with screening. This prevents you from being burned by the electrical heating cone. Please take particular note of this if you will be working with children or inexperienced assistants.

Using the same heating cone, you can get smoke by using ammonium chloride instead of the pellet.

If you want smoke to come from a pipe, cigar, or cigarette, or to flow along the stage floor, you can produce it by blowing through a tube that runs through a series of bottles. Three make for the best results—one for hydrochloric acid, one for household ammonia, and one for rose water to neutralize the odor. It's possible to rent one of these units, but if you're develop-ing a permanent puppet company it's best to make or buy one (Figure 84).

Snow. Beautiful stage effects can be created by "snow." Confetti can be drifted into your scene from above, or small flakes of plastic foam, but this can be distracting if it's over-done. The Japanese use this effect with exquisite restraint: Snow is sifted down from a single source onto one area of the stage. This is enough to communicate what's happening, and the audience's imagination fills in the details.

Rain. The effect of rain can be achieved by projecting a storm scene on a continuous film strip against the cyclorama or a scrim preset downstage.

Streamers of Mylar (a patented silvery paper-like composition available from theatrical supply houses) also works well. Strips cut from the sheet of Mylar are attached to a batten (a long wooden strip that runs the length of the stage). The batten is suspended or concealed until you are ready for it, then it's lowered or uncovered and agitated. With the proper play of lights and sound effects, you'll kick up a convincing storm.

Thunder and Lightning. If your rainstorm is intense, thunder and lightning will augment the audience's belief in it.

Thunder can be recorded on your tape or you can rattle a "thunder sheet." This is a metal sheet approximately three feet by six, but sometimes rattling a radiator cover back-stage works about as well.

Lightning is possible through several means. Flashing your lights on and off is one. Streaking light across your cyclorama (if you have one) is another, or, for a third, flashing your back lighting to silhouette some object like a tree in sharp relief for a fraction of a second.

148

DISASTERS—FLOODS, EXPLOSIONS, EARTHQUAKES, AND FIRES

Floods. Floods were a mainstay of the good old-fashioned melodrama and stories like *Noah and His Ark*. In puppetry a flood is simple to arrange. One way is to unroll on cue a large window shade extending across the forestage at the proscenium line. Another is to have a length of painted wavy muslin mounted on a strip lie face down on the forestage, from one side to the other. The strip can be flipped up by a puppeteer on either side of it or raised by strings to reveal the painted waves.

Explosions. Explosions can be an important effect in many puppetry productions, but they can be dangerous if one is careless or doesn't know what he is doing. Explosions are used not only for their own sake in a play but to conceal comings and goings of the characters. While the audience is temporarily blinded by the explosive's glare of brilliant light, fairy godmothers can appear, Rumpelstiltskin can disappear, and all kinds of enchanted goings-on can occur, including quick scene changes.

Flash powder has been used for many years, and it's still around, although many theatrical supply houses refuse to carry it because of its inherent dangers. The powder is a fine magnesium compound, the same the early photographers used. If you want to use it, be careful. Children and inexperienced personnel need supervision when handling it. (*Test the following method thoroughly* before using it onstage. Know *exactly* how much powder you need—possibly about a half teaspoon.) The correct amount of powder is placed on a theatrical stage plug. Two thin strands of wire are laid across the plug's terminals. When the plug is energized, the resultant short circuit causes a spark and the powder explodes blind-

ingly. This is good for one explosion only. If two explosions are required within a short time span, two explosive units will have to be prepared. If a second explosion is called for and you'll have time to reload with fresh wire and powder, you can use the same plug.

The safest substitute for this flash-powder method is the photoflash bulb placed in the most strategic location. It's just as effective as the flash powder.

Earthquakes. Earthquakes and other phenomena causing widespread destruction (an invasion from Mars, a robot walking through walls) can be faked by making all your set pieces collapsible. (See Figure 72.) Walls cave in, plaster flies, buildings drop, and chaos prevails. Incidentally, collapsible scenery is marvelous to tour with—it packs well.

Fire. The illusion of fire today can be created by projecting a continuous film strip of flames onto specific areas. Sometimes a rotating cylinder placed over a red bulb is used partially to obscure the light and cast dancing shadows.

MISCELLANEOUS SPECIAL EFFECTS

Dreams. As mentioned in the discussion of scrims in the section on designing the set, dream sequences take on an out-of-this-world quality when they're presented behind a scrim, with only the lighted part of the set behind it being seen. Underwater scenes can be played behind a scrim the same way, or any other part of the play that should be clearly divorced from the reality of the rest of the action. It's particularly important that the lighting enhance the mood the scrim suggests: hazy, mysterious, aqueous, or remote.

Scenery Building. Building scenery onstage is a special effect that works only when the reason for it has been integrated into the plot structure. A good example could be Noah building his ark and painting it before the audience. The ark, which has been actually built by you beforehand, lies around the stage dismantled but with each piece in its proper position. All the parts are strung together and to a controller. When you pull the appropriate strings, lo! The ark assembles itself. Painting the ark is merely an illusion created by removing cloth sections that cover the pieces of the ark, revealing already painted surfaces. As you are doing this, Noah and his sons are wielding their brushes on their now shipshape vessel.

Laboratories. Whether a laboratory belongs to the Sorcerer with his Apprentice, or to Merlin, or to a mad scientist, it's a splendid opportunity for special effects. Lights can go on and off, all kinds of vials can change color or froth up (as harmless chemical reactions), and all sorts of containers can go gurgle or glug.

MULTI-MEDIA

Multi-media, the combining of two or more art forms into a unified performance, is becoming more and more a fact of everyday theatrical life. This is one area in which puppetry has never taken a back seat—either in joining several kinds of puppetry, being incorporated into the larger world of live theater, film, or television, or incorporating aspects of that world into its own.

PUPPETS AND . . .

. . . *Other Puppets.* Hand and rod puppets are often used together. Sometimes shadow puppets appear in the background. Marionettes may participate, or may replace one or two of the other puppet types. Stages #3 and #4,

are suitable for mixed puppet shows. See whether the "Multi-Media Stage" at the end of that section has possibilities for you.

. . . *People.* For the live theater, marionettes have been integrated into the action. One such production utilized a colossal puppet clown by Remo Bufano under which a live elephant could walk (Billy Rose's *Jumbo*). In the Broadway musical *Flahooley*, Bil Baird created puppets that were an integral part of the story.

Dancers, both onstage and in films, have partnered marionettes.

In the puppet theater, it has become almost a commonplace for stringed or other puppets to conduct a relationship with a live actor. Sometimes, as in the case of Fran (Allison), she is outside the puppet frame while she converses with Burr Tilstrom's Kukla and Ollie. Sometimes the live actor irrupts into the marionette world as Aladdin's Genie of the Lamp or Jack's Giant.

. . . *Light.* One of the newer multi-media tools, at least in its more modern applications, is the use of light—both as an art medium in itself and a means of enhancing traditional theater values. Light shows with a rock musical score are popular with young people. Laser-light shows with astronomical projections against the domes of planetariums attract all ages. Light shows with marionettes and other puppets are just as successful. In its more customary form, light used in rear screen projection can eliminate extensive scenery. Films or slides against a translucent screen can set a stage fully and convey emotional overtones. Combining the action of light and actual marionette movement can be striking: projected clouds boil across the sky, and a marionette demon springs to life on the stage.

Puppeteers have been utilizing some of the

properties of light for generations. Shadow puppets have fought naval engagements or marched in regiments against a large rear screen, on which they were silhouetted in moving colored light. Fireworks and other spectacular light effects have concluded rousing performances.

Aside from frontal and rear projections of film or direct light, there's another way to achieve effects to hold an audience spellbound, particularly if the light and music are synchronized. If you put a liquid water-based paint on a tray and add an oil-based dye that won't mix with it, the chemical reaction gives exquisite moving patterns that are never the same twice. Above the tray an overhead projector enlarges the image and projects it onto the screen. Another spectacular effect easy to achieve is obtained by placing lights in such a way that cut-out silhouettes project as shadows in a variety of colors. With dimmers these can be cross-faded and blended into each other (Figure 75).

USING MULTI-MEDIA

Like any other technique, combining two or more art forms presents problems. These must be mastered if the technique is to serve a purpose, and the first step is always to understand what the technique can do for a production, or to it. Neophyte showmen and veterans alike can be so fascinated by the possibilities of multi-media that they forget about their basic show and dart from one splendid effect to the next. The show dies, and so do the multi-media tricks they sacrificed it for.

To utilize multi-media effects and keep the presentation in balance, we must understand whether the marionettes are to be the most important part of the production, or subordinate and supportive of other elements, or if all elements should have equal weight.

When puppetry is used for a brief scene or two in a live musical, obviously it's to expand the imagery of the live production. The puppets contribute and depart, unless they are invited back for a curtain call.

When a famous dancer shares the spotlight with a marionette, that's just what he's doing —sharing. For either to appear at his best, both must be proficient as artists and interrelate so that the audience regards the spectacle as a duet.

On the other hand, when your marionette show has a live actor as a narrator, it's important to keep a balance if your little marionettes are not to be overwhelmed. If a live genie bursts onto the stage, convincing the audience of his enormity by the contrast in his scale with that of the puppets, sometimes this works, sometimes it doesn't. If he sustains the credibility of the *marionettes*, he strengthens the production. If he doesn't, he destroys it.

Similarly, light used to expand the dimensions of your marionette show can make for an exciting production. Used for its own sake, or ineptly, the light can be so powerful the marionettes it's supposed to support can become the least interesting objects onstage— even an intrusion into the light show.

It's always essential to consider what you want the multi-media effects to do for your production so that you can be alert to keep them as useful tools instead of permitting them to dominate and destroy what you have gone to such pains to create—a viable, believable world of little people.

WORLDWIDE PUPPETRY

Marionettes Onstage! is a how-to book and it isn't our intent to give a history of puppetry, even a capsule version. Suffice it to say that puppetry is almost as old as mankind and that

National Shadow Theatre of Malaysia.

are frequently exquisitely detailed, often colored, with intricate silhouettes. For centuries they've been telling the epics like the Ramayana throughout the mainland of Asia and the islands of the East. Tender love stories, religious dramas, or battles between armies or between heroes and demons—the shadow puppets bring them to life for half a world. The shadow puppet reaches into Turkey, where two-dimensional Karagoz, the anti-establishment equivalent of Europe's Punch, holds his popularity.

The West has taken over shadow puppets for special sequences in plays whose major characters are living actors or other kinds of puppets. In Eugene O'Neill's *Marco Millions*, Jero Magon's shadow puppets lent a moment of pure magic to the feasting scenes. Film is a beautiful medium for shadow puppets—the flatness of the screen adjusting comfortably to the flatness of the puppets. Lotte Reiniger's work in filmed shadow puppets is considered classic. Shadow puppets can expand the marionettes' otherwise three-dimensional theater.

Bunraku. Puppetry received more from the Orient than these magical shadows. That favorite of the courts of China, the stringed puppet, developed in Japan into a remarkable form of which the Bunraku is one example. Each Bunraku figure is about two thirds life-size. The puppet is manipulated by three "trainer" puppeteers, each of whom has a specific function. One manages the head and right hand, one the left hand, and one the feet. The trainers work the puppets in full view of the audience, and, except that the operators are dressed completely in black, no attempt is made to disguise their presence or their function. The puppets weigh about seventy pounds each, and they are elaborately costumed and made up to resemble the live performers of the Japanese theater. All the voices are supplied by one

no region of the world has been without some form of it.

Your multi-media productions may combine marionettes with other forms of puppets. So many good books cover hand and rod puppets there's no reason to talk about them here, except to remind you they can be incorporated into your production easily when they are installed in a booth on either side of your marionette stage. You should know about the more exotic types to consider whether they might make a place for themselves in your marionette theater.

Shadow Puppets. The traditional shadow puppets of the Orient—China, Japan, Malaysia, etc.—antedate history. The translucent puppets

152

"Tsuri Onna" scene of great drama from classic Bunraku repertory.

reader, who is accompanied by a samisen player. The reader and the musician/musicians sit off to one side of the puppet stage, which can span a wide proscenium arch. It's instructive to watch a Western audience, so aware of the puppeteers to begin with, forget their existence as the puppet play of love or battle goes on, until it is as indifferent to their presence as a Japanese audience. The Bunraku technique is being employed outside its homeland, and it offers interesting possibilities for the experimental puppeteer. The use of black clothing has been widely adopted in America and Europe, where black-clad puppeteers manipulate their hand puppets against black curtains. And the closeness of the puppeteer to his figure in such instances has an advantage in certain presentations.

Sicilian Marionettes. The Sicilian Marionette Theater too uses puppets that weigh about seventy pounds each. They're worked from above with a steel center bar that controls the head and also is the holding point against gravity. The hands are worked by heavy ropes. The marionettes are usually caparisoned magnificently in chased armor and fastidiously detailed in every respect. These marionettes specialize in battles and spectacles that have the sweep of early Chinese dramas. Typical is their *Orlando Furioso*, the heroic tale of Charlemagne. The gory side of war is stressed, with

This is a rare photo showing an authentic Sicilian marionette being worked by Macri-Weil. *Photo: M. Richardson*

marionettes being "killed" or dismembered realistically. Heads roll, severed arms drop, blood gushes. The stories go on and on, providing an excuse for the action, which is the heart of the theater. A performance concludes with a "cliff-hanger" intended to bring the audience back for the next episode. This marionette theater, splendid in its own way, has seldom been influential outside of Sicily, and even there it's losing ground. All the emphasis has been on the craftsmanship of the figures and the technique required to make them wield swords, master horses, or engage in hand-to-hand combat. Virtually no heed has been paid to drafting good scripts or to the other aspects of modern theater—lighting, scene design, etc.

However, what is essentially the strength of the Sicilian theater, the puppets themselves, can certainly be adapted to the theater of today by anyone who may want to go in this direction —and has the physical prowess to manipulate an expatriate Sicilian marionette.

Other Puppets. For special scripts, you may want to explore some of the other authentic puppets created by different peoples. The Hopi Indians, the Nishka tribe of British Columbia, the Fiji Islanders, central Africans—these are a few of the peoples who have turned to puppetry for religious or entertainment purposes.

The world has much to offer the puppeteer, and if you explore old forms of puppetry you may find the inspiration to develop from them a form as new as tomorrow.

DIRECTION

THE LIVE THEATER DIRECTOR

In the live theater, one of the most important positions is the director's. It has been said that the director's role is to "Get 'em on, get 'em off," but there's more to it than that. The director is the artist who puts the show together.

The director begins with the script. What is the author's intent? What are the possibilities for humor? Emotion? Action? Are the characters defined and motivated? The director compensates through his craftsmanship for whatever deficiencies the script may have—but it should still be the playwright's script, not his. The director must extract all the fun from a comedy, build all the scenes to a strong, inevitable climax in a drama, and maintain suspense to the end in a melodrama. He determines the style in which the play will be staged and combines the various elements of the production to create a believable environment, whether realism or fantasy, for believable characters. He has the final word on costumes, scene designs, and stage properties, to control their fitting into the unity of his concept. He suggests to the actors interpretations of their roles that will be consistent with that concept and works with his cast in a feedback situation where ideas cross-fertilize each other and result in enriched characterizations. The director assists the actors to invent stage business that enhances the production. He stages the actors, moving them to intensify or clarify relationships and dramatic meaning.

Having collaborated with the set and costume designer, the director is always conscious of what his play looks like, including whether full theatrical use is made of the playing area. He enlists the cooperation of the lighting designer to enhance each scene not only visually but dramatically. If there's a musical background, the score may intensify emotion or drama. It may also create a sense of unreality, and it's the director who is the final arbiter.

One of the director's major functions hasn't been touched on yet: his responsibility for the pacing—that is, the tempo of the production and the distribution of energy, which are introduced at the first rehearsal. The pacing will vary according to the requirements of each production, but each has its own internal rhythms. If the production is a revue, the rhythms will call for segments of different lengths and content—a lavish production number running for several minutes and, possibly, "blackout" sketches of only a few seconds. A stand-up comic might be followed by a sentimental ballad or a skit whose aim is to present a visually beautiful effect or a novelty. To keep the show from lagging, there is a minimum amount of time between segments. If more than a few seconds are required for scene changes, a mono-

logue from an M.C. or a song or skit in front of the curtain will hold the audience's attention.

Another example: In a drama for children, the conflict should be established early and a series of episodes or adventures ensue promptly. Between the episodes, which should be of mounting intensity, there should be relatively quiet time for the audience to recover and prepare for the next. Maintaining a frenetic pace without variation is like shouting at full voice all the time; there's no way to go *up* from there for special emphasis. If the quiet moments contribute positive values to the story, the audience is held; if they're merely "padding," the tempo drags, time is wasted, and the audience is lost.

To sum up, the director assumes the burden for a total concept that, fully developed, results in a show that's unified in physical production and performance and brings the playwright's script to magical life.

THE MARIONETTE-THEATER DIRECTOR

That a director is just as important to the marionette theater is frequently not recognized. Many puppet operators, particularly one- or two-person companies, can't afford an outside director and assume the role of director also. The director of a marionette company labors with advantages and disadvantages the live-theater director doesn't share. He too must analyze his script to evaluate its ideas and isolate its production elements, but since he is often the playwright as well, the marionette director doesn't always bring objectivity to this task. He has, when he creates puppets, costumes, sets, props, lighting, and special effects himself, the advantage of not having people—

actors, designers, and technicians—of different ideas to deal with. But he loses the contribution of their thinking and skills. In a one-person show, everything onstage is his own product—ideas, physical production, tempo. The one element he can't always furnish is perspective. That has to come from outside the production. An intelligent, theater-wise person can be invited to sit in on your rehearsals before your production is set. Look for suggestions rather than approval. You aren't bound to follow them, but at least consider without defensiveness whether they have application to your show.

Now, let's be specific about how you, as the director of your own production, go about doing everything we've been discussing. You have a script. If you've written it yourself, you have no legal problems; if you are using someone else's material either as it comes or with adaptations, your producer self will have cleared it with the publisher, if necessary. You decide the time and place in which the play will be set and the style in which you'll stage it. How many puppeteers will you use? How many of them are to be involved in design and/or construction of marionettes, costumes, scenery, sets, props, stage, lighting? Can you use an existing stage or does the show require a new one? And what are you going to use for money? The conferences on budget between your producer and director selves may be frequent and prolonged.

In designing marionettes, costumes, sets, and props, small drawings are the beginning. These little sketches will indicate what you'll need for the high spots of your several scenes. If you can develop your drawings in scale, then you can make more elaborate plans that will plot how each aspect of the production will look as it relates to the stage. Only after the final draw-

ings are completed do you execute the physical components of the show.

As you've worked out the colors for your costumes, sets, and props, and considered the dramatic elements of the play, you've been thinking of the lighting. It's a good idea to set the lighting plan down on paper in as much detail as you have ready. The "Lighting" section goes into this.

REHEARSALS

When the designs are completed and the construction under way, you're ready for a first rehearsal. Whether you're alone or with a partner or a company, as director you discuss with the puppeteers just what you expect of them as their contribution to the ultimate production. Everyone has to understand the style of the play, its mood, its purpose. A first reading of the script is helpful, and the tempo is explored. You have already cast your play with puppeteers whose voices fit the characters of the puppets they are to manipulate. However, in some instances it may be that one will manipulate the puppet and another speak for it. This does not excuse the manipulator from knowing the script as thoroughly as the speaker.

As soon as the marionettes are built and costumed, the actors coordinate their dialogue and manipulation under your watchful director's eye. Props and sets are added as they're completed, and the lighting is subject to constant review and possible alteration. Whenever an element is added, rethink and possibly redirect the cast in the pacing so as to make the most of each new contribution.

From this point on, all rehearsals are built around the script. If as director you make changes in the script, note them carefully in every area: working scripts for manipulators (and speakers), stage manager, lighting design, etc.

Rehearsals must be disciplined. They're not social occasions. Performers must be ready for work at designated times, but don't call them until they're needed. Not everyone has to be present at all times—just those who are participating in the scenes in rehearsal.

Discipline is reflected in every phase of your production, the back stage as well as the front stage (a term to differentiate between the technicians and the performers). In puppetry it's not always possible to make a distinction, but everyone involved in each aspect of the production shares the same goal—to make the show a success.

Establish a schedule for production and rehearsal and adhere to it as closely as you can. It won't always be easy. Sets and props may be held up in completion for reasons beyond your control. Or a cast member may fall ill or be otherwise unavailable for good cause. But it's rehearse, rehearse, until the acting and stage mechanics are smooth and the pacing is tight.

Rehearsals are always trying times. Everyone is edgy. Nothing goes right. The words don't fit. The sequences are too long or too short. Marionettes sag or jiggle, or a joint unhinges, a chip falls off the leading character's face, and a string breaks. You want to chuck it all and raise bananas on a tropic isle. But think positively! Appreciate how much you've already accomplished and how far you've come. Suddenly everything falls into place—the manipulation, the verbal comprehension, the sound, the lights—even the sets and props are ready.

An aid for your performers in reaching this state is to tape their voices from time to time. Hearing what they sound like will speed up their responses to your direction. If you are able to video-tape a late rehearsal, this could be enormously helpful. Even though the tape may look dull, it can point up weak spots in the production. But don't judge the appearance of a staged show, lighted for the theater, by a video tape, another medium for which your production isn't designed. Video-tape equipment may be borrowed from friends or rented, and it is often available from school audiovisual departments as well as from commercial sources. The final video tape is a good record for work purposes and a good public-relations device.

THE SHOW GOES ON!

When you feel you've gone as far as you can, your show is ready!

Don't think your job as director is over now, because it's not. When you take your show to an audience, no matter how busy you are with other responsibilities, the director in you must note audience reactions. Observe when an anticipated laugh doesn't come off or comes in the wrong place. Listen to the audience. Are sympathies misdirected? Is inattention or boredom indicated by inordinate coughing, foot-shuffling, or conversation? With children, is the "bathroom brigade" out in force? As soon as you have a free moment, jot down your notes.

Rethink. Rework. Clarify. Tighten. Rehearse. Try out before another audience. It may take a while to pull your show into final shape, particularly if you're reluctant to abandon a cherished character or effect that contributes insufficiently to the production. Suggestion: Don't go to friends for advice. Almost invariably they tell you what you're doing is wonderful. Perfect. Whether they don't know what perfect is or whether they don't want to hurt your feelings, although they may ease your bruised spirit, they won't help your show. Only an objective, talented director can do this, or a trial-and-error period before audiences. One way or another, you should end up with the fine production that's been your goal.

PUTTING ON THE SHOW

Much of what this section covers has been touched on earlier. In Part One we mentioned the necessity of allowing enough time to arrive at the place of performance with a safety margin and enough time to set up. However, some points mentioned only briefly in preceding pages are expanded on here, and some topics are added which have not been gone into at all. Until you've built up your own experiences in performing, these observations and suggestions may make it easier for you to launch yourself as a producer-puppeteer.

PREPARING THE PREMISES

To make the most of the magic of your marionette theater, you want that sense of magic to influence your audience even before your presentation begins. If you are on tour and putting on your show in premises operated by the organization that has booked you, there isn't very much you can do about decorating the theater or its personnel. However, if you are playing in your own resident theater—whether a basement playroom or permanent quarters in a room in a community center or even a real theater—you have the opportunity to expand the glamour or the fun of the audience's theatrical experience.

Furnish your auditorium with as comfortable seats as your budget and other circumstances allow (according to the lease or rental terms). Curtain your windows with attractive, opaque draperies to control the light. Carpeting will cut down the noise of foot-shuffling and contribute to an air of luxury. Of course you can give a show, and a good one, with children seated informally on the floor or on benches, and if you can't eliminate outside light altogether your show will have to take that into consideration, and you can do without carpets. But the more distractions you can eliminate (children shoving each other, light, and noise) the better concentration your production will receive. Decorate the walls and ceiling to add to a sense of merriment (balloons, paintings, festoons, etc.) if your marionettes will be performing comedies, or to lend an air of importance to your marionette drama. If you have an outer lobby you could set up a display featuring your company or the subject of your presentation or marionettes in general.

Your ticket seller, ticket taker, and ushers could carry this idea further by being costumed to evoke the spirit of your play (clowns, animals, wooden soldiers, etc.). For adult audiences we suggest a distinctive but more sophisticated costume treatment.

When the audience enters the lobby or the auditorium, background music could be playing. *Background* music—creating a happy atmosphere in which people settle down to await the show, not an earsplitting din that prevents conversation and antagonizes the hearers.

As an alternative, strolling minstrels could welcome the audience or a barbershop quartet could put everyone in a holiday mood. Goblins could dance around, or pirates stalk through the aisles. Most young people love these extra touches, but if you come across a child who is frightened, have your costumed entertainer back off and turn his attention elsewhere immediately. Educate your entertainers in this respect.

Your attractive proscenium curtain should

greet the audience with soft lights on it that remain while the house lights dim to indicate the start of the show. Or if you'd prefer a more spectacular effect, you can project several colors of light across the curtain in geometric forms, interwoven and bridged by dimming from one to another (Figure 75). These colors remain on low when the house lights fade. The house should never be blacked out totally unless the script calls for it during the course of the play, particularly if there are young children present who may become panicky in darkness.

If you have an adult audience, you may want printed programs. For children, who don't care who the performers are or who can't read, printed programs are not only a waste but a potential hazard to your presentation. Programs make excellent paper airplanes, and there's no telling when a child will decide to fly one through the house or onto the stage during performance. A large sign or poster listing the credits and possibly some photographs, set up conspicuously in the lobby, may be used instead of or in addition to printed programs. This holds for touring shows as well as for your resident theater.

CURTAIN TIME

Usually the curtain goes up five minutes after the announced time to allow stragglers to be seated without disturbing the rest of the audience. In inclement weather, where people may be coming considerable distances, it's permissible to grant another five minutes' leeway. More than that is unfair to the audience that made an effort to arrive promptly. Not only that, if the audience is mainly children, it's unwise to keep them cooling their heels. Children come to the theater in a state of high expectation that is in itself tiring. To have

them wait more than a few moments means that they can come down from their happy anticipation into an irritability that may not entirely dissipate when the curtain finally rises.

There may be occasions when a backstage emergency occurs to delay the curtain, or a busload of children is overdue and you want to allow extra time. In such a situation, go before the curtain, or have one of your entertainers do it, and tell the audience what the trouble is and approximately how long the wait will be. Then until your show can begin, provide some sort of activity to keep the audience occupied. A community sing, a comic routine, a storyteller, a folk singer—anyone in your company with a talent that can be utilized is pressed into service. When you're ready, thank the audience for being patient and on with the show!

PERFORMING OUTDOORS

If you will be performing at a picnic or in a bandstand in a park, you will have factors to deal with that won't present themselves indoors, and some will be out of your control.

Which way should your audience face and which way should you set up your stage? If the seats are built in, or you're assigned a spot to set up, the question doesn't arise, but there may be times when the decision will be yours. Try not to have the audience squinting into the sun, although this will mean that *your* back is to the sun and the puppet stage will be in your shadow. Try not to have the sun shine directly into your stage, because this will put the sun in *your* eyes and make it difficult for you to function, and if the bright light penetrates your curtains, it may shatter illusions you are depending on. If you can set up so that the light falls sideways across you and the audience, this is the best compromise.

159

Steve Hansen is one of the last remaining one-man puppet showmen complete with his own musical accompaniment—Toots and Horns. It is a wraparound stage and he performs around the world on the city streets and parks. Hand puppets—Punch and Judy.

Be prepared for inclement weather. Have a lightweight nylon or plastic tarpaulin large enough to enclose your entire stage in the event of rain. And have ropes and stakes to lash your stage down if there are gusts of wind.

If you are setting up your stage on the grass or operating from a truck equipped with a puppet stage, be sure you are based on level ground. Scenery and props have an embarrassing tendency to fall over unless they are placed vertically. If the ground isn't level, come prepared to fill in under the feet of your stage.

If there's no way to prevent the audience from roaming around behind the stage, it's a good idea to bring screens or rig up some kind of curtain to close off the back of the stage. This may discourage meddling with your marionettes and other equipment before, during, and between performances, and it could reduce damage or pilfering.

Much meddling can be laid to curiosity about the marionettes and their manipulation. In circumstances where it's possible, you could add a few minutes to your regular performance to demonstrate the kinds of puppets you're using and how you operate them. This might reduce forays into your gear.

Of course, you'll have checked into available electric power and, if there isn't any, come with a battery-operated cassette for your sound. For night performances where there's no electricity, you'll have made arrangements with a number of car owners to shine their headlights onto your stage on signal.

AUDIENCE PARTICIPATION

Directors understand that adult audiences are involved in a production when they sit quietly, not coughing or scuffing their feet or mumbling. When tensions are released in a burst of laughter or a sigh of relief, the performers feel the intensity of the involvement.

Where children form the audience, theater people—writers, directors, performers, and reviewers alike—tend to equate involvement with active physical participation. They find difficulty in accepting that boys and girls can be engrossed in a performance without bouncing in their seats or shrieking. Accordingly, they solicit "audience participation" by giving the children roles in the presentation. From time to time characters in the play turn to the audience and ask, "Which way did he go?" "Should I do it?" "What is the magic word?" Or they exhort the kids to "Clap to make the fairy come!" "Say it louder. I can't hear you!" "Howl like coyotes!" There's nothing wrong with this, particularly for very young children, but it's fraught with insufficiently appreciated perils.

To begin with, this kind of participation is a gimmick, and, like any gimmick, if overdone or used for its own sake it can demolish the structure it is employed to enhance. It's easier to hold the children's attention by calling for a verbal or physical response, no matter how inane the stimulus, than it is to command attention by crafting an intelligent script and providing competent direction. If the writer and director don't understand that the children are being cheated in the first instance, not comprehending that the audience is being treated with contempt, they will continue to put on the drivel that has given entertainment for children such a bad name among those who care for children and entertainment.

Next, "participation" may lose the production's control of the audience. It's simpler to work children into semi-hysteria than it is to stop their screaming and yelling. Also, it doesn't do the show any good if, after the children have calmed down, they wait for the next opportunity to let off steam instead of interesting themselves in what is happening in the show to provide it. If a device of some kind is used to snap the audience back into a receptive state, this device must be at least as logical in the context of the script as the participation is.

Moreover, while all the hooting and hollering are going on and the director is pleased that the audience is so worked up, the show is going down the drain. Generally, the first thing is that the pacing of the production is wrecked. Timing is off all down the line while the audience carries on, or if the show is bound

to a tape and proceeds on its inexorable way, no one can hear anything happening onstage. The second result is that illusions are shattered. All the work that's gone into constructing an environment in which the little people can live believable lives is wasted when what is occurring in the audience is more important than what's onstage.

And one thing more: The puppeteer must be able to lead the audience to give the desired response. However, if the audience delivers an unexpected response to a question asked by a marionette, the puppeteer must deal gracefully with it. Nothing is more insulting to children than to have their solicited opinions ignored when they run counter to a rigidly preset script.

We feel the whole matter of audience participation needs rethinking. Isn't it indicative of a fundamentally condescending attitude toward children when we presume they are so much less than people that they can't participate actively in a well-written, well-staged production through their intelligence and their emotions? Is it fair to children to encourage their extroverted response during performance with the idea that this is theater?

The factor that can prevent excesses in participation as well as in other areas of production is that of respect. If you respect your audience you will expect it to have the capacity to enjoy your production without extraneous participation, overly broad acting, and other evidences of contempt. If you respect the material you've selected, you have confidence in its ability to involve the audience without the necessity of warping its plot or characterizations for cheap laughs. If you respect yourself as a craftsman, you'll never give any audience—children's or adult—less than your best.

161

AUDIENCE RELATIONS

We've talked about audience participation and respect, but there are other aspects of the two-way communication between audience and performer. Some of these may be within your control, some may not.

Circumstances will differ, depending on the kind of situation in which you'll be putting on your show. If you are performing in an intimate gathering for a four-year-old's birthday party, your approach to the audience would be very different from the way you would handle three hundred children from the stage of a school auditorium. With young children at close hand, you'd have to show a warm, gentle, non-threatening personality. If a child seems wary, don't force yourself on him. Ignore him, or step back a pace or two before continuing. If a child engages in conversation with the marionette and you can carry on a friendly colloquy, this could be a delightful touch. On the other hand, if he or other members of the little audience get smart-alecky, explain that it's time to quiet down so that the show can go on.

Order in the audience is a concern wherever you perform. There may be several reasons why a children's audience is noisy or inconsiderate to the performers.

The experience of going to the theater may be new to the children. All they may know is their Saturday kiddie movies, where they are confined to one part of the orchestra under the eye of a matron who doesn't care how much racket they kick up. These children may not realize that the marionettes are manipulated by live persons to whom they owe the respect due to artists. A way to handle this is to have one of the puppeteers come before the curtain and speak to the children. Not lecture them. Explain that this isn't a film that was made

long ago; what is happening onstage is happening now. Unlike the film, the actors onstage can hear the audience as clearly as the audience hears them, and distractions prevent them from giving their best. Also, the only way everyone in the audience can see and hear is to sit down and not talk during the show, because marionettes, being little, have little voices.

The natural exuberance of childhood is another factor. When the boys and girls come in from outside, they may not be ready to settle down immediately. This can be dealt with by having someone play a game with them—Stretching games, or clapping in rhythm—it doesn't much matter as long as there is an excuse to let off steam.

Children tend to grow disorderly if they can't hear well—check your amplification system, if you have one—or see well. In seating children, try to keep their view of the stage from being blocked. Unless you have a steeply raked house floor, it's advisable to seat children in front and adults in back rows or along the extreme sides. If there are children who are uneasy at being separated from their parents, seat them next to a parent at the side or on a lap at the back. If a child's crying disturbs the rest of the audience, the parent should be asked to take the little one out, and the house manager will offer to refund the price of admission if necessary.

Another factor influencing audience reaction is the age of the audience in relation to the age range your show was designed for. It was your responsibility to let the sponsoring organization (the booker) know that the show is for, say, fours, fives, and sixes. If the organization insists on selling tickets to ten- and twelve-year-olds, the older boys and girls can't be blamed for being irritable. All you can do is present such a great production that, hopefully, those who are bored by the content will be charmed by the technique.

No matter how noisy the audience is, you must remember you are there to entertain, not impose martial law. The secret of success is to capture the attention of the audience from the very beginning. You must be careful when trying to establish order not to lose the sympathy of the majority. Making it fun for the children may enlist their cooperation: Pit one half of the auditorium against the other or the girls against the boys to see who will be quiet more quickly. This is all *before* the show starts. Once it begins, it's the production itself that must hold attention by its quality.

When the matter of a booking comes up, the way the audience is supervised is of legitimate concern to you. If you know the circumstances are such that it will be impossible to establish order and that distractions will prevent the audience from concentrating on your offering, it is unprofessional to accept the date —regardless of the fee involved.

In most instances, you won't have problems of audience control. Generally children come prepared to enjoy themselves and to meet you more than halfway. When the pleasure you give them lives up to their expectations, you as well as they have a wonderful time.

One more thing: Either you or the sponsoring organization may want to make the occasion even more memorable for the children by giving each boy and girl a balloon or other toy, or a small bag of candy, or a lollipop. *Never* pass these out to the audience as it enters. Balloons will be sure to block someone's view of the stage, or one will break, or a toy will fall and roll three rows of seats away, or a child will gulp his candy and envy his neighbor's slowly savored share. Whatever happens, it's bound to cause disruption. The time for handing out souvenirs is at the end of the performance, as the children are leaving. If a balloon bursts or candy is stepped on, let it happen somewhere else.

In connection with candy or toys, two cautions: If you give away anything from the stage during a performance, be sure you have enough for every child or don't give away anything. The world's greatest show is no compensation to a child who sees someone else get a balloon when he doesn't. And if a parent shakes his head "no" when you offer a child a lollipop, don't argue. Go on to the next child. It's the parent's decision, not yours.

So far we've been discussing performing for children, but you may be booked to do some performances in a bank or supermarket or shopping mall. Here the best you can hope for is to attract passers-by who may stop and give casual interest to your production. They may see the show from the beginning or they may wander by when it's almost over. If they smile, laugh, or applaud, you may consider you've done very well. If any come back to see a complete show, this is the highest form of compliment from a shopper who is willing to be shoved around and stand for fifteen or twenty minutes with an armful of packages.

Nightclub audiences are notoriously difficult. You will have an introduction by the master of ceremonies and the assistance of a darkened playing area with a spotlight on you, and then you're on your own. For nightclub clientele you need a ready wit and a skin thick enough to stand possible heckling from not necessarily sober patrons. You have one great advantage: If you engage in repartee with a heckler, you can get away with saying through your marionette what you could never say for yourself.

The customer who may start out belligerently, after a round or two with the marionette may be so charmed or amused he'll allow the show to proceed without further disturbance.

EMERGENCY EQUIPMENT

Whenever you perform, you must be prepared for accidents. If you are on tour, you can depend on no one but yourself to supply what you need to repair damage or minor personal hurts. Therefore, you should take with you basic kits to provide for emergencies.

Tools:
Hammer
Screwdriver
Gas pliers
Long-nosed pliers
Cutting pliers
Small saw (coping or jig)
  or blade with small handle
Awl
Matte knife
Scissors
Metal measuring tape

Equipment:
Fuses
Friction tape
Masking tape
Assorted screws and nails
Screw eyes
Cup hooks
"S" hooks
Assorted hinges
Touch-up tempera paint (the colors of
  your marionettes, props, scenery)
Baling and electric wire
White glue

Toothpicks or small pieces of wood
  (white pine is best)
Nylon or cotton heavy-duty thread
Assorted needles
Plastic wood
Extra light bulbs
Extra electrical plugs
Extra controller

First-Aid Kit

SAFETY

The safety precautions you carry out in your everyday life should be carried over into your puppetry.

Personal Safety. Many accidents are caused by fatigue, so be well rested before you perform. Allow enough set-up time so that you can relax a little before going on. We've suggested black clothing, but this has been for aesthetic purposes. What's important as to safety is that your clothing have no projections or flaps on which something may catch, throwing you off balance. Proper shoes are important—slip-resistant rubber soles and no high heels.

The Stage. If you have a fear of heights, design your marionette bridge at a distance off the floor that will let you work comfortably, bearing in mind that the audience must be able to see with minimum obstruction. In any event, the bridge should be sturdy and a substantial backrail to enclose you will contribute a feeling of security. Sometimes a "kick plate," a bar at the back edge of the bridge floor, helps since it lets you know where you are without having to look down. All protruding objects should be flagged to keep heads from running into them.

Electricity. Understand how your electrical stage equipment works and see that it's properly maintained. Constant handling, even frequent plugging and unplugging of extension cords, can wear down insulation and wires. Make sure connections are properly joined and grounded and that all "Underwriters Code" regulations are followed to the letter. Don't overload the capacity of your fuses.

Tools. Learn the use of each tool and how to employ it properly. Be particularly alert with high-speed electrical equipment and don't try to save time by working more quickly than your ability to control the operation permits. Don't overheat light-duty machinery with too much stress. *Always* cut *away* from yourself. When inserting screws, *don't* use your hand as a vise or workbench; if the worked-on item must be held down, secure it with a vise or clamps before you lean on the screwdriver. Yankee screwdrivers are dangerous for the inexperienced carpenter, so go a little slowly until you master their techniques. When sawing a board, be careful not to cut past it into the saw bench.

Lights. All bulbs must be vented when covered by filters so that heat can escape. Be careful not to let anything flammable fall over or cover a lighted bulb.

Heat. When technical processes require that something be heated over a stove or a burner, keep an eye on it. Don't wander off and forget about it.

Chemicals. When you combine chemicals, be sure you know what you're doing. When you put chemicals away, be careful to see that their containers are properly labeled.

Children. Anything sharp or poisonous or otherwise potentially hazardous should be kept out of the reach of children, both in your workshop and backstage.

General. Don't place objects at the edge of tables where they can be upset and fall off. Or on steps or other work areas where they can be stepped on, not only to their own damage but to the bodily harm of whoever falls over them.

PART THREE

PUPPET THEATER MANAGEMENT

INTRODUCTION

In common with live theater, opera, dance, and films, puppetry shares a distinctive feature. All, besides being performing arts, are also businesses. They must be operated with a degree of efficiency if they are to present their artistry to the public.

As an amateur puppeteer or a full-time professional employing many marionette companies, you must be businesslike in your approach to performing. We're spelling out for you in Part Three, "Puppet Theater Management," what our experience has taught us to do or not do. Read it through at least once and then turn back to it as a guide when the need arises. We may not tell you everything you want to know to meet a problem, but we've set down what the practice is and, in some instances, our suggestions for improving on the practice.

In 1971 on television, after Jim Henson's *Muppets on Puppets*, an appeal was made to children to join the Puppeteers of America. One reply in particular to Olga Stevens, Executive Secretary, sums up the response exactly in the words of the child:

Dear Puppeteers of America: How are you doing? Can you give us information about string puppets? Are they easy to make? How many people does it usual take to have a good puppet show? How much money does a puppeter get monthly and yearly? When is the vacation? How long does it take to be a puppeter? Can you tell us when we're going shomewhere? You don't have to answer but I am in a rush. Bye now."

Some of these inquiries have already been answered in Parts One and Two. Much of the balance is covered by Part Three.

One point not taken up—the matter of vacations. Puppeteering can be a time-consuming activity and it may not leave you much leisure for a vacation in the ordinary sense of the word. However, you wouldn't be so involved in puppetry if you didn't love what you're doing. A vacation can be a state of mind, a change of pace to permit you to do for a short part of a year what the daily grind prevents you from the rest of the time. But if you're doing what you love best all year 'round, for a change of scene, you can consider that you're vacationing when you take a show on the road.

We wish you success in any course of puppetry you choose to follow and we are happy indeed if *Marionettes Onstage!* can contribute to it.

WHERE DO YOU GO FROM HERE?

WHAT DO YOU WANT TO DO?

Of course, you'll continue to enjoy your marionette theater, but when you become truly skilled as a creator and manipulator of your little people, several options will be open to you.

Amateur Puppetry. You can go on the way you are—as a talented amateur. You may be a dilettante, going to your marionettes when the notion strikes you, entertaining yourself and a few friends, and then putting your puppets away carefully until the mood to work with them seizes you again. Or you may be very businesslike about your hobby, inviting groups in for scheduled performances or contracting to take your show to schools or hospitals, either free or for just an honorarium to cover out-of-pocket expenses. Puppetry can go on being a satisfying recreation for you into advanced old age.

Part-Time Professional Puppetry. You can continue with your regular means of livelihood and become a professional puppeteer on a part-time basis. What's the difference between an amateur and a professional? They may be equally proficient, but the professional is paid according to the value he sets on his services and he is highly responsible in fulfilling the terms of his contracts. With a nine-to-five, five-day-a-week job, there's no reason why you can't find bookings for evenings, Saturdays and Sundays, and holidays. It's possible to supplement your income to a substantial degree by playing for Sunday-school classes or church suppers or even nightclub dates. You may be short on sleep, but you'll get around, you'll learn a lot, and you won't be bored.

Part-time puppeteering can be a valuable experience, whether as an end in itself or a test to see if you enjoy your marionettes as much when you are committed to perform as you do when it's just for fun. If you don't, then you certainly wouldn't want to make marionettes your primary career.

Full-Time Professional Puppetry. There are puppeteers who fall more in love with their marionettes the longer they perform, and it's these who end up as full-time professionals. If

171

this is what you want for yourself, you may be able to make a comfortable, if not luxurious, living out of puppetry. But before you abandon other vocations, there are some practicalities to appreciate. It takes time to build the kind of following you can count on to book you frequently and regularly. You should allow a *minimum* of three years to build up your business to a point where you can depend on it to sustain you. During this interval, even a partial income from a steady outside source could keep you going. Possibly you should remain a part-time puppeteer until you reach the stage where you can rely entirely on puppeteering. Or you might give thought to working full time with an already established puppeteer. This way you'll learn the ins and outs of show business. However, you'll be expressing your employer's viewpoint and personality, not your own. Depending on whether it's necessary for you to express yourself from the beginning, this may or may not be a satisfactory arrangement to you. If you want to establish your own marionette company with *your* puppets in *your* stories, then plan for it—but be practical. Marionettes don't need to eat. You do.

TO DO IT YOURSELF OR NOT

If you've decided to turn professional, then you must operate your enterprise in a business-like manner. Being businesslike means obtaining revenue from bookings or from admissions, keeping accurate bookkeeping records so that you know not only your income but what every phase of your operations costs, and attending to the myriad details of contracts, travel, office routine, publicity, etc. You have two choices. One is to do everything yourself. The other is to find one or more persons who can take care of those details or responsibilities you have neither the time, inclination, nor ability for.

Many persons, particularly those who are interested in the so-called artistic elements of the theater, insist they have no head for business.

Are you one? Before we go on, let's pause to consider if this is so and, if it is, why. Maybe you were never interested in the details of business before because it was someone else's business. But this would be yours, and that might make all the difference as to how you feel about it. Perhaps you've pushed away the business aspects because you were afraid to try to deal with them, fearing ultimate failure. It's possible you don't know everything you're capable of. You didn't know you could be a puppeteer when you began; how do you know you can't keep your own simple books or talk to a newspaper editor? Try. Before your business grows to be too large for a one-person operation, learn all you can about every phase of it so that even if others run it for you, you will understand what they're doing and remain in control.

Company Manager. When you take a company on the road, you serve as the manager of that company. If someone else is appointed as manager, he is your representative and acts for you. He travels with the company and is in charge of all phases of the production, including the deportment of the other members of the company. He may also serve as stage manager, overseeing the performances.

The company manager also takes care of all financial obligations relative to the production.

The company manager assumes the same functions in a resident company, and whether you take the functions on yourself or someone else does, it's one of the most important positions in any theatrical group.

The job requires a knowledge of puppetry, familiarity with your show, sound judgment, an ability to get along with people, and fiscal integrity.

Business Manager. Certainly when you're starting out as a professional puppeteer you won't have enough business to warrant even a part-time business manager or enough income to pay for his services. An accountant can set up the simple books you'll need, and the rest is just a common-sense approach to doing what has to be done. Unless you're fortunate enough to find a benevolent volunteer willing to contribute managerial services, you'll have to take care of everything yourself.

As your business grows and you find your time more occupied with the construction, rehearsal, and performance of marionettes, you may need someone to assist you with "office" duties or even take them over. This means either a full- or part-time employee or a partner. Possibly a member of your puppeteer company could be promoted to partner, with the understanding that while each is concerned with what the other does, the business is the other partner's sphere and the artistic direction is yours.

Do You Need an Agent? Let's think about how you find booking dates. You can go after them yourself or work through an agent or manager who locates jobs for you and charges you a percentage, based on what his services include, of the fee you receive for your performance. When you first start out, the matter of an agent may be purely hypothetical, since most agents won't work with any but established performers. When you've been around long enough to become known, you may be approached by agents or managers willing to add you to their roster of clients.

What can a good agent do for you? A lot. He can keep you so busy with performance dates you don't have time to look for additional business. He can book you into places you would never think to try. He can work with your material and suggest ideas that would attract a new classification of show-buyers to you. He might be able to get you more money for a job than you could. He can be a consultant, a manager, a friend.

But not all agents are good, so don't be hasty in deciding you need one or, having decided, don't be in a rush to sign with one until you have investigated him. What do you know about him? How long has he been an agent? What is his financial rating? Who are his other clients? What is their caliber? How does he get along with them? How much business does he do for them? How do his charges for services compare with those of other agents?

Does your prospective agent want to tie you up with a long-term, exclusive contract that will prevent you from accepting bookings except through him, or require you to pay commissions on all your business, even those contacts you had long before he came into the picture? Or will he be satisfied, at least to start out, with taking commissions on only those bookings that came clearly through him?

If you or a member of your marionette team has the time to go after business, then an agent is a convenience, not a necessity. Should you be successful in your attempts at bookings, you could agree with one or more agents to pay a commission on dates they give you that are clearly outside your regular bookings. Booking yourself has one great virtue: You are sometimes the only judge of how your production would fit into a given performing situation and you would know best when and where to perform and in what circumstances.

Volunteers—and Others. As a puppeteer you're engaged in an activity that many people consider fascinating. When you need help in the several aspects of your production—bookkeeping, publicity, sales, etc.—these individuals may often be glad to put at your disposal their talents along these lines. Sometimes they will work as unpaid volunteers for the fun of sharing an exciting enterprise. Sometimes an older man or woman, retired or semi-retired, will contribute an enormous amount of experience and good judgment on a part-time basis for a fraction of the salary that know-how might otherwise command.

Unreliable or incompetent volunteers will be of little use to you. Discourage them gently, expressing your thanks, but letting them know you don't need help any longer, or that you've made other arrangements—anything rather than hurt their feelings.

Dependable and able volunteers are something else again. Treasures. But don't take advantage of them. If you can pay them, do so. At the very least, give them what they want— participation in a form of theater that has its own kind of magic for those on the inside. Make the job more interesting than the money.

OPPORTUNITIES TO PERFORM

Once you've been around long enough for word of your company's proficiency and repertory to spread, individuals or organizations of many types may come to you and ask you to perform. In most instances, though, it will be up to you or a member of your team to solicit business actively. You may have to suggest an idea to possible clients or to the advertising agencies of possible employers, explaining its advantages for *them.*

Where can you perform?

If you have a house you can rig up a theater in your basement playroom or your garage, or arrange for shows in your garden or on your lawn. (See discussion of permits under "Business Procedures.") However, if your ambitions go beyond the few people who could attend in those circumstances, there are other possibilities.

Marionette shows are often welcomed by nursery schools, for elementary-school assembly programs, and by colleges, orphanages, hospitals, nursing homes, golden-age centers, libraries, museums, and parks. Women's clubs, fraternal and business organizations, Boy and Girl Scouts, community centers, Y's, and others are often willing to book in a production to liven up a monthly meeting or render a community service by offering good entertainment. Many times these organizations have their own money to pay for a performance. Sometimes they're affiliated with groups that will contribute payment on their behalf.

There are times when a program embodying the organization's ideas is an asset. A show with the theme of preventing forest fires, extolling a local hero, supporting the police, or fighting drug addiction, venereal disease, juvenile delinquency, or tooth decay might be just what the Parks or Fire Department, the local historical society, the Public Health Association, the Knights of Columbus, or the local dental association are looking for. Even though they may not realize it until you call it to their attention. All kinds of non-profit and trade organizations exist for causes of politics, religion, health, safety, and social service. Alcoholics Anonymous, the American Automobile Association, bicycle clubs, Kiwanis—some might incline toward the notion of incorporating your production into their public-relations campaigns.

Summer camps may welcome your production as a break in the routine, particularly if they offer puppetry courses to their campers. Private parties—birthdays, Halloween, Christmas, St. Valentine's Day, Independence Day—are a source of bookings, and if you've nothing else scheduled, you can always take to the street or the playgrounds and then pass the hat or not. Just check on local ordinances if you take up a collection.

A lucrative source of employment is businesses or organizations that employ entertainment to attract crowds of potential customers or voters or to advertise their products or services: eating places, department stores, shopping centers, bazaars, fairs and expositions, hotels, banks, flea markets, public utilities. And the manufacturers of merchandise consumed by children—ice cream and other dairy products,

peanut butter, candy, toys, clothing—are not to be overlooked.

Theaters, nightclubs, cabarets, ships—these are excellent areas for entertainment for children or adults or both.

And if you want the prestige of being a cultural asset to the community, perform with a symphony orchestra, a chamber-music group, a ballet or modern dance company, or a "little" theater. Develop an idea of how to use puppetry to support their art form and broach it to the company's business manager or artistic director.

SELLING THE SHOW

Whether you want the public to turn out in vast numbers to attend your theater or whether you want sponsoring organizations to flock to book your presentations, no one will do anything until you spread the word of your existence.

An ongoing public-relations campaign will be one of the most important operations of your business. The line between public relations and direct selling of your productions can be blurry, and we're not going to force an arbitrary distinction in our discussion of them.

SELLING IN PERSON

A most effective way to sell a show is to go to meet the buyer yourself or to send a salesman. Don't drop in without an appointment and expect the utmost in courtesy and consideration. Aside from the fact that you may be interrupting someone who won't appreciate your visit, it's possible you might not even be speaking to the right person. Set up an appointment by telephone or letter. If you state your business clearly and concisely, your inquiry will be directed to the proper official or department so that you won't waste your time or anyone else's. If you can come recommended by a mutual acquaintance or member of the community, this can sometimes get you through the front door a little more quickly, but once in contact with the right party, you have to sell the show on its merits.

You create the first impression of the show by how you conduct yourself. Be prompt. Dress in accordance with the circumstances. You can get away with blue jeans and sneakers if you're talking to a summer-camp director, but with a conservatively dressed bank president you should dress quietly and neatly too. Know the merits of your production and discuss them confidently, but don't oversell or come on too strong. Be prepared to answer any questions about your shows and about your company.

How long does the show last? What is it about? What are the highlights? To what age does it primarily appeal? How many people work the performance? Do you have any special technical requirements? Be brief, but make your points. Some publicity stills showing the marionettes in action, or some of especially attractive costumes and sets, give a very clear idea of what the production looks like. Explain why your show will answer their needs—it's educational, it will draw a crowd, it deals with what they manufacture. Don't make any statements the show won't support—that the show is for all children, two to twelve, for instance, when it's for fours through sixes. The booking will backfire in its results if obtained on misrepresentation.

As for your company—how long have you been in business? Where have you played? What's been the audience reaction? Bring your press book and letters of recommendation. You may exaggerate a little, but it shouldn't be

necessary. It's no disgrace to be starting out, and it's the performance that counts. If you or your salesman could whip out a marionette at this point and give a bit of a demonstration, this could be persuasive.

Discuss what you'll provide by way of promotional materials and services in possible cooperative ventures to publicize the show—preview demonstrations, lectures, exhibits, talk-show appearances, etc.

Handling the matter of price is discussed in the pages on "Negotiations."

SELLING BY TELEPHONE

When it comes to contacting organizations, either to persuade them to book your show into their theaters or to buy large blocks of tickets to yours, few means yield such satisfactory results as a phone call. The call is either preceded by a mailing or followed up by one, but the clincher is the direct person-to-person communication.

Telephone selling has two drawbacks. First, it consumes an enormous amount of time. To begin with, you don't always reach the right party. When you do, a long explanation is often necessary. You may have to call back again and again before any conclusion is arrived at. The person at the other end of the wire may be a compulsive conversationalist. Also, if you operate in a community where the telephone company charges for every call or for every three minutes or both, the end of the month may bring you a bill even a highly successful performance can't cover.

If you have a volunteer who enjoys talking to people and doesn't care how long a call lasts, and if the phone company doesn't charge for local calls, telephone selling can be profitable. But if you're paying for this service by the

The Performing Arts Program of the Asia Society presents

The Awaji Puppet Theater of Japan

in association with The Carnegie Hall Corporation and The Department of Cultural Affairs, The City of New York

Wednesday, February 6, 1974 at 8:00 p.m.   Thursday, February 7, 1974 at 8:00 p.m.

CARNEGIE HALL

Tickets: $6.00, $4.50, $3.50

Tickets available at Carnegie Hall Box Office or by mail (up to two weeks before concert). Make checks payable and mail to:
Carnegie Hall Box Office, 154 West 57th Street, New York, New York 10019. Please enclose a stamped self-addressed envelope.

KAZUKO HILLYER Presents

NATIONAL SHADOW THEATRE of Malaysia

Bureau pres
Opera Theatre
unter College P
gton Avenues,
er 23rd, 1970 to December

— Fairy opera by Engelbert Humperdinck
Wette from Grimm's fairy tales

oth
"d
nds
in
hey
n de
e, "c
en h

good spir
people." He inquires for the
have been sent into the woods to pick berries is grea
Ilsentein lives the wicked crunch witch who lures
magic cakes "a witch of hoary age roams in the fo
and mother hurry out in search of Hansel and Gret

Hansel and Gretel. The children are alone and working.
They soon leave their tasks trying to forget their hunger by dancing
and singing. Gretel says "Suse, Suse, what rattles in the straw." And

PUPPET CARNIVAL

PUPPETRY GUILD OF GREATER NEW YORK, INC.

PROGRAM ★ MAY 11, 1974

MUSEUM OF THE CITY OF NEW YORK, 103rd & 5th AVENUE

The Cow and the Donkey from "THE RABBIT AND THE FOX"

"Milovsoroff's style in sculpture is strongly individual, always with a touch of humor. He loves color and music and uses them with striking effect."

DANCE + DRAMA OF THE ORIENT

HUNTER COLLEGE CONCERT BUREAU announces A FAMILY SPECIAL Engelbert Humperdinck (The original one) Fairytale Opera

HANSEL and GRETEL

with SUIB'S MARIONETTES and the HUNTER OPERA THEATRE

COLORFUL, TUNEFUL—A DELIGHT FOR THE YOUNG AND THE NEVER OLD

ALL SEATS $1.00—available at Box Office and at all TICKETRON outlets. For information and group rates call 535-5350
8 PERFORMANCES ONLY! Fri., Sat., Sun. Nov. 27, 28, 29 at 1:00 & 3:00 P.M. and Saturday, Dec. 5 at 1:00 & 3:00 P.M.
HUNTER COLLEGE PLAYHOUSE
E. 68th St. between Park and Lexington

hour and the company charges per call, this can be an expensive operation in terms of results unless your employee knows how to keep a call short, pleasant, and to the point and your list of prospects has been gone over carefully beforehand to cull only the most promising.

SELLING BY MAIL

Should you decide to wage much of your sales campaign by letter-writing, the first thought that arises is to whom? Buying a list of names, as many businesses do, probably wouldn't do you much good because there is too much of a turnover in PTA committees, den mothers, and other volunteer personnel to be sufficiently current. There's no substitute for the telephone company's classified book for your territory and for areas adjacent to it. Browse through it for names and addresses of summer camps, banks, supermarkets, civic and fraternal organizations, and other possibilities for bookings. An up-to-date directory for your school district can supply valuable information, and there are other municipal and county directories covering parks, public health, etc.

There's no hard and fast rule about what you send out. It might be an attractive letter that would encompass on its one page everything you feel the recipient should know about your company and your production. Or it might be a brochure that describes your shows in considerable detail. Or it might be a letter and a brochure. It's a good idea, if your budget can stand it, to enclose a postage-paid reply card on which you don't have to pay postage until it's sent back to you. And then you don't mind if it's a legitimate inquiry about a booking.

There are those who use direct mail who feel everything should go first-class postage. First-class is delivered more quickly and recipients pay it more respect. Other users feel it's ridiculous not to avail themselves of the savings of third-class mailing. They merely mail earlier to have the letters arrive on time, and recipients don't care about the class of postage.

For single mailings of an ounce or less, the charges for first- and third-class mail are the same. However, if your mailing is over one ounce and not more than two, this second ounce is included in third-class without additional postage being required. Third-class mail must be marked as such on the face of the envelope if the letter is sealed but not if the flap of the envelope is tucked in.

A bulk-mailing permit is available for a charge, plus a charge for your permit number. The permit runs for the calendar year—January 1 through December 31. To avail yourself of the lower postage rate this permit allows, your mailings must be of two hundred letters or more, each of which is identical in appearance and number of enclosures, zip-coded and presorted by zip code.

One of the benefits that accrue to a nonprofit tax-exempt organization is that the post-office bulk postage rate for this category is about 30 percent of what a commercial corporation or an individual or partnership pays. The permit and permit number cost the same, and the other conditions also apply, the only difference being the considerable reduction in postage charges.

When you've developed a good list of prospects, figure what percentage of replies you need for a profit and do a test mailing. If it isn't successful but you feel this is still the most practical method for you, perhaps a mail consultant can help you. If you can't find one on

Togo from Rufus Rose Marionette Variety.

your own, the Direct Mail/Marketing Association, 6 East 43rd Street, New York, N.Y. 10017, can refer you to one of their members in your area.

PUBLICITY FOR WHOM?

As a puppeteer, you may be operating a resident theater. In such a case, all your publicity, directly or indirectly, is geared to bringing audiences to see your performances. Should you be a touring puppeteer instead, your publicity would be aimed at potential sponsors to persuade them to book your shows into their premises.

We believe the following sections are self-explanatory as to which market the contents apply.

When your show has been booked by a sponsoring organization, the sponsor generally has the full responsibility for attracting an audience, and this includes publicity. Of course, you'll cooperate in supplying background information about your company so that the sponsor will have material to pass along to the press for announcements or possible feature stories, and you'll supply one or two photographs, a sample flyer the sponsor may reproduce, and possibly a few posters. Don't furnish more than a minimum amount, because some sponsors won't use the material you give them and it will be wasted. On the other hand, some sponsors may request a large amount of publicity material, and you must decide—taking into consideration what the material will cost you and how much the performing fee is—how far you can go in complying.

If you are booked into a commercial theater, your contract spells out whether the management is responsible for publicity or you are and to what degree.

PUBLIC-RELATIONS DIRECTOR

If you have a knowledgeable public-relations director, amateur or professional, part-time or full-time, you are fortunate indeed. But if you have to be your own PR director, along with all your other positions, these pages will start you off right.

Even if someday you'll be able to afford the services of a professional public-relations representative, don't forget that no one knows as much about your organization as you. You have a right to expect a competent publicity job, but your knowledge and creativity are to be channeled *through* the public-relations director for action, not to be replaced.

Don't expect even the most professional PR director to bring in top results with every mailing or every appointment or release. It's a truism in the publicity business that half one's efforts are wasted. The trouble is, no one knows which half. But a representative who is good develops a feel for a particular enterprise and improves on the 50 percent after a while.

THE APPEARANCE OF PUBLIC-RELATIONS MATERIAL

The cost of printed material advertising your production may be one of your major expenses. Everything emanating from your company represents you as much as the shows themselves do. Your publicity may create your first impression on its recipient, and the effect may be lasting. It has to be a good impression or all the time, money, labor, and concern you've invested in it will be worse than a waste. Further, the material must be attractive enough to make a prospective patron or news editor want to read it through.

PUPPETEERS
OF AMERICA

Quaker Village Puppeteers
Philadelphia

Chicagoland
Puppetry Guild

THE
PUPPETRY
GUILD
of
Greater
New York

Puppetry Guild of
Greater New York

San Francisco Bay
Area Puppeteers

UP-A-TREE PRODUCTIONS

CHILDREN'S ENTERTAINMENT
Guitar...Puppets...Songs...Fun!

LOGO

It's helpful if everything coming from your organization bears a *logo*, a printed symbol, that instantly identifies it as yours.

If you or any of your friends are artistic in the area of graphics, you don't need to go to a designer for a logo. The design you create could be made up of the initials of the name of your marionette company, or it could be a little puppet or other figure that would convey the spirit of your organization. Bear in mind that while you are not bound to keep the same logo forever, every letterhead, envelope, advertisement, flyer, poster, program, and press release you send out is educating the public to identify it with you. Also, since the logo may be painted on your trunks, car, and van, and possibly over your proscenium arch, it could be a costly proposition to change it. You can appreciate, therefore, that whatever logo you select at the beginning should be flexible enough to be appropriate if the direction of your operations changes subsequently.

PRINTED PUBLIC-RELATIONS MATERIAL

Every piece of printed material coming from your organization must have specific information about your operations.

You can be extravagantly impractical and spend a mint for four-color print jobs on heavy coated stock, but don't. Eye appeal isn't necessarily dependent on lavishness. Color helps, yes. But color can be obtained either by using colored paper or by using one or two colors of ink, or using colored paper *and* colored ink. Weigh the value of coated stock against a good quality of ordinary paper and decide whom you have to impress. Frequently, coated stock is of value primarily when superb color reproduction is desired. An uncluttered appearance with carefully arranged written material in type faces that enhance your message, and possibly a photograph or some line drawings—this could be very handsome indeed as a flyer or brochure.

Outside of your own professional public-relations director, your best source of help is a good printer. Investigate the printers in your area and see the kind of work they have done for others. They can suggest layouts, colors, type faces, stock, sizes, and innumerable other details and show you what you can do yourself and what must be done by them.

If a commercial printing is more than your budget can stand, don't despair. Taste and artistry and a good mimeograph machine can turn out acceptable results.

As to the content of the printed matter, make sure that all information is set down in clear, unambiguous language. Put the copy aside for a day or two until you have some perspective on it and then read it back. How does it sound? Clear? Interesting? Would you buy the show after reading it? Has anything important been left out?

How many to order is frequently a problem. Five thousand copies of a brochure ordered at one time cost appreciably less than five separate orders of a thousand each, and the temptation is strong to take advantage of the saving. Before you do, ask yourself some questions. How many shall I use *now*? When will the next opportunity arise to use them and how many shall I need then? Will the circumstances be the same then so that the copy may stay unchanged? If new material will be needed before this order is exhausted, will the leftovers be usable elsewhere? Unless you are quite certain that you'll really be able to dispose of the entire run profitably, err on the side of caution in purchasing your printing.

Posters and Handbills. A poster or handbill can be displayed on a school bulletin board, in a merchant's shop window, in a laundromat, in supermarkets, in a church recreation room, or anywhere you can persuade someone to let you put it up. Commercial movie houses often give a shop owner a pair of passes for the privilege of placing a poster in the window, a custom not universally observed by other showmen.

Three rules apply to posters and other throwaway material: They must be attractive to look at. They must contain all necessary information. They must be relatively inexpensive to reproduce in quantity. Since your paper stock will be the least costly that will take ink, your layout will have to be eye-catching enough to compensate.

Volunteers are frequently willing to post your promotional material. If you can convince them of the merits of your production and its value to the community, Boy and Girl Scouts will do it for points toward merit badges for community service. Or they might be happy to stand on corners and pass out your handbills. If the volunteers are young, insist that they go out in pairs and stick together at all times.

Handbills and posters are an effective way of reaching the public for a neighborhood performance.

RADIO AND TELEVISION RELEASES

When you're sending promotional material to broadcasters, this can take two forms. In both instances, double- or triple-space your copy and type it all in capitals, using no lowercase.

A news release/feature story goes to the news director. Submit an interesting article that has "hard" news value—something beside the fact that you exist, are about to perform, or have just performed. Are the mayor and his wife planning to attend with a group of handicapped children? Is the library running an exhibit in conjunction with your performance? Did the fire department honor you for promoting fire safety? Keep it short but factual and make it lively. Be available for an air interview.

Spot announcements go to the community service director or, if the station is a small one, to the program manager. Send the station three separate releases under different headings:

"20-SECOND SPOT," "30-SECOND SPOT," and "60-SECOND SPOT." Start with an attention-grabbing announcement and then go on to give precise information about your coming performance, the name of the show, the time and place of performance, the auspices, ticket cost, and telephone number for further information. Include your name and as much background story as can be fitted into each release, read at normal speed and timed carefully. When there is available time between programs, an announcer may read one or more of your spots as is.

In each instance, check beforehand to ascertain how much advance notice the station needs and be sure to send in your copy early.

Make up a press file and include in it the special requirements of each station.

NEWSPAPER AND MAGAZINE RELEASES

If you're trying to get a feature story in the press, such a story could have two forms. One is the hard-news kind of story, referred to under "Radio and Television Releases." If the editor thinks the story newsworthy enough, it could make the front page of a small city daily or weekly paper. In most instances you'd be better off trying for a human-interest story on the inside of the paper. Any unusual anecdote about the company or production could be the basis of the feature. Tell it briefly but entertainingly and leave some sort of "teaser" at the end to pique the editor's curiosity and make him want to know—and pass along—more about you. If you have some good photographs, enclose one or two. In any event, be sure to include in your release all pertinent details about the performances. The five W's—when, where, what, who, why—plus how much tickets are

and where the editor can reach you for more information or an interview.

Often an editor will not bother to rewrite material that crosses his desk. He may print as much of what you've sent in as he has room for and then stop when he runs out of space. Accordingly, it's important to put the most essential facts in the lead paragraph. Follow this with facts you think are next in significance, and so on in order of descending weight.

For announcements that your production will be playing shortly, prepare a one-page release that shows the name, address, and phone of the "contact"—the PR director or someone else able to answer and follow up inquiries. List the name of the production, the name of the company, the date of the performance, the time, where it will take place, the price of admission, and, if you have received support to develop the production or present it, give the names of your benefactors. We don't mean to list a hundred people if they've each given you five dollars—only those who have made substantial contributions. (Sometimes the donation of a substantial contribution is a newsworthy story.) A brief paragraph or two that will make your production sound exciting is all you can fit onto the page.

A point to keep in mind always: Often people will do you favors, including giving you publicity, if it doesn't cost them anything. If your contact shows an out-of-town telephone number that might cost an editor a toll charge, he could have second thoughts about publicizing your production. Therefore, it's vital that your material be complete and accurate in all details that an editor might question.

Newspapers and magazines vary in the amount of prior notice they require before publication and also in the person to whom your release should be directed. Check into each and record this information in your press file so that sending out your releases to obtain maximum results from them will become routine.

Beginning with one month before a performance, you might want to have three releases appear in the press.

PERSONAL APPEARANCES

Personal appearances are among the most effective public-relations techniques you can employ. Women's clubs, service organizations, PTAs, and a multitude of other groups have regular meetings—as often as weekly, as seldom as two or three times a year. A featured speaker at these meetings is frequently welcome, particularly if the speaker doesn't charge, comes with a marionette or two, and gives a demonstration. You don't have to push your productions actively at these affairs. A talk on marionettes in general, or some specific aspect of them slanted to the particular interests of the members, together with a little display of their capabilities, should be enough to enthrall your audience. If you have questions from the floor about your own work, of course you can talk about yourself. But even if you don't, the members get the message. And when they decide to put on a formal entertainment, either for their own amusement or to sell tickets, most likely you'll be the first one they think of.

Although puppetry helps make a television appearance visually lively and you should take every opportunity for TV coverage, radio appearances are also productive. In either medium, try not to think of the thousands of people who are giving you their attention. Consider only the interviewer and the handful of studio audience who may be present. Know what you're going to be talking about—the dates, times, place of your next show or whatever else the topic is. If you are thoroughly prepared and concentrate only on the persons in the room with you, you won't be nervous. The one thing interviewers—particularly inexperienced ones—dread is "dead" air, when you aren't saying anything and the interviewer can't think what to ask next. Be prepared with some chatter on the subject of marionettes or something funny that happened with a puppet show, but don't force it if the interviewer has the situation in hand. The second thing interviewers don't like is a guest who takes over.

Don't begrudge the time you give to personal appearances. Make the time count. When you address a business luncheon or a school-board meeting, it's not being pushy to leave a supply of flyers on a table for the members to help themselves to. With the permission of the members, you might make arrangements with a local newspaper to send a reporter or photographer to cover the event. And your own public-relations director would send a story to all outlets about your presence at the luncheon or meeting.

A couple of pointers: Don't accept an offer to speak unless you're sure you can be there and *on time*. If something unavoidable comes along to prevent your showing up at the last minute, arrange for a substitute speaker. Don't leave the membership high and dry. And after you have spoken and displayed your marionettes and gone home, write a letter to the chairman expressing your thanks for being allowed to participate in their activities. Even though you have done them the favor, say thank you. This is your public and you can do as much business by being Mr. or Ms. Nice as you can by being a great puppeteer.

EXHIBITS

An exhibit of your puppetry is an eye-catcher that has few peers. If your office is large enough for you to set up some marionettes, photographs, and posters, it's an attractive way to sell your show to a visitor without saying a word. A permanent revolving exhibit in your theater lobby or auditorium gives the audience a topic to talk about on entering or leaving. However, if you have valuable or fragile objects on display, we suggest you show them behind glass. All unprotected marionettes, props, stage models, etc., should be under constant super-vision or hung above arm's reach or behind enough of a barrier to discourage pilferage or vandalism.

When you play an outside theater you might, wherever it's practicable, lend the sponsor or manager some marionettes and other paraphernalia to display for a week or so before the performance—provided you're satisfied with the measures taken for their safety.

Libraries, which usually have excellent facilities for protecting property, are enthusiastic exhibitors—especially if an exhibit of your work coincides with the arrival of some new puppetry books, or your production tells a tale that is on the library shelves, or your show ties in with a civic activity with which the library is cooperating.

There are many opportunities for you to call attention to your company through exhibits that carry a neat placard: "Through the courtesy of Y.O.U.R. Marionette Company." A display of firemen puppets in a fire house during Fire Prevention Week; doctor and nurse marionettes during a hospital drive; farmer and animal figures when the Four-H has its judging . . .

An exhibit doesn't necessarily have to be limited to showing what your company does. Spectators may be constantly reminded that puppets are performers by what you display and how you display it.

Puppets or photographs of puppets from around the world can fill one panel, together with sketches or paintings that supplement your printed explanation.

Marionettes can be set up so that they appear frozen in a moment from a play. Scenes from a current production can catch particular attention. A bird or angel puppet can be suspended from the ceiling. More mundane marionettes may sit on a ledge and look the spectator in the eye. Props for the puppets should be presented along with them to reinforce the sense of scale and help create the marionette's world.

The exhibit should be three-dimensional wherever possible to foster the illusion of life in the marionettes themselves.

Another panel can hold the many materials of which puppets can be constructed: plastic foam, wood, cloth, cardboard, wire. These can be accompanied by working drawings, elevations, or photographs demonstrating construction.

Only your imagination and your time limit

you in using exhibits to promote your theatrical presentations.

SHOWCASES

The best of all possible methods of selling a good show is to give prospective purchasers a look at it. Every time you perform, consider that you are presenting a showcase. You never know who in the audience may be a potential buyer of entertainment.

When you play your own theater, you should reserve a block of seats for the press and for other guests you invite from a list you've been compiling: PTA heads, recreation directors of Y's, community centers, homes for the aged, etc., librarians, business leaders, agents, theater managers—anyone who could book your show or give you leads to additional bookings should be sent a pair of tickets. If the show is for children, the parents need enough tickets for the family. We're not suggesting that you invite everyone to the same performance; you won't have seats left over to sell to the public. However, if in your immediate community and in surrounding towns there are a large number of those who ought to see your production, why not give a special gala showcase performance just for them? Invite enough, and you may have a good attendance.

When you perform on tour, you may request a reasonable number of seats from the sponsor so that you may invite prospects from that area to see your show. What's reasonable depends on the circumstances. Twenty tickets in a house that seats two thousand is reasonable. In an auditorium of two hundred that could sell out, that's excessive.

It's not always easy to persuade prospective sponsors to come to see a production. If you have a children's show that runs an hour or a

nightclub spot that lasts twenty minutes, the sponsors' travel time could exceed the performance's, and many, particularly business people, are reluctant to tie up a major part of a day for only a single possibility. Sponsors are less reluctant to extend themselves for a showcase that offers several opportunities for the same effort on their part.

Let's suppose you've built up a repertory of three productions for children that are each under an hour. You'd invite everybody for miles around who buys entertainment for young people to a showcase that will include the best of your presentations full length. If you have additional shows and you want to give the sponsors an idea as to what they are like, then give excerpts from each—preferably sections that can stand on their own feet with-

out a lot of explanation about what happened before and what happens next. Between plays or excerpts, come before the curtain and, while the stage is being reset, answer questions about the productions. In the literature you supply to each guest include the suggested age range for each show, special requirements (a microphone, a totally dark house for U.V. effects, minimum ceiling height), etc. Unless your prices will be strictly uniform to all sponsors, don't list them. And don't discuss prices of shows from the platform. Tell sponsors when the subject comes up, as it surely will, that too many variables are involved: travel distance, whether more than one show a day is booked, whether several productions are booked and over how long a span of time, etc. Since PTA heads would probably be a major part of your audience and many would have children coming home for lunch and after school, the best time for a showcase would be mornings. Begin about nine-thirty and try to keep to two and a half hours maximum.

In the case of adult-oriented puppetry material, the situation is somewhat different. Your audience would be largely comprised of theater managers, agents, representatives of women's clubs, professional recreation personnel, business-committee representatives, and the like. Since many of these would include your showcase as part of their regular working day, early afternoon is a good time to begin. This will let them take care of mail and business routine in the morning and get back to their desks for an hour or so at the end of the day. As for housewives who are delegates from various clubs, if you don't go past three-thirty or four, they can still arrive home in time to prepare dinner.

Now let's say you want to bring prospective buyers in from a wide radius but you have only one or two productions to offer and you fear this may not be enough of an attraction. Or you haven't been successful in building up the right kind of mailing list. Or you want to hire a theater or concert hall and can't bear the entire expense. What do you do? You invite other producers to participate.

You have many options. If you are specializing in children's entertainment, you may invite other puppeteers whose work is very different from yours to come in with you. You share mailing lists, expenses, publicity chores, and other duties and invite your guests to a private festival of puppetry for young people. On the other hand, you may wish to be the only puppeteers, so the other participants could be a producer of "live" fairy tales, a folk singer, a group of ethnic dancers, or a mime company. This kind of variety is also successful in drawing audiences of children's-entertainment buyers.

With adult material, the procedure is analogous. You could split the expenses and obligations with those whose specialty is like yours (e.g. a ventriloquist) or entirely different (a stand-up comic, a folk singer, an instrumentalist, a combo, dancers).

Even though it's not cheap to put on a showcase, it may give you the most return for your public-relations dollar, *once you're sure of attracting the sponsoring organizations.*

Before you become involved in setting up a showcase, look around to see if there is one already existing you may join. Agents often run showcases of the talent on their roster. Professional organizations, some concerned with theater in general and some with puppetry in particular, keep track of what's happening regionally, and inquiries directed to them can result in information on showcases in your territory. (See pages on "Professional Affiliations.")

A puppet of George Bernard Shaw by Ralph Chesse. Shaw was always a good friend of puppetry.

In any showcase situation, it's important to know who the other entertainers are, who will immediately precede you in the spotlight, and who will follow. Because your marionette operation takes time to set up, the act before you—or even two acts before you—should be the type that can perform in front of the curtain, giving you the opportunity to get organized as quietly as possible behind it. The act after you will also need to play on the apron so that you can clear out. You have to make arrangements when you discuss coming in on the showcase for the time you need and also for the marionette stage to be positioned advantageously. A showcase that displays you to buyers at less than your best is more of a liability than an asset.

When all the participants in the showcase are puppeteers and everybody has a stage, this is a whole different proposition technically. An excellent solution is to have all puppet stages set up before the audience enters. The stages are lined up against the walls of a large room, with the audience seated in the center. Instead of moving the stages, the audience turns to face whichever stage is performing. This arrangement has another good feature: Since virtually no time is lost between shows, everything goes smoothly and swiftly. It might even be possible, depending on the number of puppeteers involved, to give some or all of them a second slot for another excerpt.

Even though people promise to see your show, they don't always come. With agents and managers it's wise to phone them and get a personal commitment, either for a showcase or for a regular performance. Ask them to let you know when to expect them and how many complimentary tickets should be left at the box office. Request that they see you after the performance and you be prepared to discuss a business arrangement.

Almost invariably agents and managers want some changes made in your production. Make it longer, shorten it, stress the dramatic elements more, alter a characterization . . . Listen without defensiveness. Are the criticisms intelligent, sensitive, in line with your basic thinking, feasible? Or do you feel that modifying your show to accord with them would destroy your concept or cost you more work than the show is worth? In the former instance you might

be so lucky as to find an agent who can not only bring you bookings but can augment your company with his own professional know-how. In the latter case, you'd be making a mistake to align yourself with someone whose thinking and practicality are foreign to yours.

CRITICS

What critics have to say about your production could be a major factor in the number of tickets you sell or the interest potential sponsors take in your work. But critics can't say anything at all if you don't invite them to a performance —usually the first official performance so that they can get their reviews in early enough to affect your audiences for later performances. Often, however, your run is limited and might be finished before the criticism could appear in print or be aired. In that case, invite the critics to a preview or a dress rehearsal.

If you are doing a show for adults, it's customary to send each critic (press, radio, TV, special reviewers) a pair of tickets with an invitation to use them. You have no guarantee that the critic will come, but hold the seats until curtain time. Occasionally a critic will ask for an additional seat or two, and if you can manage, by all means set them aside. For a performance for children, it's a good idea to call the critic, invite him or her with wife or husband, and ask whether they wouldn't like to come with their children, however many. Critics will frequently attend a show for their children's sake when they might not go to satisfy their own curiosity or out of their sense of duty.

At the conclusion of the performance, should you recognize any critics, merely thank them for coming. *Don't* ask them what they thought of the show. You may inquire what issue of the paper the review will appear in or what time to listen for it on radio or TV, or ask for a transcript (for which you supply a stamped, self-addressed envelope).

You are free to quote in your publicity releases anything that has appeared in print or gone out over the air.

PUBLICITY PHOTOGRAPHS

The time to start taking pictures of your show is from the very beginning, when you start constructing stages, creating marionettes and costumes, and go into the full swing of backstage preparation. Why? To build up a record of how the show was put together. Continue making these photographic records until the presentation goes on and the audience applauds—not missing any pictorial aspect of the operation. Eight-by-ten glossies will be the most serviceable.

These photographs serve several purposes. They can be enclosed with news releases or letters to prospective sponsors. An exhibit of your marionettes can be enhanced by a display showing them in construction. A feature-story writer for a newspaper or magazine might devote more space to you if you could supplement the interview with striking visual material. The photographs would be a major feature of your impressive press book. And, of course, later on through them you'll relive the fun.

Sometimes a newspaper will send its own photographer to take pictures of your performance or of your audience. Usually, many more pictures are shot than ever get published. It's often possible to obtain a good print of what appears in the paper, either free or at nominal cost. If you want prints of other photographs, these may be obtained from the photographer at a reasonable price.

When you send out your photographs, don't forget to caption them so that everyone in the

Felix Mirbt of Montreal working his unusual Eskimo marionette. Mirbt's work is serious and fully experimental. *Photo: M. Richardson*

picture is identified. If pertinent, include the name of the production and always the name of the company, your address, and telephone number. This information is usually put on the back of the photograph. *Never* write on the back of the print with a ballpoint pen, a hard pencil, or anything else that could push through onto the face of the picture. The safest method of furnishing the information is to type it on a gummed label and paste it on the back.

TESTIMONIALS AND ENDORSEMENTS

As soon as possible, start collecting laudatory notices about your productions. If you appear at a school and the principal praises your performance, ask him to put it in writing in a letter. If the performance was attended by someone who outranks the principal in the school system, try to obtain a letter from him as well. When the director of a golden-age center thanks you for your show, get a letter. When the president of the bank compliments you on your appearances there, get a letter. And with every letter, secure the writer's permission to quote from it.

Letters of this kind, together with feature stories clipped from newspapers and comments from critics, constitute an important segment of your publicity base. The promotional material (flyers, brochures, posters) you make up can include the most flattering of the quotations from the names that will mean the most in your community.

A particularly effective form of testimonial is the mail schoolchildren send you or that their teachers collect for you about your shows. When these letters are reproduced with their frequently original spelling and obvious sincerity, they can convey a charm not easily matched.

PRESS BOOK

An effective tool for the selling of your productions is an oversize scrapbook with pages made of clear plastic into which can be inserted testimonial letters, photographs, feature stories, critical comment, and flyers about your current and past shows. Anything on paper that is attractive and makes your marionette company appear to be the greatest that ever was can go into the plastic pages.

When you go out to sell your show to theater managers, PTAs, or whoever, take the press book along. Even if the prospective buyers are experienced enough not to be overwhelmed by

the glowing tributes to your artistry and professionalism, they'll be interested in seeing what you've done and what's been said about it.

PAID ADVERTISING

You'll be approached by newspapers and perhaps by radio and TV salespersons to take out paid advertisements through them. Approach this suggestion cautiously. Ask yourself questions. What can an ad do for me that I can't do without it? If I don't pay for an ad, will other departments of the paper/radio/TV still print or air my releases, still do an occasional feature on my productions? Or is this "free" publicity contingent on my going along with

the advertising department? How many tickets do I need to sell to pay for this ad? Is there any realistic hope of selling that many?

When you have answers to these questions, ask some more: If I have to spend $X for newspaper/radio/TV coverage, could that money possibly be spent more profitably elsewhere? On phone calls, posters, throw-aways?

There are further considerations. Dollars and cents may not be the only factors. Would an ad in a big-city newspaper or over a prominent radio or TV station give the show more prestige than other forms of publicity? What would this be worth in the long run?

After you've considered all the angles, you'll be in a position to know whether you should pay for advertising and, if so, how much.

PERSONAL RELATIONSHIPS

Entertainment is a people business, and your relationship with the people you meet every day may have a profound effect on your marionette theater. Aside from the obvious—that

word-of-mouth advertising is an important part of your public relations—there are more subtle influences affecting your image and that of your company.

Develop a reputation for punctuality. Whether you are speaking informally to an association of camp directors, or meeting a photographer for some press shots, or giving a demonstration to a troop of Brownies, be on time. When you are due at a theater at a given hour, be there. Be at the radio or TV station not even five minutes later than you're expected for your talk-show interview.

Develop a reputation for reliability. If you make a commitment, oral or written, and someone is relying on you, keep it. If it is truly impossible, give as much notice as you can and offer to find an adequate replacement.

Develop a reputation for being pleasant to get along with. No outbursts of temperament, either before your company or before the public. No bullying your crew or throwing your weight around. No backstage grousing on the part of the crew in the presence of outsiders. If anything is wrong, keep it in your professional family. Be as agreeable to the porter as to the manager or the sponsor—and exact the same standards of behavior from your company.

Develop a reputation for professional standards. This means, among other considerations, that the show comes first. No matter how easygoing you may be with other people, this is not at the expense of your production. You have a right to insist that your stage be placed properly, that box-office arrangements be ready on time, that you be able to set your lights to best advantage, etc. You mustn't let your firmness of purpose be confused with lack of concern for the problems of others, but you are present to give a first-class performance, and you are entitled to have your basic requirements seen to.

Build up a rapport not only with the people who book you but also with those who can influence public opinion on your behalf. Get to know the local newspaper editor, the head librarian, the school board, the banker, and other business and civic leaders. They can become your friends and you can be theirs with a bond of mutual respect.

BUSINESS PROCEDURES
PERMISSIONS

In today's world, the best things in life aren't necessarily free, and even when they are free we may have to obtain permission to use them.

Performance. You may think all you have to do to be a puppeteer is to put on a show, and in some communities that's true. But there are others where, if you charge admission or a fee for performing, you may have to secure a permit from some municipal or county authority. The permit probably won't cost anything—at most a couple of dollars—but it's a formality you have to go through.

Theater. If you convert a room of your house or your garage into a little theater—be careful. There's undoubtedly some statute or other that states that a theater seating more than X number of patrons must have two approved exits and separate washroom facilities for males and females. One way around this is to declare that your enterprise is a club and that admissions are contributions toward dues. Regulations about clubs are looser.

Playscript. When you build your show on someone else's literary or dramatic property, the original author has rights that must be honored. The front part of the book names the copyright owner. Write to the owner in care of the publisher, requesting permission to convert the property to a marionette production.

Do this *before* you put any work into your play.

You'll be notified that (1) the material is in the public domain and its use is not restricted, or (2) dramatic rights are controlled and you may not use the property, or (3) you may use the property in stated circumstances, with or without a fee.

It's important to go through this because misuse of copyrighted material is a violation of federal law that carries severe penalties. The Library of Congress, Washington, D.C. 20540, will send you a pamphlet on copyright laws that goes into a more detailed explanation.

Music. When you wish to use music in your show, the licensing of the music rights is reserved to the copyright proprietor, normally the publisher. The theatrical or "grand" rights are not handled by any of the usual licensing societies such as ASCAP (American Society of Composers, Authors, and Publishers) or BMI (Broadcast Music, Inc.). Take the matter up directly with the copyright proprietor, whose name is generally indicated on the record or the sheet music. If you have difficulty in locating the proprietor, ASCAP (One Lincoln Plaza, New York, N.Y. 10023) or BMI (40 West 57th Street, New York, N.Y. 10019) can probably help you.

BUILDING A REPERTORY

If you're in earnest about making a living out of puppetry, you'll have to take into account that your productions must be salable. In Part Two under "Playscripts" we've discussed known "titles" as against original material from the standpoint of marketability. But there are many other possibilities to consider.

Churches, synagogues, and religious schools like Bible stories. Stories from the New Testament generally appeal only to Christians, but if you have enough business from churches and affiliated Sunday schools, you may be busy enough not to look for additional business elsewhere. Stories from the Old Testament can play churches and synagogues both and sometimes other institutions that regard Old Testament stories as non-denominational and non-controversial. David and Goliath, Noah and His Ark, and Daniel in the Lion's Den come at once to mind as being excellent puppetry material with a wide appeal. The Story of Esther, while also from the Old Testament, seems to be more popular with Jewish than non-Jewish groups, particularly around the Purim holiday, the Feast of Esther. The Story of Jesus goes well in almost every church, especially around Christmas time.

Schools like programs that have educational values as well as entertainment. It is simple to check with the school or the board of education to see what the different grades study and the months they cover the subjects. By offering a classic or a historical episode at the same time the school is teaching it, you are making a virtually irresistible appeal to the principal or the PTA or the school board. Rip Van Winkle, Daniel Boone, Hiawatha, The Midnight Ride of Paul Revere, The Story of Lewis and Clark, Harriet Tubman, Abraham Lincoln, Martin Luther King, The Story of Cotton— all are potential good sellers.

We've already talked about fairy tales and classics. If you have questions about the age ranges for which a story might be suitable, check with a children's librarian. Most librarians are very willing to discuss children's preferences and can be of great assistance. Two books on children's literature are listed in the Bibliography.

A variety program—with an identification figure—can broaden a repertory. Based on a circus or vaudeville theme, with clowns, animals, monsters, come-apart-skeletons, acrobats, and assorted variety acts, the same act could be used for children's and adult audiences, with different dialogue and possible modification of some of the routines.

Fraternal, philanthropic, and social organizations may be in the market for general entertainment, but they would almost certainly be impressed by a marionette show that tells the history of their association or of one of its founders. A play or playlet on such a subject could have as many performances as there are lodges or temples of the order. Why not sound out one of the officials before you prepare your script and puppets? The order can supply you with your research materials if it is enthusiastic.

A repertory theater needs a stock cast. For a children's fairy-tale repertory, you want to build up a cast of marionettes that can be adapted quickly to a specific story: a princess and a prince, a girl and a boy, a mother and a father, a witch, a giant, a fairy queen, goblins, elves, and an animal or two. These can be created in your relatively idle moments and held in readiness until you select a story and mount a new production.

Similarly, depending on the kind of audience that is your target and the type of show you're planning to produce, you can set up your "stock company" to be almost instantly on call.

THEATER MANAGEMENT

When you play a commercial theater, there are facts that you should know about the way its operation is structured. This knowledge will be useful to you as a producer-performer, and it may give you some ideas that you could apply to the operation of your own theater in the future.

Every city has many types of auditoriums for public use. Legitimate theaters and film theaters may be available when regular shows are not scheduled, and a marionette stage should be able to use even the limited stage space before the screen of most movie houses. Museums, churches and synagogues, Masonic temples, community centers, Y's, hotels, civic auditoriums, and many others have space they'd be glad to rent on a variety of bases. Essentially they all function the same way, the degree of complexity being determined by how many rentals they make and whether they rent primarily to theatrical or non-theatrical groups. If all they have is an occasional speaker, naturally they don't need the elaborate personnel or procedural policies we'll dissuss next.

PERSONNEL

The *theater administrator* or *manager* is the top official. A large theater may give him one or more deputies or assistants. If there is a *deputy administrator*, he'll probably be your liaison with management, see to your needs, and hand you your check. Either he or the administrator is most likely the one who contracted for your services in the first place. If there is no deputy, all your dealings are directly with the manager. It's important for your relations to be cordial and that he understand that your demands are for the purpose of the best show possible. These are the theater officials with whom you make the arrangements for set-up time, storage of your stage equipment, etc.

If the manager is merely renting the facilities to a performing company (yours) and has no financial interest in the production other than the rental fee, he has no obligation or incentive to help sell seats. If you and the manager are sharing receipts on a predetermined basis, his *public-relations director* will probably cooperate with you in selling the

house. While the PR person can do a great deal to attract audiences, you'll have to give him the information he needs about your performance and your company.

The *house manager* oversees the operations of the theater. He sees that the house is clean and in order, lighted properly, and open on time, with the programs ready. He sets the curtain time and has the box-office people, ticket takers, and ushers set to go on schedule.

The *head usher* works directly under the house manager, and the *ushers* work directly under the head usher.

Box-office personnel are responsible to the administrator or manager.

Backstage are three union members—the *head electrician*, who lets you know where to plug in your equipment, explains the fuse loads, and gives you the general safety requirements; the *head carpenter*, who advises you how to place your equipment within sight lines and curtain operations and about any idiosyncrasies the house may have; and the *property man*, who tells you about the availability of tables, chairs, benches, and such you may need to accommodate your own equipment. The *stagehands* work under these three.

You may need extra help in unloading your van and loading it again in due course, and this is something to be specified in your contract. If you are playing a college theater or a fraternal organization's hall, this assistance may be contributed by volunteers. But in a union house, the union decides how many stagehands will be required for the operation and for how long a period. The theater may be compelled to hire four or five union stagehands—needless to say at union rates—and this is a factor to be considered when designing your equipment in the first place and when negotiating a contract. Who pays for this? Neither the management nor the puppeteer could justify the cost for a single performance but allocated over performances for a week or two, it's possible to absorb it.

The *security personnel* consists of a stage *doorman*, private *police*, and a *night watchman*—or any one of these.

PROCEDURE

When you arrive at the theater at the date and hour set forth in your contract, check in with the deputy administrator or whoever else has been designated as your contact. He will either take you or direct you backstage, where the head stagehand will take charge of unloading your equipment and bringing it into the theater. You'll have discussed with your contact what your place is on the bill and about the set-up and striking time you need. If the time is less than you require, your stage may be set up on a wheeled platform known as a "wagon stage" so that it just gets pushed on and off when your turn comes.

If your stage remains set up for the entire series of performances, you must insist on full security for everything connected with it. Your tape recorders, lighting equipment, and other property with a ready resale value should be locked away in a closet or a storage room. Never leave anything of value in the theater except what is directly connected with your production.

Even though you are fully set up and ready to go, it's still a good idea to arrive at the theater at least an hour before every curtain so that you can deal with any emergency that may arise.

You'll have been shown where the dressing rooms are and their proximity to the stage. One or more will have been assigned to you and the members of your company. In the likelihood of your sharing a dressing room with a stranger, don't impose on your roommate's space or personal property. Keep your portion of the premises as neat as you'd like his to be.

When the time comes to perform in a "real" theater, you'll discover you have nothing to worry about with a first-rate professional show and even this much information about procedures.

NEGOTIATIONS

Whether you are conducting business in person, over the phone, or by correspondence, there are two areas where selling your show can be fouled up. One is your contacts, the other your price.

We presume you have initiated your dealings with the right person—the artistic director or business manager of an orchestra, the head of the entertainment committee for the PTA, the public-relations officer of a department store. If matters seem to be going smoothly, be careful that other dealings don't bring you into conflict with your first connection.

Let's give some examples of what not to do. You have started the wheels going around with the vice-president in charge of consumer relations for the X Manufacturing Company. He appears interested but hasn't reached a decision. Meanwhile, you approach the Y and Z Public Relations Company with the same proposition for using marionette shows, hoping to interest them in the idea for some of their clients. The Y and Z PR go to their client, the X Manufacturing Company, full of enthusiasm about a stupendous new original advertising scheme they've concocted—using marionettes. The vice-president doesn't think it's so original; he heard it from you last month. Y and Z are furious and won't have anything to do with you, and the vice-president isn't going to antagonize them by dealing with you directly, and you're out.

Or the head of the entertainment committee

of the PTA has been discussing a possible marionette show with you. Meanwhile, to put pressure on her, you go to the president of the PTA. The committee head is outraged at your going over her, and the president won't interfere. The moral of these two little tales? Be careful not to get your wires crossed. Don't go to a second party unless you are sure your first source is hopeless and you have nothing to lose.

Price—the second area to be particularly careful about—requires consideration from several angles. If you've been accurate in your bookkeeping, you know what the show is costing you. You know what profit margin you require. But what is the price of other puppeteers' productions that run the same length and use the same number of operators? If your price is substantially higher than theirs, you won't be able to compete unless your show is markedly superior. If your price is substantially lower, go over your books to verify whether you've included all your expenses. It stands to reason that if they can't function economically on less, you can't either unless you are able to operate more efficiently, are using unpaid volunteers instead of paid personnel, or are waiving your profit. There's no quicker way to go broke than to charge too little.

With all this in mind, set a base price for one performance and then go up or down from there, depending on negotiations. The price goes up if the booking is more than two or three hours away, which means you will be using more gas, putting more wear and tear on your van, paying tolls, buying meals for your crew, paying overtime, possibly paying for motel accommodations. Or the sponsor could ask for something extra that will make your show twice as long or call for writing in a new marionette that entails added rehearsal time. The price goes down if the sponsor wants more

than one show the same day, or contracts for X number of other performances of the same production or others within a specified period of time, or sets up booking dates on your behalf with other sponsors in the area.

Sponsors who are new at booking entertainment often go into shock when they hear the price of a production. "You mean a puppet show costs more than $25.00? That's what my sister gave the man who performed at her little boy's birthday party!" When you get this reaction, don't fluster and don't apologize. And don't patronize. Explain that you are a professional performer. Your other puppeteers, if you have them, are also professionals. You have had to pay for the time and material that went into constructing your stage equipment, you have royalties and other standard theatrical expenses to meet, there is the cost of your transportation, etc., etc., and all this can't be equated with a soloist who comes for a half hour with some balloons and one puppet in a suitcase. If they want your show, this is the price.

The next move is usually the sponsors'. "But we are a non-profit organization. What is your reduced price for non-profit organizations?" This *is* your reduced price. For commercial organizations you charge 10 to 15 percent more. If the sponsors panic and say they can't possibly afford you, find out how many seats their house holds and what they are selling tickets for. Sometimes with the right kind of publicity, which you might help them with, they can cover their expenses if they sell out. If they can't afford you really, offer them a less expensive show, if you have one, but don't cut your price. The sponsors may be very grateful for a reduction, but gratitude won't keep them from telling other sponsors how they got you to give them a discount. You could have trouble for the rest of your professional life.

Sometimes a theater or other organization

offers you a percentage deal. This could be attractive, *always* providing there is a minimum guarantee to cover your expenses. Without a minimum, no—unless you are prepared to pay all your costs as a contribution to the theater or the organization's cause. On a percentage, it's important that the contract spell out who is responsible for what in the way of duties and responsibilities for selling the show and what charges will be allocated to whose account. Otherwise, whether the split is made gross or net, there can be hard feelings if each party feels the other made unjustifiable charges that cut into the shares.

Price is almost always the first or second question a sponsor asks. Whether you're dealing with the PTA, a Masonic temple, or the controller of a manufacturing company, always be prepared to discuss it and to justify differences in charges by explaining the circumstances.

A theater manager may approach you with a percentage offer that may be for performances for a large number of weekends or solid weeks over the Christmas or Easter holidays. Look into the kind and quality of other shows they've brought in. What condition is the theater in—clean and in good repair or grimy and shabby? What security do you have if he defaults on his contract? (And over an extended period you might have given up alternative bookings.) Are you free to work elsewhere during this period as long as your dates don't conflict with the theater's? Or are you precluded from working in the same territory for the duration of your agreement? More subjects for possible negotiation.

CONTRACTS

Many people are under the misapprehension that a contract must be a piece of paper containing writing in legal form setting forth a mutual obligation. A contract may also be a verbal agreement, and it can be just as binding as the most official-looking document. The advantage of a written form is that it spells out the obligations of all parties. Therefore, a contract that states who will be performing where, at what time, and for how much, is a useful paper. It may also mention the person in charge of the function, the admission to be charged, when the fee is due, travel expenses, information about the theater, and travel directions. However, this same information in a letter from an authorized individual, confirmed by you, has the same strength.

Pictured are three sample contracts: between the agent and the puppeteer, between the puppeteer and the sponsor, and between the agent and the sponsor. A sample confirmation from the agent to the puppeteer is also enclosed. In addition, for your information as to how a sponsor operates, we're showing forms used by the Saturday Theatre for Children, an organization whose members are a large number of public elementary schools. The first is a page from its instructional manual showing procedures of interest to puppeteers. The second is a confirmation-of-booking form sent to producers to be signed in duplicate, one copy to be returned to the STC office. Saturday Theatre for Children has been in operation for many years. It has never used any more of a contract than this confirmation in its dealings with some thirty producers a year, and it has never run into any difficulties, nor have the producers.

Each party to the contract should retain a copy signed by each of the other parties.

In an agreement between puppeteer and sponsor, there are no other parties, so there is no commission for the puppeteer to pay. In an agreement between the agent and the sponsor, the puppeteer is obligated to give the agent a cut. If the agent is also the artist's personal representative, he shares a higher percentage because the representative does more than merely book the performance. He may make travel arrangements, handle publicity, and any other details that go into a more successful appearance.

The most important ingredient in any contract, oral or written, is the faith both parties to it have in each other. If either party breaches the agreement and the other chooses to litigate, the expenses are likely to equal, if not surpass, the amount claimed. And even if it is financially worthwhile suing, it probably won't be in terms of nuisance value.

You'll find, as you go farther afield to accept bookings, that the entertainment world is small in one sense. Everybody in it knows everyone else. Sponsors talk to other sponsors and to other performers and agents, and it's amazing how fast the word gets around when someone feels taken advantage of. A good reputation travels also, albeit more slowly, so a reputation for integrity is one of the greatest assets any producer could have.

XYZ AGENCY

ARTIST'S PERSONAL REPRESENTATIVE

Address
Phone

CONFIRMATION

Artist: _____

Date: _____ Time: _____

Auspices: _____

Place of Meeting: _____

_____

_____

Contact: _____

Dress: _____

Remarks: _____

We will send a check covering your appearance and we will remit your fee of _____
_____ immediately after collection is made on the check.

IMPORTANT: Please notify committee or designated representative of exact time of arrival in their town. Please verify best routes to place of performance.

Please acknowledge receipt of this instruction sheet by signing and returning attached copy.

(from agent to performer)

ABC PUPPET COMPANY

Address
Phone

AGREEMENT:

The Sponsor agrees to engage the professional services of the ABC Puppet Company according to the following arrangements:

The Sponsor is: _____

name   address   phone

Place of performance _____

_____

date   time   age of group

Performance is to be shared with _____

group   type of performer

The performance _____

title   length of performance

ABC will need _____ hours to set up and _____ to take down and require _____ space for proper performance.

minimum dimensions

The Sponsor must arrange for _____ of electrical power necessary for a

120 volts (amp)

proper performance and service should be within a reasonable distance to the set-up.

The Sponsor is responsible for all financial arrangements related to the auditorium and any advertising, tickets and program expenses. The Sponsor agrees to pay the fee of _____ for the above performance plus _____ for traveling expenses.

Both parties must sign this agreement to make it valid. The date reservation cannot be held for more than _____ days and if finalization is not realized within this period of time both parties are free of any contractual obligations.

For ABC Company _____

name   date

For the Sponsor _____

name   date

(from performer to sponsor)

XYZ AGENCY

ARTIST'S PERSONAL REPRESENTATIVE

Address
Phone

AGREEMENT

This agreement made the _____ day of _____ by and between XYZ personal representative, hereinafter called Manager and _____ hereinafter called the Sponsor.

WITNESSETH:

In consideration of the mutual and dependent covenants hereinafter set forth, the SPONSOR engages the services of _____ hereinafter called ARTIST to appear in _____ on _____ at _____.

1. SPONSOR agrees to pay ARTIST on the date of performance, and prior to performance, the sum of _____ by certified check or accepted draft on a _____ bank payable to the order of XYZ, Manager. Such draft is to be delivered to ARTIST or mailed to MANAGER as MANAGER may direct in writing.

2. SPONSOR agrees to furnish at his own expense a suitable theater, hall or auditorium, well heated, lighted, clean and in good order, with spotlights, benches, and all electrical equipment and background curtain necessary for the performance of ARTIST, a clean comfortable dressing room near the stage for ARTIST, and to pay for taking show in and out, furnishing all necessary attaches, license if license is required, and any newspaper advertising SPONSOR chooses to use.

3. ARTIST will furnish or cause to be furnished to SPONSOR copy of the program to be performed, and SPONSOR agrees, at his expense, to print and distribute a sufficient quantity of house programs to conform with the material furnished by ARTIST.

4. MANAGER shall not be held responsible for the non-appearance of ARTIST where such failure to appear is caused by illness, accident, or any other unavoidable cause beyond the control of the MANAGER, and in event of such failure to appear each party shall bear its own expense or loss and have no claim against the other.

5. SPONSOR agrees to prevent the broadcasting, recording or reproduction by radio or any other device of ARTIST's performance or any part thereof unless such arrangements have been negotiated.

6. A porter should be at the disposal of the performing troupe to aid in bringing in equipment from the street or loading area to the place of performance and aid in every way possible in the setting up of equipment.

7. Please advise as to the best place for unloading.

8. The primary requisite is an electrical outlet at place of performance, a wall socket or extension cord the power of which must accommodate a minimum of _____ amperes. Otherwise, two outlets that can divide this electrical requirement.

(*continued*)

9. This agreement represents the full understanding between the parties and ARTIST shall not be bound by any terms or undertakings other than those contained herein.

_____
Sponsor

_____
Artist

_____
Manager

Auditorium _____ Seating capacity _____

Location _____ City _____

Subject _____ Time allotted _____

Best hotel _____ Arrival time _____

Artist is to contact _____

IMPORTANT: Performing troupe will need the stage_____ hours before scheduled curtain time.

(from agent to sponsor)

204

XYZ AGENCY
CONFIRMATION OF BOOKING
PLEASE FILL IN ALL DETAILS

Address

Phone

Date: _____

Artist: _____

To Appear on _____ Hour of Appearance _____

Auspices _____ Age Range of Audience _____

Person in Charge _____

name   address   business phone   home phone

Invoice to Be Sent to _____

Place of Performance _____ Seating Capacity _____

Address

City _____ Zone No. _____ State _____

Nature of Sponsorship   Program Shared with

Subject or Program   Length of Program

Terms plus travel expenses per mile

Hotel Reservations at _____

Directions for Reaching Place of Performance from _____

                                                               town landmark

Other Remarks:

Artist's Copy   Signed _____

                                                   for XYZ

Please keep this copy in your file   Signed _____

                                                   for Artist

Payment: Check for fee and expenses payable to XYZ, is to be handed to Artist on the day of appearance. Please Mail Check Immediately to Agency.

(from agent or manager to performer)

SATURDAY THEATRE FOR CHILDREN

131 LIVINGSTON STREET, BROOKLYN, NEW YORK 11201 • TEL. 834–8027

1. SECURING APPROVAL OF PRINCIPAL AND PARENTS' ASSOCIATION

Successful programs need the enthusiastic endorsement and cooperation of the principal and the Parents' Association. The following advantages can be mentioned:

a. Children are exposed to varied theatrical experiences such as ballet, mime, drama, operas, *puppetry*, modern and ethnic dance programs, folk singing, concerts and magic shows.

b. The creative excitement sparked by the STC program stimulates the children in all areas of communication, oral and written.

c. These productions come directly to your school either on Saturday mornings or after school on weekdays.

d. All productions are booked and confirmed by the STC secretary.

e. The admission charge is nominal. These same productions often cost several times more at midtown theaters.

f. All productions on the STC circuit have been carefully previewed and are of the highest quality available.

g. Tickets and publicity material are provided free by STC.

h. Most of the programs have study guides which are available for use by the teachers as an extension of their educational program.

i. Community involvement with the school can be sparked via STC program.

j. To enlist support, a film titled *Saturday Is for Children* and/or a sound filmstrip titled *Bring on the Show* is available free for showing to parents and teachers.

k. Our Community Coordinator is available to address groups of parents or teachers about the program.

2. HOW TO JOIN

a. Secure the endorsement of your principal and Parents' Association.

b. Obtain application form from STC office.

c. Have your principal and designated representative of the sponsoring organization (Parents' Association or other) sign form.

d. Upon receipt of completed form, your school will be considered a member of STC.

e. There is no fee for joining.

206

SATURDAY THEATRE FOR CHILDREN:
131 Livingston Street
Brooklyn, New York 11201
Tel. No. 834-8027

Date Sent _____

Producers' Booking Confirmation

Name of Production _____

Name of Producer _____

Address _____

Telephone No. _____

The following is a confirmation of performances booked for your production through the Saturday Theatre for Children. Please sign in duplicate and return one copy to us promptly. It is our sponsor's responsibility to contact your office at least one week before performance. However, should our sponsor's representative fail to do this, it will be up to the producer to make sure that his requirements for the production are met by telephoning the school representative.

Date of
Performance

      Time

      School

      Address

      Borough

Contact's Name and Tel. No.

      Remarks

Signed _____

Date _____

207

ACCOUNTING, BUDGETING, COSTS

The marionettes may be the heart of your operation, but a good bookkeeping system is its brain.

Good financial records will enable you to budget your enterprise and to compute the charges you make for your services so that they cover your expenses at the very least. And if you receive grants, gifts, or allocations of space or materials, the donor may be entitled to look into your books to see how the contribution was spent. If you are acting as a partnership or a corporation, you have financial accountability to the other members of your organization.

What are categories that might be included under income? Ticket sales or contractual fee for performances. Sponsorship underwriting, grants, donations. Program advertising. Concessions (candy, puppets, toys, etc.).

Under expenses, make a distinction between direct expenses (those having to do directly with production) and indirect expenses (overhead and non-specific items). Direct expenses are the costs of making and costuming the marionettes; construction of stages, scenery, props, and controllers; tools; supplies; lighting equipment; royalties for script and music; theater and workshop rental; salaries, taxes, and insurance of puppeteers and theater personnel; rehearsal costs; promotional material, postage and other costs that can be ascribed directly to the productions; and travel expenses of the shows (including rental or amortization of car or truck, gasoline, tolls, food, lodging, and insurance). And one more a lot of people don't allow for: cleaning, repairs, and maintenance of the marionettes and the other theatrical properties. Taxes on tickets also fall under direct costs.

Indirect costs take in the charges for the operation of the office end of the business—rent for the office; insurance; telephone; electricity; stationery; postage; promotional expenses having to do with the business as a whole rather than specific shows; administrative and office personnel; general business and realty taxes; professional memberships and subscriptions.

If you're running a simple one-person operation, it isn't necessary to worry about what charges go where as long as they're all included. But if you should expand to where you have several companies out simultaneously, each with one or more puppeteers, it will be important that all charges be allocated exactly, even if one employee's time, for example, should be shown as charged 20 percent to production A, 20 percent to Production B, and 60 percent to overhead. Without keeping careful track of what every part of the operation costs, you won't be able to tell what a production has entailed, how much you should charge for it, and whether it's paying its own way or being covered by the profits of another show.

Under your assets go the worth of your stages, scenery, marionettes, props, lighting and sound equipment, your car or van if owned by the business, or any other salable property, not overlooking your office furniture and equipment. Assets also include cash on hand and in the bank, any substantial amount of postage, and a reserve that you should be accumulating from revenues that can be a contingency fund in the event of a financial shock or as the basis for your next production.

Under liabilities, list outstanding debts in the form of borrowed money, unpaid bills, and anything else that could affect the net worth of your company.

Any good accountant can start you off right; after that it's a matter of following through consistently. Discuss with your accountant what depreciation allowance you're entitled to and how to show it on your books. This allowance should be for your van or car as well as for the marionettes, stages, etc., and it can also apply to your office equipment (typewriter, adding machine, addressing machines, etc.) and furnishings.

Unless you put a dollar value on your time and charge the company for it, the biggest expense item won't be listed. Every laborer is worthy of his hire—and so are you. The time spent in developing your talent and your company is your investment. From this point, you should be reimbursed for further efforts, just as any skilled mechanic is for a job. When you evaluate what your time is worth, be reasonable as well as realistic. You know what the budget is. Don't become too expensive to afford yourself.

Traveling can be a major item, particularly if you're taking other puppeteers with you and are responsible for their food and lodging while on the road. You must make sure your performance fee is adequate to cover it. Incidentally, if you are performing as a hobby and no fee is charged, the insurance company covering the liability on your car will look on your operations as being a hobby and therefore under the provisions of the "pleasure and business" clause of the policy. Even if you take a very occasional paid booking, the company probably won't quibble. But if you have an accident while engaged in carrying puppeteers and equipment and the insurance company discovers this is a frequent activity, your use of the vehicle may be deemed "commercial" and problems could arise. If you intend to use your car often to tour your production, we suggest you notify your insurance carrier and have your policy amended, even though there will be an increase in the rate.

There is no hard and fast rule about what anything should cost or how much of your budget should be allowed for it. But if you want a general guide to expenses, you might allow, roughly, one third for the physical production (puppets, stage, etc.), one third for actors'/puppeteers' salaries, and the final third for overhead and profit.

If your business set-up is such that you'll be paying taxes, your accountant will let you know about deductions. Broadly speaking, you'll be allowed to depreciate the stages, marionettes, etc.; that portion of your home used exclusively for your work area, or your studio or office if you own them; and your car, van, or station wagon, to the extent that it is used in the business. These are written off over expected useful life of each item and are considered legitimate deductions. (Expendable items such as bulbs, recording tapes, props that wear out quickly, chemicals for special effects, string, fabrics, lumber. Promotional costs such as business cards, photographs, programs, news releases, advertising, solicitation and commission fees, design expenses, etc. Travel expenses such as mileage (not otherwise compensated for), repairs, tolls, meals, lodging, professional memberships, subscriptions, books. And child-care expenses for your own children connected with your show.

PROFESSIONAL ETHICS AND CONDUCT

Those puppeteers who look on puppetry as a business are bound by the ethics of the market place. But those who regard puppetry as a form of theater, as an art, even as a way of life, are held to higher standards. Ethics enters into every area of your operations. There are instances when "ethics" as applied to principles and "conduct" as applied to business can be one and the same thing.

You and Other Puppeteers. Ethics affects your relationships with your fellow professionals. Price-cutting for the simple purpose of taking a booking away from another puppeteer is considered underhanded and so is denigrating another puppeteer. Puppeteers know that one of the best sources of bookings is a sponsor who is pleased by the latest show. If a sponsor has exhausted your repertory and wants additional puppetry, don't hesitate to recommend someone whose work you respect. You undoubtedly will receive recommendations from other puppeteers. The better shows all puppeteers give, the more lucrative the field is for everybody. This is something not sufficiently understood by many in theater who look on everyone else as being in competition rather than cooperation. If your company is stricken with flu, you can call on another puppeteer, with the sponsor's permission, to fill in for you. You may be called in to fill in for someone else. If you can do a favor for another puppeteer or he for you, help each other. A professional puppeteer can step into someone else's shoes with a minimum of rehearsal in an emergency, let you know who sells equipment you may need—or may even rent or lend you his. Young puppeteers should be encouraged. When a school child after a performance asks you how some particular movement was performed, if you can possibly spare the time, demonstrate it. Encourage interest in puppetry in those who might be tomorrow's fellow artists.

You and Your Show. Your first loyalty as a professional theater person must be to the in-

tegrity of your production. The highest standards of performance are expected of you. Those who know your work have a right to dissatisfaction when they see less than your best.

As a practical matter, what does this mean? It means that your seal of approval by way of a performance goes on nothing that fails to live up to your best expectations of yourself. It means that if you can't afford to put on a big, splashy, expensive, good show, you put on a small, modest, inexpensive but professional production within your ability and your budget. It means every production goes out at all times clean, in good repair, and well rehearsed. If you can keep two dozen plays in your repertory and see to it they all are in tip-top condition, you're a better puppeteer than most. So don't maintain more in your active repertory than you can care for properly. Similarly, if you have twenty puppet companies touring several states simultaneously, all supervised by competent stage managers who refuse to lower your standards, you're not only a good businessman or -woman, you're a fine artist. But if those companies become careless in their presentation, improve them or drop them.

In order to see that the show appears at its best, it is sometimes necessary to be firm about your requirements with sponsors or theater managers who don't always have all details set up as specified in the contract or who don't see what difference it makes that the curtains aren't drawn or that backstage electrical outlets you need are blocked. Your show needs it; you need it. Don't be obnoxious or temperamental but explain and persist.

You and Your Own People. No better way has ever been found to develop loyalty in those you work with than to make loyalty a two-way street. Treat them with the respect one professional accords another. Let them know as long beforehand as possible when their services will be required. Pay them promptly. Don't take advantage of them. (You may be willing to contribute your services to a benefit for a cause you're enthusiastic about. You have no right to contribute theirs.) Share the spotlight and the applause with them. And let them express their own creativity as long as it's consistent with your goals in theater.

If you have an agent or a business manager to whom you have financial obligations, don't keep him waiting for his money. Or for your approval, if this is necessary, of any bookings he has tentatively set up for you. If he expects you to check in from time to time, do so in order that he'll know where he stands. There's no reason why colleagues can't be friends, but to have a friend you must be a friend.

Actually, of course, that's the basis of all ethics—doing unto others as you'd have them do unto you.

You and the Sponsor. You and the sponsor both know what's expected of you according to the contract, but there are reciprocal obligations that are implied as well.

If you have agreed to be at the theater two hours before curtain time, the sponsor has a right to expect you then. You should be admitted to the theater on your arrival and not wait around until the sponsor arrives half an hour late with the key.

You and your company are neat, clean, and presentable, and your equipment is in good repair and safe for your company and other backstage persons.

If you've contracted for *Cinderella,* show up with *Cinderella,* not *Jack and the Beanstalk.* The sponsor will have to apologize to the audience and explain away weeks, even months, of contradictory publicity. Deliver the production agreed on in every respect, including quality.

You are responsible for the decorum of your employees and for the effect your own demeanor creates on the sponsor.

You have a right to expect the sponsor's agreed-on compliance with your setting-up procedures and, though not spelled out, the sponsor's cooperation in establishing decorum in the auditorium before the show begins. Once the curtain goes up on a quiet house, it's your job to control the audience by your performance.

A professional company strikes its set and moves out of the theater as specified. The sponsor may owe a fee if the theater is occupied past a given hour, or another show may be following you and needing the facilities. When you leave, see to it that the backstage and dressing-room areas are no more untidy than when you arrived.

When the sponsor hands you your check or cash at the end of the show, don't suddenly announce extra charges because the trip took longer than expected, or for any other reason. The price was settled beforehand, and unless it was adjusted beforehand, it holds.

All this comes under the heading of professional conduct—ethics. Proper professional conduct will encourage the sponsor to continue doing business with you.

You and the Public. Much of what you owe the public has been touched on in what you owe the production and what you owe the sponsor. But there's one thing you owe the public not mentioned yet, and that is respect. We touched on respect in the pages on "Playscripts" in Part Two and elsewhere, but it can't be stressed too strongly that your attitude toward your audience is reflected by your production. Children have an instinct for detecting condescension. An adult audience can sense if you think they're idiots. There are intelligent people out there in that sea of nameless faces, and you owe them what they've come for—your best.

Benefits come up for discussion under the subject of professional ethics. All sorts of individuals and groups will approach you, asking you to give them a free show for some worthy cause. Remember, everyone is entitled to ask, so don't be high-handed. You do owe the public something, and an occasional benefit is reasonable. But when you discuss this with the head of the benefit committee, there are points you should bring up. Puppetry is your livelihood, and you can give only so many free performances a year. You may decide to contribute your services and your own out-of-pocket expenses (hiring of van, etc.), but you can't ask your company to work free when they might be accepting paid work from someone else for that time. And even though you give of yourself, you may not be able to defray out-of-pocket expenses and you need to be reimbursed for your costs, which include your players' salaries. If they're willing to go along with you on your costs, there are certain other conditions to be met having to do with the performance. You'll need to know where you'll appear on the program and whether there will be time for you to set up properly and strike your set afterward. You must insist that if your show doesn't look good, not only will the audience not enjoy it but you can do yourself much harm by earning an undeserved reputation for a slovenly production. You want as many possible bookers or agents to see your show, so, particularly if you are in a territory you've never played

before, make a certain number of tickets for your guests part of your negotiations. Proper exposure is always a major part of your operations.

So far as your general business relations are concerned, answer your mail and pay your bills promptly. Be generous and effective as a performing artist, and you'll find that this course of professional conduct will earn you a reputation that will insure a growing number of persons eager to attend or book your productions.

PROFESSIONAL AFFILIATIONS

Every mature profession has an organization that encourages higher standards in performance and ethics and serves as a resource and a channel of communication for its members. For marionette people there are two such types of organization—one concerned primarily with puppetry and with theater as puppets have a place in it and the other essentially with theater and with puppetry as being one aspect of that.

The Puppeteers of America, Inc., is the national organization for puppeteers and the friends of puppets. Its bimonthly *The Puppetry Journal* publishes informative articles and news of puppetry festivals, workshops, and other relevant events. It also lists addresses of the regional guilds or chapters in the United States and Canada. For information about the Puppeteers of America, write to Olga Stevens, Executive Secretary, P.O. Box 1061, Ojai, California 90323. Its annual summer conferences, held each year in a different city, allow all kinds of puppeteers to meet one another, see what's being done in puppetry by various companies or individuals, learn, and socialize.

UNIMA (Union Internationale de la Marionette) is the international organization of puppeteers. Its worldwide membership doesn't meet every year, but from time to time it holds puppetry festivals in different countries. UNIMA'S attendance is drawn from more than fifty nations. UNIMA publishes a journal and is a member of ITI (International Theatre Institute) and UNESCO (United Nations Educational, Scientific, and Cultural Organization). For information write to its General Secretary, 132 Chiquita Street, Laguna Beach, California 92651.

Many puppeteers also belong to groups that share an interest in theater as such. Under the general heading of American Theatre Association, the following deal with specific aspects of theater or with specific age ranges or services:

American Community Theatre Association
Children's Theatre Association
Secondary School Theatre Association
University and College Theatre Association
Army Theatre Arts Association
University Resident Theatre Association

Each of these is a national organization with a regional structure, and any inquiries should be directed to 1317 F Street, N.W., Washington, D.C. 20004. These associations maintain cordial relationships with the Puppeteers of America.

ASSITEJ (Association Internationale du Théâtre pour l'Enfance et la Jeunesse), or the International Association of Theatre for Children and Youth, holds biannual conferences in countries around the world. Performing-arts groups are invited to appear so that delegates from the various nations can see their work. If you'll be performing abroad, ASSITEJ might be useful to you. To learn more about ASSITEJ, write to the American Theatre Association.

The International Theatre Institute of the United States is not a "professional affiliation," but it is a research center, a resource, and a service organization, like a library specializing in one subject. It is helpful to foreign theater people in this country and to American theater folk—including puppeteers—going outside. Its address is 245 West 52nd Street, New York, N.Y. 10019.

INCORPORATING AND FUNDING

These pages of *Marionettes Onstage!* may strike you as something to skip over, but if you intend to be a professional puppeteer, we urge you to read them carefully. If you have no immediate need for the information they contain, read them anyway so that you'll know where to refer in the future if it should become important.

Why are these sections vital? Because in today's world performing companies have discovered it can be cold and cruel out there, financially speaking. In order to survive or grow or deliver their services to those who can't afford them, these companies need more than admissions or performance payments can bring in. Whether they're huge symphony orchestras or small dance groups, live theaters or puppets, playing for adults or for children, they have had to turn themselves into the kinds of organizations that could appeal effectively for grants, funding, or subsidies—*money*. If you don't need money—wonderful! We hope this blissful condition obtains forever. Or if you can adjust your dreams and schemes so that you can function within your receipts, great. But if insufficient money is an artistic or professional straitjacket, these sections of the book may help you.

INCORPORATING

Why. When you decide to turn your marionette hobby into a profession, you might want to consider forming a corporation. There are several reasons for incorporating, but the main one is the same as for any business: The corporation assumes the responsibilities of the business and relieves you of legal liabilities for debts and other contractual obligations in the event the business fails.

To form a corporation, consult an attorney.

Commercial vs. Non-Profit Corporations. A commercial corporation has an important advantage over a non-profit corporation if the operations are very successful. All the profits belong to the stockholders—and you would most likely be the major stockholder, perhaps even the only one. However, a non-profit corporation could be advisable if you are seeking funding from foundations or governmental divisions, which can't allot funds to "ordinary" corporations.

Non-Profit Corporation. If you decide to go nonprofit, there are some regions where you can get free legal advice. Your local bar association or state arts council can let you know whether your state has a group of lawyers who donate their services to the arts. (The Volunteer Lawyers for the Arts operate in New York City.) Legal Aid societies throughout the United States offer general legal assistance, either free or at low cost.

As a puppeteer performing in schools, hospitals, prisons, old-age homes, etc., you would be eligible for non-profit status if your corporation were formed ". . . exclusively for a purpose or purposes, not for pecuniary profit or financial gain . . . no part of the assets, income, or profit of which [the corporation]

is distributable to, or enures to the benefit of, its members, directors or officers. . . ." This is taken from the law of the State of New York, but the requirements are substantially the same in all states. The corporate charter is granted by your state.

Some foundations and some governmental funding authorities give grants to non-profit corporations regardless of whether they have tax-exempt status. Others consider only those that are tax-exempt.

Your corporate income may derive from grants and other gifts, admissions, and booking revenue. From this are paid the expenses of the corporation—e.g., rent, etc., construction costs, royalties, and reasonable compensation by way of salaries to the business manager, puppeteers, and others whose services are required.

Tax-Exemption. If you've met all state conditions to qualify as an educational or a charitable non-profit corporation, you may apply to the federal government through the Internal Revenue Service of the Department of the Treasury for exemption from federal income taxes. To apply, request IRS Form 1023 for exemption under Section 501 (c) (3) of the Internal Revenue Code. This form requires an employer's number, so if you don't already have one, ask for Form SS4 at the same time. It will take about two months after you've filed all forms before you receive the decision of the IRS as to whether you're entitled to tax-exemption. There is no blanket category, every request being decided on its individual merits.

When the IRS grants tax exemption, notify your state and local governments that you have the federal exemption. They will follow suit and exempt you from city and state income and sales taxes and, in some instances, realty taxes.

As a non-profit tax-exempt charitable or educational organization you pay the same taxes as any other corporation except that you're not liable for the taxes listed above and Social Security or Federal Unemployment taxes. On behalf of your employees, you may waive the Social Security exemption if you wish.

For post-office privileges to non-profit corporations, see discussion on selling by mail.

Taxes on income from an unrelated activity would be your principal tax concern. Therefore, if you should accept a booking date that would be obviously commercial in nature, it would be a good idea to check with the IRS to see if this could impair your tax-exempt status. If this should be a problem, it might be advantageous to sign the contract not on behalf of the non-profit corporation but as an independent producer outside the sphere of the organization, or even as an officer of a separate commercial corporation.

These tax exemptions are important, but what may be even more vital is that tax-exempt status allows individuals to claim deductions for donations to your corporation on their income-tax declarations under Section 170 of the Internal Revenue Code. And of course those foundations and governmental bodies that can't fund corporations that are non-profit only may do so when those corporations are also tax-exempt.

FUNDING

Foundations. Let's suppose now that you've been operating your marionette company for some time—long enough to have established a "track record" as a responsible, creative artist. At this point either you've run into financial difficulties or you want to mount a new experimental production or a production of such magnitude your reserves can't finance it or you want to present your production free or at nominal cost to schoolchildren or shut-ins who can't afford normal admission charges. You need money. One place to go for it is to foundations.

There are an estimated 26,000 grant-making foundations in the United States. It's impossible to contact all of them, and it would be a waste even if you could. There's no point in appealing to a foundation concerned with the Pittsburgh area exclusively if you operate out of Dallas. Or asking for $2,000 from a foundation that rejects applicants who need less than $100,000. Or turning for help with performing arts to a foundation interested only in indigent seamen.

How do you find those foundations whose interests and yours are the same? An invaluable resource is *The Foundation Center*, an independent not-for-profit organization dedicated to the gathering, analysis, and dissemination of information on philanthropic foundations. It endeavors to be useful to anyone interested in applying for funds to grant-making foundations. It doesn't direct applicants to particular foundations, but it can be of help in selecting foundations that are relevant to your needs. Its Foundation Directory (beginning with Edition Five) lists foundations geographically. Since it's always advisable to look to local sources for funding, this is a good place to start. Look, then, to the purpose of the foundations to see whether you can find common ground. The Foundation Center has collections and information offices throughout the country. To learn the address of the location nearest to you and the full extent of the services available, we suggest you write to The Foundation Center at one of these addresses:

888 Seventh Avenue, New York, N.Y. 10010

1001 Connecticut Avenue, N.W., Washington, D.C. 20036

The Chicago Community Trust, 208 South La Salle Street, Suite 850, Chicago, Ill. 60604

You should know that very few foundations award grants to individuals. In nearly all instances, grants are made to non-profit corporations only, and in many cases these must also have tax-exempt status.

If you are fortunate enough to secure a grant from a foundation, don't depend on its being renewed. There are those that continue their grants, but many foundations prefer to fund another non-profit corporation when their original grant has been allocated.

Proposals and Cover Letters. A letter to the foundation describing who you are, what you want, and how you propose to spend it is the first step. Point out how your proposed project dovetails with the foundation's aims. Ask for a meeting, either on your premises or the foundation's.

The letter may be enough to launch you. In most instances, though, it's merely a preliminary. If the foundation is interested in your project, it will probably want a detailed proposal. Don't make this any longer than necessary, but include the purpose the funded program will serve, who has already given support, your corporate "track record" and that of your personnel, your income and expenses, and the names of enthusiastic references who will back you if questioned by the foundation.

The Foundation Center has two excellent pamphlets: "What will a foundation look for when you submit a grant proposal?" and "What makes a good proposal?" A paperback book that sells at nominal cost (Glide Publications, 330 Ellis Street, San Francisco, Ca. 94102), *The Bread Game: The Realities of Foundation Fundraising* (Revised Edition), is highly recommended. The information in these publications could be a valuable guide in your proposal and cover-letter writing.

Preparing a proposal can be a prolonged, agonizing experience, but if it's not done well, it can be useless. The devastating factor is that even if it *is* done well—your purpose is clearly defined, your figures make sense, and your logic is overpowering—you may still not receive a grant. Always hope for the best but expect nothing.

If you are turned down, comfort yourself with the thought that you've clarified your thinking and that most of what you've done may have to be recast with only minor modifications to be suitable for another foundation. Don't give up if you believe what you want to do is important not only to you but to your audiences.

There's an old saying that "Them as has gits." If you can match with another grant half the amount you're seeking, this sometimes works. The trick is to get the first half. If you have the ingenuity to work up a parley between Foundation A and Foundation B on the one hand and your own corporation on the other, you just might be able to swing the entire sum.

Should you receive a positive response from a foundation, don't look for your check in the next mail. The mills of the gods grind slow, and it can be anywhere from a couple of months to the better part of a year before you have the money in your hands.

Federal Funding. The National Endowment

216

for the Arts is an agency of the federal government that makes grants to organizations and individuals concerned with the arts. Under the heading of "National Program Funds," matching moneys are available to individuals and cultural organizations. Under the "Treasury Fund," the Endowment can accept a private donation earmarked for a specific group (yours?), and an equal amount is freed from the Treasury Fund. The doubled amount is then made available for the grantee to match. But all grants, including those under the Treasury Fund, are subject to review, so don't depend on approval. In general, the Endowment does *not* give grants for deficit funding, capital improvements (construction), purchase of permanent equipment, or general support. Applicants should contact the Theatre Program or Program Information, National Endowment for the Arts, Washington, D.C. 20506.

The National Park Service conducts environmental education and interpretative programs to help visitors understand and appreciate the natural and cultural values of the parks and national monuments it administers. A number of the programs have employed puppetry. If you have a concept for a marionette production that might fit the theme of a particular park or monument, contact its superintendent or inquire through the National Park Service, U.S. Department of the Interior, Washington, D.C. 20240, for suggestions of parks to contact in your region.

The Health, Education and Welfare Department of the United States, under the Elementary and Secondary Education Act (ESEA), provides federal money for a variety of projects. The funds are channeled through the states, which distribute the allocations as they deem fit, subject to HEW's over-all regulations.

There are several areas, designated as "titles," according to which projects are classified. We're listing only those titles which could pertain to puppeteers.

Title I:
provides supplementary educational assistance to children in areas having high concentration of low-income families. (Puppetry might be valuable as a tool in training teachers how to motivate diverse populations to learn; it could also motivate the children directly.) In applying, show a linkage between puppetry and progress in reading and math.

Title II:
provides for libraries and learning resources (puppetry shows or classes to stimulate reading). *After July 1, 1976, this will be covered under Title IV, (Part B).*

Title IV (Part C):
provides for innovative programs to test teaching techniques and materials. (Puppetry!)

Title VII:
provides for teacher education in bilingual education. (This could include puppetry instruction.)

Title VIII:
provides for drop-out prevention. (Puppetry classes might motivate potential drop-outs to stay in school or bring them back.)

Title IX:
provides for anti-discrimination programs to reinforce the concept of sexual equality. (A puppet play on the subject.)

In all instances, except for Title IX applications are formulated by the appropriate school district, library system, etc., and submitted to the state department having jurisdiction for review and approval. Title IX applications may be sent directly to Room 256N, 330 Independence Ave., S.W., Washington, D.C. 20201.

HEW, under the Education Professional Developments Act, may also provide funds for teacher training in puppetry, particularly for handicapped students. In this case, apply to the Office of Education, United States Department of Health, Education and Welfare, Washington, D.C. 20202.

The Follow-Through Program of the Office of Education deals with children from kindergarten through third grade. Puppetry may be supportive here as well. Write to Regional Office Building #3, Seventh and D Streets, S.W., Washington, D.C. 20202.

The Childrens' Bureau of the Office of Child Development funds prekindergarten programs. Puppetry might be particularly effective in motivating this age group to learn. Apply to this bureau at P. O. Box 1182, Washington, D.C. 20013.

The federal government funds other programs under a miscellany of organizations. The Veterans Administration and the Department of Labor are both concerned with rehabilitation (puppetry could well be part of such a program), and other bureaus may also be worth investigating for a possible interest in funding a marionette theater.

State, County, and Municipal Funding. When a performing-arts company seeks funding, frequently it turns first to some agency in the state in which it's domiciled. Usually the initial request is to the Council on the Arts or the Arts Commission, or however it's titled. Each state has some such organization, and they differ widely from each other in the amount of money they have to distribute and what they can spend it on.

The New York State Council on the Arts considers grants to non-profit corporations only (tax exemption is not a requirement), not to individuals. Its application form consists of thirteen pages in triplicate (ghastly!) asking for a description of your program and what you'll provide for the money requested. Detailed budgets, copies of income-tax returns, and other financial documents are required. A considerable amount of miscellaneous data about your corporate structure and personnel and audiences is also called for. The Council rarely funds an entire operation but intends instead to close the gap between income and deficits. This is not necessarily the case in other states, where councils may have different eligibility requirements or fund specific projects in whole or in part.

The New York State Council doesn't fund public school districts or other state agencies or departments. Again, councils in other states are not necessarily limited the same way.

If the funding you're seeking has to do with school performances or master classes in puppetry, you might apply either to your state education department or to your local board of education.

Should you want to take your marionette show to the parks or on the street, funding might be available from a state, county, or municipal department that deals with parks or recreation. Does your program deal with a medical problem, or mental health, or consumer information? Almost always there's a state or local agency into whose bailiwick these fall, and often there's possible money available. Procedures vary as to how you should apply and the kind of corporate structure, if any, required of you. Investigate the potential for puppetry under the aegis of some governmental authority. It might provide a niche in which you can find a home, grow, and fill a civic and artistic need.

The Creative Artists Public Service Program (CAPS) is sponsored by the New York State

Council on the Arts, the National Endowment for the Arts, and works in cooperation with the New York City Department of Parks, Recreation, and Cultural Affairs. This program gives grants to individuals, and individual puppeteers would be eligible to apply. The grants, or fellowships, range from $3,500 to $6,500 in the Mixed Media/Related Fields category, as puppeteers would be classified. CAPS's application form contains a full description of requirements and conditions. Similar programs are available in other states for individuals.

Business Contributions. There's nothing to stop you from going to local merchants, utility companies, banks, etc., and asking them to contribute to the support of the arts—through your marionette company. If you've formed a non-profit tax-exempt corporation, this lends dignity and prestige to your appeal and it could be important to a donor who wants an income-tax deduction.

Businesses of all kinds are becoming increasingly aware of the importance of the arts, particularly major concerns. It is no longer unusual for them to donate to any type of arts group, whether for love of the arts, out of corporate citizenship or enlightened self-interest (what's good for the community is good for the corporation), or for the public-relations value. Unlike many foundations, once a corporation has given a contribution of money or products or services, it's likely to continue to give on reapplication.

Your local chamber of commerce might be able to tell you the businesses in your territory which support the arts directly—or indirectly through schools, hospitals, or other institutions that could use your services.

The Business Committee for the Arts, Inc., 1700 Broadway, New York, N.Y. 10019, is a private, tax-exempt national organization of business leaders created to encourage business and industry to assume a greater share of responsibility for the support of the arts. Among its activities, it counsels arts organizations on more effective ways to enlist corporate involvement in and support of their activities. It is of assistance to non-profit tax-exempt corporations and individuals. The Committee won't help in any actual fund-raising, supply a list of names for you to contact, or act as a conduit for funds. The Committee *will* help with advice on your approach to business people, including the basic letter and prospectus. It maintains files on arts groups that consult them and uses the files in discussions with business people who consult the Committee. It also allows you, if you have consulted the Committee, to use it as a reference. The Business Committee for the Arts publishes a valuable little pamphlet describing fund-raising procedures to be followed and a number of do's and don'ts to which careful heed should be paid: "Approaching business for the support of the arts."

The Arts and Business Council of New York City, Inc., 130 East 40th Street, New York, N.Y. 10016, functions altogether differently. A pilot endeavor confined to New York City and its environs, it will share its knowledge of any similar organizations operating in regions outside New York. The ABC works to bring the arts and business communities together. It lists neighborhood arts programs through semiannual directories. It conducts seminars and informal meetings and offers consultation services to arts groups in preparing corporate presentations. It is involved in ethnic arts and various education programs and maintains a skills-services resource bank as a contact between corporate volunteers and arts groups in need of business skills and services. The ABC can't help individuals, but it's not concerned about your corporation's being non-profit.

Whether you decide to approach a business concern on your own or through one of these organizations, you could certainly avail yourself of the accumulated wisdom they have in the fund-raising area.

An important consideration to bear in mind is that help need not necessarily be in the form of money. The loan of space (to set up your theater), personnel (accountant, business manager, etc.), equipment (typewriter, van, lights, etc.), or the gift of theater seats or corporate products (lumber or other materials for your stage, fabrics for your curtains or costumes, etc.) is the equivalent of money, if you would have had to lay out the money to obtain these things.

Contributions from Individuals. Friends or family may be happy to donate money, supplies, and services because they want to encourage you in your enthusiasm for puppetry. But you can't expect outsiders to contribute unless you can persuade them that what you're doing is important.

Although some wealthy members of the community may donate to your marionette theater on the basis of your need or that of your audiences, this may not be an incentive that will convince others to support you. People give not so much for the benefit of the recipient as for what they derive from the giving—tax benefits (for this you must have tax exemption), community status, improved public relations (although some donors insist on anonymity), pleasure in one's own magnanimity, a common enthusiasm for your cause, or a tie-in to another in which they are already involved. If they are already emotionally concerned in charities that have to do with children, hospitals, theater, or

the like, you have a lot going for you before you start. Otherwise, you might be able to develop genuine interest in marionettes on their part by inviting them to a performance or visiting them with a private demonstration of puppetry in which they can try manipulation.

Whenever possible, approach potential patrons through a mutual acquaintance who can give you a build-up before the meeting.

Acknowledgments and Reports. It should go without saying, but unfortunately it doesn't, that all gifts should be promptly and gratefully acknowledged. Moreover, patrons who have contributed a substantial amount should be invited to performances when you play in their territory. If the donors want the publicity, their names should appear on programs, tickets, theater posters and exhibits, and anywhere else where it would benefit them. Keep the acknowledgment within the bounds of good taste, but look on this as being what the donors are entitled to.

Foundations, governmental agencies, and businesses usually require reports as to how their money was spent, and you're notified of this when you receive your grant. But it's intelligent to give such a report to anyone who donates more than a nominal amount. Demonstrating that their generosity was exercised in a successful project is the best way to encourage donors to repeat or even increase their generosity on another occasion.

FUTURE OF PUPPETRY

What are the long-term prospects for puppetry as a theatrical form?

For some generations, puppetry has been considered primarily as entertainment for children, and theater for children in the United

States has never been considered a major form of theater. But the situation is changing on two fronts.

The public is beginning to appreciate that puppetry is a technique with which anything can be said—from the most frivolously entertaining to the most profound. Full recognition hasn't yet been granted to puppetry as a mature art, but this is because so many puppeteers don't meet the high standards that the best of puppetry demands. Colleges and universities are entering the scene and hopefully will do much to improve it. Courses in puppetry are being included in theater studies, degrees in puppetry are granted, and here and there resident university puppet companies are being encouraged to develop the highest technical standards and to experiment with new ideas. As theatrical specialists emerge who take pup-

petry seriously, their skills can be put at the disposal of puppet producers who now often must handle every aspect of their operations themselves.

Critics, particularly in large cities, who write for big newspapers avoid covering any but internationally famous puppet shows, or they review them as if they are minor novelties rather than a valid expression of theater. As puppetry progresses, critics will find they must inform themselves on it in order to turn in the competent reviews that will be demanded.

The other area of change that will affect puppetry is that of children's theater. Theater for children is on the threshold of achieving in the United States the respectability it has long held in some foreign countries. Among other implications inherent in this change is that more money will be allocated to it by federal agencies, state legislatures, and boards of education. Those puppeteers who are working for children will be carried along in this new recognition.

The children in an audience don't stay children very long. Soon they're buying their own theater tickets. If puppetry continues to mature along with them, it can be assured of an un-ending supply of enthusiastic supporters.

So—what are the long-term prospects for puppetry as a theatrical form? Very rosy—but as a puppeteer, to some extent they depend on you. Your commitment to your marionettes can create a positive image of puppetry for your audience, which will go far in raising puppetry to its proper status in the theater.

APPENDIX 1

SUPPLIES & TOOLS FOR MAKING
PUPPETS, COSTUMES, STAGES & PROPS

———————————————

(Equivalents may be substituted, and some equivalents are listed below)

Materials

Cardboard
Soft pencil
Tracing paper
Carbon paper

Upholstery thread or Fishline
Straight pins
Paper clips
Shellac

Paper toweling or Toilet tissue
Gauze bandage
White glue

Fabric scraps
Stocking heel
Yarn
Sponge
Cork
Buttons
Leather findings

Tempera paints
Whiting
Varnish
Turpentine
Benzine
Acetone

Alcohol
Plastic foam
Plaster of paris
Modeling clay
Plastic wood
Celastic
Rubber
Masking tape
Lattice strips
Chicken wire
Petroleum jelly
Bailing wire, screws
Assorted nails and tacks

223

Tools

Scissors

Grommet stapler

Hole punch

Awl

Heavy needle

Brushes

Small pliers

Screwdrivers

Putty knife

Spatula

Wire cutters

Sander

Matte knife

Drill with several bits

Coping saw

Back saw

Cross-cut saw

Assorted chisels

Curtains, hardware, and lumber as required

APPENDIX 2

SUPPLIERS FOR PUPPETRY

Crafts supplies:

American Handicrafts Co., Inc., 330 Fifth Avenue, New York, N.Y. 10001 (also in E. Orange, N.J. and Los Angeles, California)

Arthur Brown & Bros. Inc., 2 West 46th Street, New York, N.Y. 10036

Fabricators:

Associated Drapery & Equipment Co., 40 Sea Cliff Avenue, Glen Cove, L.I., N.Y. 11542

I. Weiss & Sons, 445 West 45th Street, New York, N.Y. 10036

J.C. Hansen, 423 West 43rd Street, New York, N.Y. 10036

Gelatine Sheets:

Roscolene, 36 Bush Avenue, Port Chester, N.Y. 10573

(Also from above lighting companies)

General Theatrical Needs:

Theater Production Service, 26 So. Highland Avenue, Ossining, N.Y. 10562

Simons Directory of Theatrical Materials, 1564 Broadway, New York, N.Y. 10036

Lumber:

Dykes Lumber Co., 348 West 44th Street, New York, N.Y. 10036

(Also in N.J. & Long Island)

Tulnoy Lumber Co., 300 Wyckoff Avenue, Brooklyn, N.Y. 11217

Muslin & Canvas:

Astrup Co., 39 Walker Street, New York, N.Y. 10013

(also at local department stores, variety and remnant stores)

Plastics:

Plastic Wood; Boyle Midway, Inc., 685 Third Avenue, New York, N.Y. 10017

Styrofoam; Creegan Co., 508–510 Washington Street, Steubenville, Ohio 43952

Celastic; David Hamburger, 136 West 31st Street, New York, N.Y. 10001

Sound Equipment:

Masque Sound & Recording Corp., 331 West 51st Street, New York, N.Y. 10019

Garry & Timmy Harris, 236 West 55th Street, New York, N.Y. 10019

Stage Lighting:

(for rental and purchase)

William Haas Jr., 29–31 Charles Street, New York, N.Y. 10014

Ken Moses, 230 Kamena Street, Fairview, N.J. 07022

Times Square Theatrical and Studio Supply Corp., 318 West 47th Street, New York, N.Y. 10036

Theatrical Fabrics:

Dazians Inc., 40 East 29th Street, New York, N.Y. 10016

Maharam Fabric Corp., 45 Rasons Court, Hauppage, L.I., N.Y. 11787

Theatrical Hardware:

Mutual Hardware, 5–45 49th Avenue, L.I. City, N.Y. 11101

Silver & Sons Hardware Corp., 711 Eighth Avenue, New York, N.Y. 10036

Theatrical Paints:

Gothic Color Co., Inc., 727 Washington Street, New York, N.Y. 10014

APPENDIX 3

PRODUCTION CHECKLIST

Ask yourself these questions before you present your show to the public. If you can't answer them objectively, try to find someone to reply to them for you.

1. Have I accomplished my original aim?

2. Have changes from the original concept improved it?

3. Are the subject and treatment designed for puppetry?

4. Is the script tight and free of extraneous material?

5. Are the characters clearly defined?

6. Is there a character with whom the audience can identify? If the show is for children, is that character worthy of emulation or otherwise sympathetic?

7. Are the marionettes credible in movement as well as in design and concept?

8. Can the marionettes communicate without dialogue, which could be eliminated?

9. Do the marionettes, costumes, scenery, props, lighting, and sound effects communicate directly and quickly without the necessity for further explanation?

10. Are there complicated movements that could be simpler and more effective?

11. Are the voices, music, and sound effects clear and effective?

12. Is the pacing good, are the lines delivered smoothly, is there brisk forward movement, and are there quiet (not dull) moments for variation?

13. Is there unity in the production that allows the audience to accept the basic premise and final situation?

14. Is everyone connected with the production conducting himself professionally?

BIBLIOGRAPHY

Marionettes

Abbe, Dorothy, *The Dwiggins Marionettes*. New York: Harry Abrams, 1970.

Fling, Helen, *Marionettes: How to Make Them*. New York: Dover Publications, 1973.

Fraser, Peter, *Puppet Circus*. Boston: Plays, Inc., 1971.

French, Susan, *Presenting Marionettes*. New York: Van Nostrand Reinhold, 1964.

Whanslaw, H. W., and Victor Hotchkiss, *Specialised Puppetry*. Redhill, Surrey: Wells Gardner, Darton and Co., Ltd.

Non-Stringed Puppets

Ando, Tsuro, *Bunraku*. New York and Tokyo: Walker/Weatherhill, 1970.

Boylan, Eleanor, *How to Be a Puppeteer*. New York: McCall Publishing Co., 1970.

Efimova, Nina, *Adventures of a Russian Puppet Theatre*. Birmingham, Michigan: Puppetry Imprints, 1935.

Engler, Larry, and Carol Fijan, *Making Puppets Come Alive*. New York: Taplinger, 1973.

Fraser, Peter, *Punch & Judy*. New York: Van Nostrand Reinhold, 1970.

McPharlin, Paul, and Marjorie Batchelder McPharlin, *The Puppet Theatre in America*. Boston: Plays, Inc., 1969.

Obraztsov, Sergei Vladimirovich, *The Chinese Puppet Theatre*. London: Faber & Faber, 1961.

———, *My Profession*. Moscow: Foreign Language Publishing House, 1957.

Pasqualino, Antonio, *Pupi Siciliani*. Rome, 1970.

Speaight, George, *Punch & Judy*. Boston: Plays, Inc., 1970.

General Puppetry

Baird, Bil, *The Art of the Puppet*. New York: Macmillan, 1965.

Batchelder, Marjorie, *The Puppet Theatre Handbook*. New York: Harper & Row, 1947.

Boehn, Max von, *Dolls and Puppets*. New York: Cooper Square Publishers, 1966.

Fraser, Peter, *Introducing Puppetry*. New York: Watson-Guptill, 1969.

Joseph, Helen Haiman, *Book of Marionettes*. New York: Viking, 1936.

Malik, Dr. Jan, and Dr. Erik Kolar, *The Puppet Theatre in Czechoslovakia*. Prague: Orbis, 1970.

Niculescu, Margareta, ed., *Marionettes of the World*. Boston: Plays, Inc., 1969.

Costumes

Davenport, Millia, *The Book of Costume*. New York: Crown, 1964.

Klepper, Erhard, Introduction by James Laver, *Costumes Through the Ages*. New York: Simon and Schuster, 1967.

Laver, James, *Costume in the Theatre*. New York: Hill & Wang, 1967.

Motley (pseudonym), *Designing and Making Stage Costumes*. New York: Watson-Guptill, 1972.

Tompkins, Julia, *Stage Costumes and How to Make Them*. Boston: Plays, Inc., 1969.

Stage Design and Production

Bay, Howard, *Stage Design*. New York: Drama Book Specialists, 1974.

Burris-Meyer, Harold, and Edward C. Cole, *Scenery for the Theatre*. New York: Little Brown, 1972.

Cornberg, Sol, and Emanuel L. Gebauer, *A Stage Crew Handbook*. New York: Harper & Row, 1957.

Gorelik, Mordecai, *New Theatres for Old*. New York: Samuel French, 1940.

Heffner, Hubert C., Samuel Selden, and Hunton D. Sellman, *Modern Theatre Practice*. New York: Appleton-Century-Crofts, 1969.

Nelms, Henning, *A Primer of Stagecraft*. New York: Dramatists Play Service, 1968.

Parker, Oren W., and Harvey K. Smith, *Scene Design and Stage Lighting*. New York: Holt, Rinehart, Winston, 1973.

Rowell, Kenneth, *Stage Design*. New York: Van Nostrand Reinhold, 1968.

Simonson, Lee, *The Stage Is Set*. New York: Theatre Arts Books, 1964.

Warre, Michael, *Designing and Making Stage Scenery*. New York: Van Nostrand Reinhold, 1966.

Stage Lighting

Bentham, Frederick, *The Art of Stage Lighting*. New York: Taplinger, 1969.

Fuchs, Theodore, *Stage Lighting*. New York: Benjamin Blum, 1963.

McCandless, Stanley Russell, *A Method of Lighting the Stage*. New York: Theatre Arts Books, 1958.

————, *A Syllabus of Stage Lighting*. 11th Ed. New York: Drama Book Specialists, 1964.

Pilbrow, Richard, *Stage Lighting*. New York: Van Nostrand Reinhold, 1971.

Rubin, Joel E., and Leland H. Watson, *Theatrical Lighting Practice*. New York: Theatre Arts Books, 1954.

Wilfred, Thomas, *Projected Scenery*. New York: Drama Book Specialists, 1965.

Sound

Burris-Meyer, Harold, and Vincent Mallory, *Sound in the Theatre*. Mineola, New York: *Radio* magazine, 1959.

Technical journals.

Theater Administration

Cavanaugh, Jim, *Organization and Management of the Nonprofessional Theatre (Including Backstage and Front-of-house)*. New York: Theatre Student Series, Richard Rosen Press, 1973.

Ham, Roderick, *Theatre Planning*. Toronto: University of Toronto Press, 1972.

Langley, Stephen, *Theatre Management*. New York: Drama Book Specialists, 1973.

Lounsbury, Warren C., *Theatre Backstage from A to Z*. Seattle: University of Washington Press, 1968.

Young People's Literature

Arbuthnot, May Hill, *Children and Books*. 4th Ed. New York: Scott, Foresman, 1972.

Carlsen, G. Robert, *Books and the Teenage Reader*, Revised Edition. New York: Harper & Row, 1972.

Huck, Charlotte S., and Doris A. Young, *Children's Literature in the Elementary School*. New York: Holt, Rinehart, Winston, 1968.

Pilgrim, Geneva Hanna, and Mariana K. McAllister, *Books, Young People, and Reading Guidance, Second Edition.* New York: Harper & Row, 1968.

Funding

The Bread Game: The Realities of Foundation Fundraising, Revised Edition. San Francisco: Glide Publications, 1974.

The Foundation Grants Index. New York: The Foundation Center, 1973.

What Will a Foundation Look for When You Submit a Grant Proposal? and *What Makes a Good Proposal?* (pamphlets). New York: The Foundation Center.

General Reference

Hartnoll, Phyllis, ed., *The Oxford Companion to the Theatre.* Third Ed. London: Oxford University Press, 1967.

GLOSSARY

Act curtain: see *Curtains.*

Apron: that part of the stage floor forward of the proscenium curtain.

Arena theater: theater in the round, a stage area surrounded on all sides by the audience.

Auditorium: that part of the building from which the audience views the production.

Backcloth or *backdrop:* see *Curtains.*

Backing flat: a flat set outside a scenery opening to conceal the view beyond.

Backstage: the offstage area; also the crew that operates the mechanics of the show.

Barn door: metal flaps hinged to a frame in the forward housing of a Fresnel to confine the spread of light.

Batten: a pipe or wood strip usually running the length of the stage, to which hangings are attached.

Blackout: an instantaneous cutoff of all onstage lights to complete a segment of a performance; often used in place of a curtain.

Book or *Booked flat:* a twofold hinged piece of scenery or set piece resembling a book.

Border: see *Curtains.*

Box office: that part of the theater from which seats are sold; also the receipts.

Box set: a set in which the stage is enclosed by three walls (the fourth is invisible) and a ceiling to form a realistic interior.

Brace: a support for a set piece attached to its back at one end and to the stage floor by a screw or weight at the other.

Breakaway: scenery or a prop designed to come apart.

Bridge: the area of a marionette stage on which the puppeteers stand and operate the puppets.

Bridgerail: the crossbar forward of the bridge from which backdrops are hung and on which the puppeteer rests his arms.

Bridge backrail: the crossbar at the rear of the bridge from which marionettes are suspended while inactive.

Broken bridge: the working area of the puppeteer's stage, divided to increase the mobility and depth of the playing area.

Built stuff: all carpentered three-dimensional objects.

233

Caliper: an instrument for measuring three-dimensional objects.

Cassette: a small tape recorder.

Cinemoid: a trade name of a lens color filter.

Contour curtain: see *Curtains*.

Control: in lighting, the device that governs the intensity of illumination.

Controller: the apparatus to which the marionette strings are attached and which the puppeteer holds. (British English: perch.)

Cross-fade: to reduce illumination in one area and illumine another simultaneously.

Cue: a reference point in the working script that indicates action, a spoken line, or a change in the lighting or the set.

Curtains: all hanging draperies. Usually referred to as "soft goods."

> *Act drop*: an inner proscenium curtain, part of the production; the removable fourth wall of a box set; lowered to indicate the end of acts or scenes.

> *Backcloth* or *backdrop*: the curtain hanging at the rear of the performing area and forward of the bridge.

> *Border*: a narrow strip used to conceal the top of the stage from the audience.

> *Contour curtain*: the "Austrian" type of curtain, pulled up in shirred loops.

> *Draw curtain*: a curtain divided in the center and pulled to the sides of the stage.

> *Front* or *House curtain*: the proscenium curtain, part of the permanent stage rather than the production.

> *Grand drape*: a hanging that decorates the proscenium arch, like an elaborate valance across the top and possibly down the sides of the front curtain.

> *Legs*: curtain panels at the sides of the stage, used to frame the set and conceal offstage business.

> *Rising curtain*: an up-and-down curtain with a fixed upper stop.

> *Roll curtain*: canvas attached to a horizontal pole, raised and lowered like a window shade.

> *Safety* or *fire curtain*: a fire-retardant curtain behind the "grand drapery" in the proscenium arch; sometimes called the "asbestos."

> *Scrim*: a seamless translucent curtain used as a screen for special effects; lights behind the screen permit visibility.

> *Tabs* or *tableau curtain*: a curtain raised from the sides with diagonal pull cords for a draped effect.

Curtain set: a stage set with various curtains only, without scenery.

Cyclorama: *Cyc* for short. Sometimes a curved wall with an unbroken surface built at the back of the stage; a partial or shallow cyclorama is more frequently used; also the curtain farthest from the stage. Used for sky effects or as a large screen for multi-media projections.

Dim: to reduce the intensity of light.

Dimmer: the rheostat or auto transformer that controls the intensity of light.

Divider: an architectural and construction instrument for measuring architectural drawings.

Dolly: a wheeled platform or rollaway wagon on which set pieces can be placed.

Downstage: that area immediately behind the proscenium curtain line; divided into left, center, and right.

Draw curtain: see *Curtains*.

False Pros.: wings and a top border used to fill in and reduce the size of the proscenium-arch opening.

Flat: a canvas-covered frame used as the structural unit forming walls, etc.; usually rectangular, the basis of the box set.

Flies: the space above the stage where, out of view of the audience, scenery can be "flown" or raised.

Flood: wide spread of light.

Fly floor: the level on which the crew stand to "fly" scenery.

Focus: the adjustment of lighting equipment to the area of coverage.

Follow spot: a spotlight manipulated so as to illuminate a performer as he moves about the stage.

Footlights: a series of lights in the floor in the front of the stage; rarely used today.

Forward bridge: the downstage part of a marionette stage on which, with their back to the audience, the puppeteers work the marionettes.

Frames: the metal holders used in lighting instruments for gels and Cinemoid.

Fresnel: a type of spotlight used primarily for area lighting. The small Fresnel is an "inkie."

Front curtain: see *Curtains.*

Front lighting: illumination from instruments forward of the proscenium.

Front of house: the staff and those parts of the theater servicing the audience—the auditorium, lobbies, bars, box office, etc.

Front view: a silhouetted outline of any object, seen from the front.

Gelatins or *Gels:* the colored transparent sheets placed before the lens of lighting instruments.

Gobo: a metal patterned disc inserted into a Leko for a projected light design.

Grand drape: see *Curtains.*

Greenroom: the room offstage in which the actors gather with their friends before a performance or after it.

Grid: a framework above the stage, hidden from the audience, from which stage gear can be suspended.

Ground cloth: on a marionette stage, a fabric on the stage floor that cuts down reflected light and gives the marionette feet better purchase than the bare floor.

House curtain: see *Curtains, Front curtain.*

Hanging rods: small metal arms on the bridgerail from which to suspend puppets and props.

Incidental music: in a production not primarily a musical, the background music or occasional musical selection, which enhances the presentation but which is not essential to it.

Inkie: a baby spotlight (a three-inch fresnel).

Inner proscenium: a portable, adjustable proscenium frame to reduce the size of the stationary proscenium arch; used in touring. Sometimes called a "portal."

Iris: a metal unit that reduces the area of light coverage by adjusting the size of the aperture through which the light passes.

Jog: a narrow flat set at an angle to a larger flat, to produce a "return."

Key light: the main source of light, usually from a "motivational" source—the sun, a lantern, etc.

Keystoning: the distortion of a projected light caused by the angle of throw.

Lamp: the bulb of a lighting instrument.

Legs: see *Curtains.*

Leko: a spotlight with a plano-convex lens and an ellipsoidal reflector, used for specific lighting. The pin spot adaptor converts the Fresnel into a Leko.

Lens: a glass unit placed in front of a lighting instrument to alter the direction of the light rays.

Line: a rope on which scenery is hung to be raised or lowered.

Lobsterscope: a device in front of a spotlight causing regular intermittent obscurity of the light for staccato effects.

Machinery: all mechanical equipment having to do with the backstage production.

Mask: to conceal backstage areas from the audience.

Offstage: Backstage, immediately outside the playing area.

Onstage: the area in which the actors appear before the audience.

Papier-mâché: a mixture of paper, paste or glue, and water.

PAR: a specially designed bulb with a built-in parabolic reflector.

Pin spot adaptor: a device that converts an inkie into a Leko.

Practical/practicable: functional, operating—as a door or window that works, opposed to one that is merely painted.

Preset: to ready a subsequent light cue or scene before its time onstage.

Props: stage properties; anything in the production except costumes, scenery, and furniture. In the marionette theater, the puppets are actors, not props.

Proscenium: the wall between the stage and the auditorium, with an opening through which the play is seen.

Proscenium arch: the opening in the proscenium wall.

Rake: the slope of an auditorium or stage floor.

Ramp: an inclined approach.

Return: a narrow flat set at an angle in the walls of a box set to break the line or mask the sides of the stage.

Reveal: a construction piece framing an opening in a flat that gives an illusion of thickness.

Revolving stage: a mechanical contrivance sometimes set into the stage floor that turns, permitting several sets to be erected simultaneously; scenes are changed by moving the turntable to show one scene or another with minimum time between changes.

Rising curtain: see *Curtains.*

Roll curtain: see *Curtains.*

S-hooks: S-shaped metal devices from which to suspend objects.

Safety curtain: see *Curtains.*

Scale: relative dimensions without difference in proportions.

Scenery: the structural appurtenances, either painted or three-dimensional, that create the environment in which the play occurs.

Scrim: see *Curtains.*

Set: the total of scenic pieces and their arrangement on the stage at a given time.

Set pieces: the flats or three-dimensional units of which the full scenery is assembled.

Sharp focus: a narrow beam of light cleanly cut into a specific area.

Shutters: the metal discs on a Leko that create a hard distinction between light and darkness.

Side view: a profile of any object or marionette.

Sill iron: a flat strip of metal for bracing an opening in the bottom of a flat.

Spike: to mark the stage floor for the placement of set pieces.

Stage door: the back or side entrance to the theater.

Stage floor: the area where the action of the presentation takes place.

Stage peg or *screw:* a piece of hardware used to secure units to the stage floor.

Strike: to remove scenery; to break down set units or the marionette stage itself.

Strip lights: group lights that create evenly distributed illumination for area lighting.

Strobe light: an instrument for staccato lighting effects.

Switchboard: the electrical unit that controls the lighting instruments.

Tabs or *Tableau curtain:* see *Curtains.*

Teaser: the proscenium border.

Theater in the round: see *Arena theater.*

Toggle rail: a reinforcing bar across the back of a canvas flat.

Top view: an outlined plan looking on the stage from above; a floor plan of set or scenery.

Tormentors: the lights placed vertically downstage on either side.

Trap: a device by which onstage actors or set pieces can be dropped through the stage floor or by which they can be placed onstage from below.

Trim: a mark for the placement of units onstage.

Ultraviolet or *U.V. light:* light filtered to allow only the ultraviolet to illuminate the stage; only specially painted objects are visible.

Upstage: that part of the stage farthest from the audience.

Wagon stage: a low-wheeled platform on which a set or a puppet stage can be placed for quick moving on or off the stage floor; similar to a dolly.

Wings: flats on either side of the stage to mask in the offstage areas and frame the stage picture; "in the wings" means immediately offstage.

INDEX

Accounting procedures, 208–9
Adults, as audiences, 73–74, 79, 163–64
Advertising, paid, 193–94
Agents, 174–75, 211
Allison, Fran, 150
American Theatre Association, 213
Animal marionettes. *See also* Ruff
  based on Ruff, 93
  music for, 130
  scale of, 93–94
  in scripts, 72–73
  variety of, 80–81
  voices of, 96
Arc lamp, 122
Ark-building, as illusion, 150
Arms. *See also* Hands
  module assembly of, 13–15
  movement of, 35
Arts and Business Council of New York City, Inc., 219
ASCAP, 195
ASSITEJ, 213
Associations, professional, 212–13
Audience participation, 160–61
Audience relations, 73–74, 76–80, 162–64, 211–12

Backdrops, 116, 119
Baird, Bil, 150

Begging manipulation, 46
Benefit performances, 212
Birds, 93
  music for, 130
Bird trick
  in script, 59–60
  stringing for, 29
Black light, 126–27
Blackouts, 98
BMI, 195
Bowing manipulation, 35
Bridgerail, 49, 53
Bufano, Remo, 150
Bunraku puppets, 71, 152–53
Business aspects of puppetry, 173
  accounting procedures, 208–9
  agents, 174–75, 211
  contracts, 200–1
    examples of, 201–7
  employees, 175, 210–11
  funding, 213–14
    business contributions, 219–20
    Federal, 216–18
    foundations, 215–16
    individual contributions, 220
    local, 218–19
    incorporating, 214–15
  managers, 174, 211
  negotiations, 198–200
  permissions, 195
  professionalism and, 209–12

repertory-building, 195–96
reports, 220
selling. *See* Publicity
theater management, 196–97
  personnel, 197–98
  procedures, 198
Business Committee for the Arts, Inc., 219
Business manager, 174, 211

Cardboard, for construction, 5
Card trick, 53
  in script, 59
  stringing for, 29
Celastic, for construction, 85, 86
Changelings, 146
Children
  as audience, 76–80, 162–64
  and audience participation, 160–61
  music for, 129–30
Chorus lines, 92, 144, 146
Cinemoid filters, 123, 125, 126
Clay modeling, 83–86
Color
  of controllers, 27–28
  of costumes, 89
  of curtains, 50
  in lighting, 54, 125–26
  of scenery, 118–19
  of skin tones, 17–18
  of strings, 28

"Come-apart" skeleton, 144–46
Company manager, 174
"Computerized man" puppet, 147
Construction. *See also* Controller; Costumes; Stringing
    of changelings, 146
    of Kandu, 5–29
        controller, 27–28
        facial features, 16–17
        hair, 18
        module assembly, 7–15
        painting, 17–18, 21
        pattern tracing, 5–7
        skin wrapping, 15–16
    of lights, 123–24
    modeling, 83–86
    of props, 121
    of Ruff, 38–44
        controller, 44
        fur covering, 41–44
        module assembly, 38–41
    scale of, 82
    of scenery, 116–18
    sculpting, 85, 86
    for special effects, 144–47
Contour curtain, 98
Contracts, 200–1
    examples of, 201–7
Controller. *See also* Manipulation
    "double airplane," 27
    for Kandu, 27–28
    manipulation of, 29, 33
    for Ruff, 44
    tandem, 92, 144, 146
Corporations
    commercial, 214
    non-profit tax-exempt, 180, 214–15
Costumes. *See also* Construction
    appropriateness, 87–89
    changes of, 90–91
    color of, 89
    construction of, 21, 90–91
    fabrics for, 21, 89–90
    importance of, 86–87
    for Kandu, 21
    research on, 87
Creative Artists Public Service Program (CAPS), 218–19

Critics, 191–92
"Curtain Rod and Chairs" stage, 49
Curtains, 49–50
    materials for, 50
    types of, 98
Cycloramas, 155

Dances, 70, 128, 150. *See also* Music
"Desk-and-Table" stage, 49–50
Dimmers, for lights, 53, 124–25, 126, 151
Directors
    and lighting procedure, 127
    in live theater, 154–55
    in marionette theater, 155–58
Doorways, in scenery, 111–12
"Double airplane" controller, 27
Draw curtains, 98
Dreams, as special effect, 149
Drops, 111

Ears (animal)
    movement of, 46
    stringing of, 44
Earthquakes, as special effect, 149
Education Professional Developments Act, 217–18
Elementary and Secondary Education Act (ESEA), 217
Employee relations, 175, 210–11
Endorsements, 192–93
Equipment. *See also* Stages
    emergency, 164
    lighting, 122–26
    portability of, 50, 62–63
    sound system, 138–39
Ethics, professional, 209–12
Exhibits, as publicity, 187–88
Explosions, as special effect, 149
Eyes, 86
    movable, 83, 146
    painting of, 18

Face. *See also* Heads
    painting of, 17–18
    paper-sculpted, 16–17
Fairy tales, as scripts, 76–80

Feet
    modular assembly of, 13
    painting of, 21
    weighting of, 33
Fingers. *See also* Hands
    grasping illusion of, 142–43
    movable, 86
Fire, as special effect, 149
Fish illusion, 146
Flash powder, 149
Flats, 117
Floodlights, 54
Floods, as special effect, 149
Flora, 92–93
Flower-in-lapel trick
    in script, 61–62
    stringing for, 29
Flower pot trick, 52, 57
Flying, as special effect, 143–44
Focus, of lighting, 125
Fog, as special effect, 147–148
Follow spot, 121
Foundation Center, The, 215–16
Foundations, 215–16
Fresnel (light), 122–23, 125
Funding, 215–20
    business contributions, 219–20
    Federal, 216–18
    foundations, 215–16
    individual contributions, 220
    local, 218–19
    and reports, 220

Galloping manipulation, 46
Gels, 123, 125, 126
Gesso, 84
Gestures, as special effect, 144
Gluing. *See also* Construction
    of facial features, 17
    of hair, 18
    over skin wrapping, 16
Gobos, 126
Grasping, as special effect, 142–43
Grommets, 7

Hair. *See also* Head
    materials for, 18, 41–44, 85
    paper-sculpted, 17
    for Ruff, 41–44
Hand puppets, 150, 152
    stages for, 97, 98

Hands. *See also* Fingers
  module assembly of, 15
  special construction of, 86
Hand trick, 52
  in script, 58
Hanging, of marionettes, 15, 27, 28
  devices for, 47
  of flora, 93
  and wrapping, 36
Hats, as costumes, 91
Hat trick, 53
  in script, 58–59
Head movements
  of Kandu, 35
  of Ruff, 46
Heads. *See also* Face
  modeling of, 83–85
  module assembly of, 7
  paper-sculpted, 16–17
  sculpting of, 85
Health, Education, and Welfare
  Department, 217–18
Human marionettes. *See also*
  Kandu
  as casts of characters, 80–83
  scale of, 82
  variety of, 80–82
Humor, in puppet theater, 72, 79, 133

Illusions. *See* Magic tricks;
  Special effects
Incorporating, 214–15
"Inkie," 122–23, 125
Internal Revenue Service, 214–15
International Theatre Institute
  of the United States, 213
Interviews, 186

Joints, covering of, 86–87, 90
Juggling, as special effect, 144

Kandu (magician marionette).
  See also Human marionettes
  construction of, 5–29
  facial features, 16–17
  hair, 18
  module assembly, 7–15
  painting, 17–18, 21

  skin wrapping, 15–16
  controller for, 27–28
  costume for, 21
  manipulation of, 29, 33–35
  props for, 51–53
  script for, 55–62
  stringing of, 28–29
  tricks for. *See* Magic tricks
  voice of, 38
Kick plate, 164
Kneeling manipulation, 33–35

Laboratories, as scenery, 150
Labor Department, 218
Legs, modular assembly of, 11–13. *See also* Feet
Leko (light), 122, 125, 126
Lighting, 53, 121–22
  color in, 125–26
  control of, 124–25
  and costumes, 89
  equipment for, 122–26
  focus of, 125
  mood and motivation in, 122–24
  in multi-media, 150–51
  outdoors, 160
  procedure for, 127
  and safety, 127, 165
  special effects in, 126–27
Lightning, 53, 148
Lullabies, 130

Magazine releases, 185–86
Magic tricks, for Kandu. *See also*
  Special effects
  bird trick, 29, 59–60
  card trick, 29, 53, 59
  flower-in-lapel trick, 29, 61–62
  flower pot trick, 52, 57
  hand trick, 52, 58
  rabbit-in-hat, 53, 58–59
Magnets, for special effects, 143
Magon, Jero, 152
Mail campaigns, 180–81
Managers
  business, 174, 211
  company, 174
Manipulation. *See also* Controller; Stringing
  as body communication, 94–95

  of Kandu, 29, 33–35
  of Ruff, 46
Marching music, 131
Marionettes. *See* Animal marionettes; Human marion-
  ettes
Military music, 131
Milovsoroff, Basil, 85
Mist, as special effect, 147–48
Modeling, in clay, 83–86
Module assembly
  of Kandu, 7–15
  of Ruff, 38–41
"Mop Handle and Drapery"
  stage, 47
Mouth, movable, 83, 146. *See
  also* Face
Multi-media effects, 150–51
Music, 54, 128–29
  catalogues of, 137
  historical periods of, 136–37
  for moods, 132–35
  permissions for, 195
  popular, 137
  record collections of, 135, 136
  situational, 129–32
  taping of, 142
  unity of, 135–36
Mustache illusion, 146
Mylar, 148

National Endowment for the
  Arts, 216–17
National Park Service, 217
Negotiations, 198–200
Newspaper releases, 185–86
New York State Council on the
  Arts, 218
Nightclubs, audiences in, 163–64
Noah's ark illusion, 149–50

Office of Education, 218

Painting
  of controllers, 27–28
  of marionettes, 17–18, 21
  of scenery, 118–19
Paper-sculpting, 16–17
Papier-mâché, as construction
  material, 83–85, 86
PAR bulbs, 53

Performances
  and audiences, 160–64
  benefit, 212
  body communication and, 94–95
  lighting of, 127
  opportunities for, 175–76
  outdoor, 159–60
  permissions for, 195
  preparation for, 47–54, 158–59
  and professionalism, 210
  safety of, 164–65
  script for, 55–62
  special effects for, 147–50
  taping of, 54, 138, 139–42
  timing of, 54, 139–42
  voice communication and, 95–96
Permissions, 195
Personal appearances, 186
Photographs, publicity, 192
Plaster casts, and clay modeling, 84–85
Plastic foam, as construction material, 85, 116
Plastic wood, as construction material, 85, 86
Playscripts. See Scripts
Press book, 193
Price negotiations, 198–200
Professionalism, 194, 209–12
Programs, 159
Props, 119–20. See also Scenery
  construction of, 121
  for Kandu, 51–53
  materials for, 120
  scale of, 120
  stringing for, 29
Publicity
  advertising, 193–94
  appearance of, 182–84
  critics, 191–92
  exhibits, 187–88
  mail campaigns, 180–81
  personal appearances, 186
  personal contact, 176–77
  personal relationships, 194–95
  photographs, 192
  press book, 193
  printed material, 182–84
  and public-relations director, 182

releases to the media, 184–86
  showcases, 188–91
  telephone contact, 177, 180
  testimonials, 192–93
Punctuality, 194
Puppeteers, 171–72, 210
  clothing of, 122, 152, 153, 164
  professional organizations of, 212–13
Puppeteers of America, Inc., 212
Puppetry
  future of, 220–22
  part-time, 171
  professional, 171–72. (See also Business aspects of puppetry)

Rabbit-in-hat trick, 53
  in script, 58–59
Radio releases, 184–85
Rain, as special effect, 148
Rehearsals, 62
  direction of, 156–57
  of illusions, 142
Reininger, Lotte, 152
Releases, publicity, 184–86
Repertory-building, 195–96
Restringing, 36–38
Robot puppet, 147
Rod puppets, 150, 152
Roll-away curtain, 98
Royalties, 80, 195
Ruff (dog marionette). See also Animal marionettes
  construction, 38–44
  controller for, 44
  manipulation of, 46
  in script, 60–61
  stringing for, 44
  voice of, 46

"S" hook, 28
Safety, 63, 127, 164–65
Scale
  of animal marionettes, 93
  of human marionettes, 82
  of props, 120
  of scenery, 112–13, 116
Scenery, 110–13. See also Props
  color of, 118–19
  construction of, 116–18

design of, 113–16
  and lighting, 121–22
  painting of, 118–19
  scale of, 112–13, 116
  in special effects, 149–50
Schwann-2 Record and Tape Guide, 137
Scrims, 115–16, 149
Scripts
  for adults, 73–74, 79
  animals in, 72–73
  for children, 76–80
  for Kandu and Ruff, 55–62
  permissions for, 195
  sources of, 80
  structure of, 69–71
  violence in, 78–79
Sculpting, 85, 86
Seasonal music, 132
Shadow puppets, 150, 151, 152
Shoes, painting of, 21
Showcases, 188–91
Shows. See Performances
Shrinking illusion, 144
Shutters, 125
Sicilian marionettes, 153–54
Silhouettes, 151
Sitting manipulation
  for Kandu, 33
  for Ruff, 46
Skeletons, "come-apart," 144–46
Skin
  colors for, 17–18
  for Ruff, 41–44
  wrapping of, 15–16
Smoke, as special effect, 147–48
Smoking, as special effect, 143, 147
Snow, as special effect, 148
Songs, 70, 128. See also Music
Sound effects, 54, 128, 137–38, 142
Sound systems, 138–39
Special effects. See also Magic tricks
  construction for, 144–47
  in lighting, 126–27
  stringing for, 29, 94, 142–44
  theatrical, 147–50
Spotlights, 54, 122

Stages
  areas of, 50
  basic
    "Curtain Rod and Chairs," 49
    "Desk-and-Table," 49–50
    "Mop Handle and Drapery," 47
    "The Trunk," 50
  condition of, 50–51
  for hand puppets, 97, 98
  multi-media, 98
  permanent, 97–98
  portable, 96–97
  revolving, 114–15
  safety of, 164
Steam, as special effect, 147–48
Storage, of marionettes, 36, 62
Storms, as special effect, 148
Stringing, 21, 27. See also Construction
  for chorus lines, 92, 144, 146
  for Kandu, 28–29
  of props, 121
  for Ruff, 44
  for special effects, 29, 94, 142–44
Strings
  holes for, 7
  materials for, 11, 28
  tangled, 36–38
Strip lights, 124
Strobe lights, 126, 144

Switchboard, for lights, 124–25
Swords, as special effect, 143

Tableau curtain, 98
Table prop, 51–52
Tail
  movements of, 46
  stringing of, 44
"Tallest man in the world" marionette, 144
Taping of shows
  complete, 138, 139–142
  and directing, 157
  partial, 54
  for rehearsal, 139
Television releases, 184–85
Tempera, as filler, 17, 84
Testimonials, 192–93
Theater management, 196–97
  personnel, 197–98
  procedures, 198
Theaters, permissions for, 195
Thread
  for module assembly, 11
  for strings, 28
Thunder, as special effect, 148
Tickets, complimentary, 188, 191
Tilstrom, Burr, 150
Tracing, of pattern modules, 5–7
Transformations, 146
Trees, movable, 92–93

Tricks. See Magic tricks; Special effects
"Trunk" stage, 50
Tubes, for special effects, 147
"Two-Table" stage, 49–50

Unima, 213
U.V. (ultraviolet) light, 126–27

Veterans Administration, 218
Videotaping, of rehearsals, 157
Voice(s)
  of animals, 96
  of Bunraku puppets, 153
  care of, 96
  of Kandu, 38
  and performing, 95–96
  of Ruff, 46
Volunteers, 175

"Wagon stage," 198
Walking manipulation
  for Kandu, 33, 94
  for Ruff, 46
Weather, as special effect, 147–48
Wedding music, 129
Wigs, illusions with, 146
Wood, as construction material, 85, 86
Wrapping (storing) of marionettes, 36, 62

Zenon lamp, 122